The Complete Guide
to Graduate School Admission
Psychology, Counseling,
and Related Professions

Second Edition

The Complete Guide
to Graduate School Admission
Psychology, Counseling,
and Related Professions

Second Edition

Patricia Keith-Spiegel
Ball State University

Michael W. Wiederman
Columbia College, South Carolina

2000

LAWRENCE ERLBAUM ASSOCIATES, PUBLISHERS
Mahwah, New Jersey   London

Lawrence Erlbaum Associates, Inc., Publishers
10 Industrial Avenue
Mahwah, NJ 07430

Cover design by Kathryn Houghtaling Lacey

Library of Congress Cataloging-in-Publication Data

Keith-Spiegel, Patricia.
  The complete guide to graduate school admission :
psychology, counseling, and related professions /
Patricia Keith-Spiegel, Michael W. Wiederman.—2nd ed.
        p. cm.
  Includes bibliographical references.
  ISBN 0-8058-3120-7 (cloth : alk. paper)
ISBN 0-8058-3121-5 (pbk. : alk. paper)
    1. Psychology—Study and teaching (Graduate) 2. Univer-
sities and colleges—Admission.   I. Wiederman, Michael W.
II. Title.
  BF77.K35 2000
  150'.71'173—dc21   99-088977
                                                   CIP

Books published by Lawrence Erlbaum Associates are printed on
acid-free paper, and their bindings are chosen for strength and du-
rability.

Printed in the United States of America
10 9 8 7 6 5 4 3 2

To our student readers and the hundreds of former students who influenced and inspired us

CONTENTS

PREFACE

This is the book we wish had been available when we stumbled our way through the graduate school application process. Although we each had one professor in particular who offered considerable encouragement and advice, most of the tasks and decision making were our own responsibility. We knew that we were missing out on information and strategies that could help us but were unsure of what they were. Both of us did make it through the process, but our paths were laden with pebbles, dead ends, and pits into which we seemed to have no trouble falling.

We set out to write the book that we had needed. This is it! We take you through every facet of the process of deciding where to apply, getting the information you need, completing certain tasks before you apply, completing the application process itself step-by-step, and deciding about the options that become available to you. In addition, those of you who have a semester or more before applications are due are offered many suggestions and strategies to enhance your chances of getting into the best possible program.

Going through this process the right way does not take less time than the wrong way, but the outcomes are very likely to be markedly different. We suggest that you first read this book from beginning to end, even if it seems like a long while before you need to make your graduate school plans. A perspective on the entire process will help keep you focused and clear-headed. Keep this book close at hand for in-depth review and specific directions for moving from one phase to the next.

Applying to graduate school is one of the most important steps you will ever take. Committing to the process now is likely to influence what you will do for the rest of your life. We know of so many people who wish that they had spent that extra time and effort to work on their graduate school plans. Some got sidetracked and never continued their education. Some lost one or more years because their choice of schools was poorly conceived and they were not accepted anywhere. Others lost time because their applications were inadequately or inappropriately prepared. And still others made choices that they regretted.

Although we cannot guarantee that you will be accepted into a graduate program, especially the program of your choice, we will help you maximize your chances.

—Patricia Keith-Spiegel
—Michael W. Wiederman

ACKNOWLEDGMENTS

We appreciate our students and colleagues who enhanced the second edition of this book. We owe a very special thanks to Patrick Cabe at the University of North Carolina (Pembroke). Pat applied his superior editing talents to early drafts of the manuscript and offered many excellent suggestions for changes and content additions. Other very helpful colleagues who provided reviews included Melissa Beeson (Ball State University, Career Center), Jeff Bryson (San Diego State University), and Joe Horvat (Weber State University).

Our students assisted with the logistics of completing the project and, in addition, reviewed the manuscript during its various stages of development to ensure that we were providing the information that contemporary students would want to learn. We owe gratitude to Leslee Throckmorton-Belzer, Marci Gaither, Kat Ajmere, and Jennifer Padgett.

Our publisher, Lawrence Erlbaum Associates, is always a pleasure to work with. The competent and personable staff provides a supportive and smooth publication process. Thank you, especially, Judi Amsel, Barbara Wieghaus, and Julie Anderson.

ABOUT THE AUTHORS

Patricia Keith-Spiegel has counseled students about their graduate school plans for over 30 years. She earned her master's and doctoral degrees from Claremont Graduate University (formerly Claremont Graduate School) and taught at California State University, Northridge, for 25 years before joining Ball State University in 1991 as Reed Voran Honors Distinguished Professor of Social and Behavioral Sciences. She has served as president of the Western Psychological Association and the Society for the Teaching of Psychology (Division 2 of the American Psychological Association). In 1994 she won the American Psychological Foundation Distinguished Teaching Award. Her writing and research areas include teaching technology, integrity in academia, ethical decision making, and moral development.

Michael W. Wiederman earned his master's and doctoral degrees in clinical psychology from Bowling Green State University. He completed a predoctoral internship and a postdoctoral fellowship in the Department of Psychiatry and Behavioral Science at the University of Kansas School of Medicine–Wichita before becoming a faculty member in the Department of Psychological Science at Ball State University in 1994. In 1999 he joined the faculty at Columbia College in Columbia, South Carolina. He has been active in the Society for the Scientific Study of Sexuality, and his research interests include sexuality, gender, body image, psychosocial aspects of health behavior, and self-report methodology.

Part I

Overview of the Pursuit of Graduate Study

CHAPTER 1

HOW DO I GET THE MOST FROM THIS BOOK?

The term *graduate school* conjures various images, both positive and negative, among those contemplating extending their education beyond the bachelor's degree. For some students, it is hard to even imagine what graduate school entails. If you wonder whether you are the only one who is confused and nervous about graduate school application, rest assured that you are not alone!

One might expect that people with a bachelor's degree (or students nearing the completion of their bachelor's degree) would be reasonably well-attuned to the emerging shape of their future and knowledgeable about the resources that would guide them toward their goals. However, many students experience bewilderment and apprehension about their immediate future. Although they typically feel a strong sense of interest in, and commitment to, their chosen field and are fairly confident they will eventually settle into a career related to that field, the issue of whether or how to seek graduate training can be overwhelming. It is not uncommon for students to feel anxious and to procrastinate.

We can help you. We believe that the large majority of students who are willing to assess their status conscientiously and realistically and then to make their decisions very carefully will be able to continue their education beyond the bachelor's level. If you are to be among these students, you must work hard on the various tasks involved to achieve this goal. We see our role as providing you with the information you need to select and apply to graduate schools. When you know what you are doing and why you have to do it, the process will seem much less mysterious and burdensome. Informed decision making will maximize your chances of acceptance because you will apply to programs for which you are well suited. Also, we tell you what common mistakes graduate school applicants often make. The majority of these mistakes are the result of ignorance or misinformation, all of which are preventable.

We also aspire to debunk some persistent but inaccurate myths, such as the following:

- You have a better chance of being accepted into a graduate program in your own town or state than outside of your own state. (The opposite is usually true.)
- If you want to get into a good clinical program, you should accumulate lots of prior clinical experience. (Too much actually can be inappropriate or counterproductive.)
- You cannot do anything with just a master's degree. (Yes, you can.)
- You cannot get into any PhD program unless you have at least a 3.5 grade point average (GPA) and very high Graduate Record Examination (GRE) scores. (The stronger your credentials the better, but there are many options for the more average student.)
- A good strategy is to keep your grades high by only taking courses in which you know you can get an *A*. (This is a really bad idea!)

In the following chapters we explain why these views are inaccurate, but please finish reading this chapter before jumping into the core "how-to" material. You will get far more out of the book if you are familiar with its game plan and terminology. We later define frequently used terms.

Target Readers

Our advice and the information we offer are relevant to students in any of several different circumstances:

- Undergraduates at any point in their education who will apply to a doctoral or master's program in any area of psychology or an allied behavioral or social science (e.g., sociology, neuroscience) or mental health (e.g., counseling, social work) field.
- Students who have already earned an undergraduate degree, including those who are currently enrolled in terminal master's degree programs and who aspire to doctoral training.
- Current graduate students seeking to change programs.
- Students who have already earned a degree, bachelor's or otherwise, and are seeking to return to academia after having been away from school for a while.
- Students whose previous applications to graduate programs have failed and who need fresh application strategies.

Our training and experience are in psychology, so we are most familiar with that field and the process of gaining admission to psychology graduate programs. Accordingly, we write primarily with applicants to psychology programs in mind, including those interested in clinical, counseling, industrial/organizational, social/personality, developmental, experimental, educational, and school psychology. However, the information and advice contained in this book also apply well to those seeking graduate degrees in some aspect of counseling (e.g., marriage and family counseling, substance abuse counseling, rehabilitation counseling) or clinical social work.

The book is woven around a dialogue between ourselves and an imaginary graduate school hopeful. We easily recognize this make-believe student, not only in the many hundreds we have counseled but in long-ago versions of ourselves as well.

Sometimes I wonder if going to graduate school is what I really want to do right now. Is there any way to be sure?

A graduate degree can be the right path for a number of reasons. One reason is simply the desire to continue studying in an area that one finds absorbing. Undergraduate training often ends when students are still only up to their ankles in the subject matter in which they wish to fully immerse themselves. There is still so much to discover and contribute, and graduate training opens up opportunities for knowledge advancement. Zest for learning, then, is a good reason to seek an advanced degree and perhaps is the one that will best sustain you.

Another common reason for wanting to earn a higher degree is to reap the employment opportunities that accompany graduate training. Job applicants with advanced degrees have an advantage over those without them, and many careers require an advanced degree to qualify at the minimum entry level. Those who want to work in a professional capacity in psychology or related fields typically will need to earn a master's or doctoral degree.

Finally, as a group, people with advanced degrees make more money— at least over the longer haul—than those without them. So, love, employment, and money are all common motivations for seeking advanced degrees.

Graduate school, however, is not for everyone. Regardless of the reason for seeking advanced training, one must be very motivated. Persistence and enthusiasm are the markers of students who complete advanced educational programs. Those who are interested in graduate school solely because of the social status that those letters after their names will bestow may not be able to endure the rigorous journey. Those who like the idea of having an advanced degree and what it can do for them, but who intensely dislike all that goes into getting it—such as reading, writing, working in the library, and studying—should reexamine their goals. Those who are attracted to a number of careers and remain confused about which direction to take would probably benefit from career counseling or taking a break until they become more focused. Otherwise, they could be among those who drop out of graduate school.

Often, though, students who doubt their graduate school aspirations are, in fact, masking low self-confidence. They want very much to continue their education but are overwhelmed with the application process or have negative perceptions of their capabilities. They may have received a negative comment about their chances of success from one of their educators, and that feedback may have had a profound impact even though it was, in fact, unwarranted. With the knowledge this book provides, we hope to pull anyone in these categories out of the rut. (For those with doctoral degree aspirations who remain unsure of themselves, we suggest considering the "master's-first" plan as detailed in chap. 5.)

If your doubts about graduate training persist, you may wish to consider taking a year or more away from school. Sometimes it is hard to go back to school after you have worked at a job, but those who are truly committed do get around to it eventually and, by that time, have attained additional maturity and valuable experience. Even first-year graduate students with gray hair are not uncommon!

Glossary of References to Survey Data and Recurring Terms

Throughout the book we refer to survey data as the basis for some of the advice we provide. This information comes from several original surveys by Patricia Keith-Spiegel conducted in 1989–1990. These surveys included questionnaires completed by faculty around the United States who were involved in graduate student selection committees, students successfully enrolled in competitive PhD programs, undergraduate faculty who wrote letters of recommendation for applicants, and administrative and secretarial staff who processed application materials and inquiries from applicants. Additionally, we extracted information from 360 applications to graduate programs in psychology in the United States and Canada. Of course, we have supplemented these data with our personal experiences working with students who are applying to graduate programs and serving on graduate selection committees.

A few terms and abbreviations, some of which may be unfamiliar in the context in which they are employed, will show up again and again. Frequently used abbreviations include GPA (grade point average), GRE (Graduate Record Examination), APA (American Psychological Association), and APS (American Psychological Society). The term *graduate school* is often used in this book to refer to the total concept of graduate training institutions, including programs and the universities or free-standing professional schools that house them. In short, *graduate school* is used when a generality is intended.

Graduate program refers to the specific program of study, usually administered within an academic department (such as the Department of Psychology or the Department of Social Work) or by a school, division, or college (such as the School of Social and Behavioral Sciences or the Division of Education), each of which is made up of several related departments. Some graduate programs are interdisciplinary, which means that several departments or schools within the university contribute to and administer the program. Occasionally, a graduate program may be cooperative, offered by two departments from two different universities. Most academic departments or schools offer more than one program, each with its own selection committee. For example, a particular psychology department may offer doctoral programs in five areas—clinical, developmental, cognitive, social/personality, and physiological—and perhaps even a terminal master's degree program in counseling.

Although postbaccalaureate (post-BA or BS) degrees involve a potentially confusing array of abbreviations, we primarily refer to the four most commonly bestowed in psychology and closely related fields: the PhD (Doctor of Philosophy), the PsyD (Doctor of Psychology), the EdD (Doctor of Education), and the MA, MS, or MSW (Master of Arts, Master of Science, Master of Social Work, or, as more commonly stated, the master's degree). A *terminal master's* (or *master's-only*) degree program is a fully-contained program created for that degree and not as a stepping stone to a doctoral degree within that same program. Most terminal master's degrees are offered at institutions that do not offer the doctoral degree. Terminal master's degree students wishing to go on to a doctoral program usually have to transfer to another school.

Professional schools are often free-standing, private institutions focusing on graduate training in one or a few select applied areas. Sometimes psychology professional schools operate in association with a traditional university, much like dental and medical schools. Growing numbers of professional schools train students at the master's and doctoral level to do applied work such as counseling and psychotherapy.

Selection committee is the general term used in this book to refer to graduate program faculty members who recommend to their all-university admissions office which applicants will be accepted into their program. Sometimes, for the sake of variation, we use the terms *evaluators* or *evaluation committees* instead. The actual programs themselves may label the selectors by yet other names, such as *admissions committee* or *graduate committee*.

People for whom this book is written are referred to mostly as *applicants* or, sometimes for the sake of variation, *candidates*. An *application essay* is a commonly requested written assignment, usually consisting of two or more typed pages, included with the application to a graduate program. Application essays that request a focus on the applicant's educational goals are often referred to as *statements of purpose*.

Referee refers to a person, typically a professor or practicum supervisor, who agrees to support an applicant by providing a letter of recommendation. *All-university* describes something that pertains to the entire campus, not just a specific degree program. For example, you will usually have to fill out an all-university application form (issued by the all-university Admissions Office) as well as a supplementary application form (issued by the department or program to which you apply).

The term *postapplication* simply means that a program's application deadline date has passed. The *preselection interview* takes place after applications have been processed and is used by some graduate programs to further evaluate applicants who appear promising. An *alternate* is an applicant who has been favorably reviewed by a selection committee but is not among the first tier of accepted candidates. As applicants who are ranked in the top group decline their offers, alternates are issued acceptance letters.

With this basic set of terms, we are armed to begin the graduate application process. That journey begins by assessing what you should do and when, which is the focus of the next chapter.

CHAPTER 2

WHAT SHOULD I BE DOING WHEN?

Having a long-range perspective with a clear sense of timing is the key to effective graduate school planning. Most graduate programs reject far more applicants than they accept, but you can greatly enhance your chances by doing the right things at the right time.

An ideal timetable can be devised easily, as we have done in this chapter. We understand that such a timetable may make you feel inadequately prepared at this point in your education. However, we provide suggestions for those who missed some of the steps. You can, to some extent, minimize certain shortcomings.

I am a first-semester senior already. I probably can't meet the requirements of an ideal timetable.

That is precisely the predicament. The ideal timetable is geared to the student who is just starting college and who has little else to do except prepare for graduate school. Needless to say, such a student probably does not exist!

This is not to say that a model timetable is useless to real students. The timetable provides a general set of activities, some of which are desirable, though not mandatory, placed in the most reasonable order. Thus, regardless of your status, we suggest that you review the ideal timetable carefully and check off everything that you have already accomplished. The closer the dates when applications are due, the more likely that compromises will be necessary. Shortcuts may have to be devised, but you should never use these if the option to do the task more thoroughly is still open. We describe how to do all of these things properly as well as how to cut corners when absolutely necessary, or how to compensate when some experiences are absent from your record altogether. Also, it is almost always acceptable to start anything you can handle earlier than the timetable suggests.

The ideal timetable is geared toward the student seeking entry into a competitive doctoral program. The items that are especially important for prospective doctoral students are marked with an asterisk. Applicants to master's programs may not have to comply with the marked items as early, as thoroughly, or even at all, although these could not help but strengthen a master's program application.

A number of the timetable items (e.g., B6, D5, and F4) describe activities that will greatly enhance your chances of finding the best program for you. Try not to shortchange these, because where you decide to do your graduate work will affect the rest of your working life. This decision deserves as much consideration as other monumental life decisions.

In chapter 3 we offer specialized information to students who are in unusual circumstances, such as a nonpsychology major who wishes to pursue graduate work in psychology or a person who has been out of school for quite a while and wants to return for graduate training. Although the model timetable may not work well for you if you fall into one of these categories, do look it over to get a feel for what is involved. No matter what your circumstances, you will need to go through many of the same procedures when you are ready to apply to graduate programs. The same is true for those who are currently in master's programs and will apply to doctoral programs. Many of the following items will apply to you, especially those items starting under the heading Summer Between Junior and Senior Years.

The Ideal Timetable for Undergraduates

A. Freshman Year Through First Term of Sophomore Year

___1. Concentrate on taking your institution's required general core courses. (Do not shy away, now or in the future, from mathematics, statistics, and science courses.*)

___2. Take any lower division required courses in your major (such as the introductory course sequence or a prerequisite statistics course). Do not load up on lower division electives in your major. (See chap. 7 for course selection strategies.)

___3. Work very hard for good grades in all of your classes, and keep up the effort. It is very difficult to pull up your GPA after getting off to a bad start. (See chap. 14 for a discussion of grades and how to proceed if your record is not strong.)

___4. Be thoroughly aware of the required course sequence for your major and map it out tentatively, perhaps with the aid of an academic advisor. (Plan to concentrate on the major requirements during your junior year, for reasons described in chap. 7.*)

___5. Learn to use the full resources available in the library, especially scholarly periodicals, computerized information search-and-retrieval systems, and the Internet. Develop a habit of looking through the major journals in your area (e.g., *The American Psychologist* or *Psychological Science*). You may have to struggle with some of the content, but you will be exposed to some new ideas and begin to feel more comfortable with the professional level of your chosen field.

___6. Seek out advisement, career counseling, and other services available on your campus.

___7. Start what should become a regular habit of attending events sponsored by your major department, such as social gatherings and talks by invited guest speakers. Do not worry if you do not yet feel like a department insider. That feeling will come a little later, after your professors see you around the department and know that you are a dedicated, committed student. (See chap. 6 for the rationale for becoming visible and active within your department.)

___8. Check the departmental bulletin boards routinely, seeking out special opportunities and information you can use.

___9. Find out what information and services are provided by your department regarding graduate study in your field. If your department has a web page, carefully examine it. (See Appendix B for a list of the resources to which we are referring.)

___10. If you qualify, participate in a departmental or campus-wide honors program.

B. Second Term of Sophomore Year

___1. If permitted, take a required upper division course or two in your major. Finish up as many core courses required by your institution as possible. If permitted, and if you think you are ready, take the required research methods course. The better your knowledge base in research methods, the more success you will have in other advanced courses.

___2. Find out about student clubs, organizations, and honor societies in your major (e.g., Psi Chi in psychology; Phi Alpha and Student Social Work Association in social work). Plan to join as soon as you meet their admission requirements (see chap. 9).

___3. Learn as much as you can about the faculty in your department. What are their scholarly interests and research areas? What courses do they usually teach? Get to know one or more highly successful and serious students who are already juniors or seniors and learn from them what you can about the department and its faculty.

___4. Start a file in which you put notes regarding activities or accomplishments that you might be able to use on your résumé or vita (described in Appendix A), announcements about graduate school or volunteer opportunities that you run across, and so on.

Save articles by professionals in the field that fascinate you. (Who knows; you might want to study with one of these authors in a couple of years.) Save all of your term papers, course syllabi, and the catalog descriptions for all of your courses. This information could be very handy later on when you are asked for specifics about your academic background. It may also be a good idea to keep your textbooks from the core courses in your major. The few dollars you get from reselling them are worth less than their usefulness when you study for your GRE or write about your academic background in an application essay.

___5. Learn about any special professional meetings that you might be able to attend. Professional conventions or conferences in your field can be excellent and stimulating learning experiences for undergraduate students and often mark the beginning of feeling a professional identity. Try to attend two or three of these meetings over the next couple of years. Deliver your own paper or poster at one of them, if possible. Also watch for meetings specifically for undergraduate students. Undergraduate conferences provide less competitive opportunities for you to get your work accepted for a presentation or poster display. Such activities look very good on your record* (see chap. 9).

___6. Begin to do outside reading about the professions associated with your field and related fields (see chap. 5).

___7. Start a personal library consisting of solid text and reference works. Professors often give students their extra or unwanted books; watch for those opportunities.

C. Summer Between Sophomore and Junior Years

___1. If you still have required general core courses to take, consider taking one or more of them in summer school.*

___2. If you need to work, find a job that relates to your chosen field or that puts you in direct contact with a population with which you might wish to work later (e.g., children, the elderly, or chronically mentally ill persons). Pursue any opportunities for research-related work* (see chap. 8).

___3. Buy textbooks for your first-term courses of your junior year, if you know for certain what they are, and start reading early (see chap. 7).

___4. If you aspire to a career in human services, consider a volunteer placement for a few hours each week in a community agency (see chap. 8).

D. First Term of Junior Year

___1. Take any required upper division statistics course if you haven't already.*

___2. Take two or more other upper division courses required in your major and consider at least one impressive course from another department in an area in which you think you can do well (such as a philosophy of science or computer science course).* Do not save all of the difficult courses for your senior year (see chap. 7).

___3. Get to know one or more professors in your major. Around this time, they will see you as a more mature, serious student and will be more interested in you and your professional development (see chap. 6).

___4. Look for an opportunity to get research experience. If possible, engage in a project that could lead to authorship credit on a paper presentation or publication* (see chap. 8).

___5. Become familiar with the resources that describe graduate programs and their requirements as well as how to access the Internet for relevant information (see chap. 11).

___6. Keep alert for opportunities to observe seniors filling out their application forms. Look over some of the materials they are processing. This will give you an idea of what you will be doing next fall.

___7. Begin to seriously consider focusing your interests in a particular program area (e.g., developmental, clinical, or social/personality psychology). Program choice issues are discussed in more detail throughout the book.

E. Second Term of Junior Year

___1. Continue with the required upper division courses in your major. Consider another impressive elective in another department.

___2. Continue to get to know professors in your major, thinking in terms of those who might be good sources of recommendation letters next fall. Be sure that these professors and other referees will not be away from campus next year. If so, see if they would be willing to write a general letter before they leave (see chap. 17).

___3. If appropriate, plan to take a second course in the fall from professors who are most aligned with your interest areas and who may be particularly good sources of letters of reference (see chap. 17).

___4. If you have not become involved in research, time is slipping away, especially if you hope to receive coauthorship on a conference presentation or publication. See if there is some research opportunity that you can become involved in now.

___5. Join a club or student organization related to your field if you have not done so already. Volunteer for activities (e.g., organizing a fundraiser, working on the membership committee), even if the work is tedious (e.g., helping out with mailings). Join one or two other professional organizations (such as APA or APS) as a student affiliate, if you qualify (see chap. 9).

___6. If you can, visit any campuses with graduate programs that inter-
    est you to get a sense of what they are like (see chaps. 12 and 15).

___7. Begin to learn about financial aid opportunities for graduate stu-
    dents if you will require outside support to attend graduate
    school (see chap. 13).

___8. Check with your campus registrar or assigned academic advisor
    to ensure that you are on the right path to graduate next spring.
    (You do not need any surprises during your senior year!)

___9. Create a first draft of a résumé or vita if you have not done so al-
    ready (see Appendix A).

___10. If your department has a senior honors program, see if you are el-
    igible for it. If so, enroll in it.

___11. Consider taking an advanced statistics course (or plan for it in
    the fall.) For traditional programs (including traditional clinical
    psychology programs), passing an advanced statistics course
    with at least a *B* is very impressive to graduate school selection
    committees.

F. Summer Between Junior and Senior Years

___1. If possible, do not work full-time at an outside job unless it pro-
    vides research or other highly valued experience relevant to grad-
    uate programs. You should spend several hours a week on the fol-
    lowing tasks as well as any ongoing involvement in research that
    you have already started.*

___2. Visit any campuses with graduate programs of interest to you, if
    possible. Under certain circumstances, you may wish to commu-
    nicate with specific faculty members in graduate programs of
    particular interest to you (see chap. 15).

___3. Study consistently and diligently for the GRE* (see chap. 10).

___4. Research graduate programs in depth* (see chap. 11).

___5. Download information from the Internet regarding programs
    that interest you. Request information and an application if these
    materials are unavailable on the Internet (see chap. 15).

___6. If required for the types of programs that interest you, schedule
    yourself to take the GRE (ideally) in September or October* (see
    chap. 10).

___7. Start creating your notes for application essays and statements of
    purpose* (see chap. 19).

___8. Line up the financial resources required to apply to graduate
    school (see chap. 16).

___9. Continue updating your résumé or vita (see Appendix A).

G. First Term of Senior Year: September–November

___1. Take a slightly lighter load than usual if the bulk of the applica-
    tions you will be filing have late December through February

deadlines. However, take at least two basic, required core courses in your major* (see chap. 10).

___2.   Complete any tasks from the summer list that you could not finish.

___3.   Take advantage of any services offered by your department or
university to help students fill out applications to graduate
school, such as a workshop or graduate school counseling.

___4.   Apply for any independent financial awards or assistance, if you
qualify. See if financial assistance forms are due early for the programs that interest you (see chap. 13).

___5.   Continue studying for the GRE, and take it (ideally) in September
or October (December at the latest)* (see chap. 10).

___6.   Create any specialized materials to distribute to your referees (let-
ter writers) and begin asking for letters of reference (see chap. 17).

___7.   Organize all applications and program materials received (see
chap. 16).

___8.   Make final decisions about where you will actually apply (see
chap. 16).

___9.   Order transcripts at least 6 weeks before each application dead-
line date. Get an official copy—and make photocopies—of transcripts of all your college-level work to include, as an unofficial
exhibit, in your application packets (see chap. 16).

___10. Order test score reports at least 6 weeks before each application
deadline date. Photocopy your own test score reports to include
as unofficial exhibits with your applications (see chap. 16).

___11. Because you may be traveling later this winter for interviews, ob-
tain a flu vaccination now (these take several weeks to take effect). Impressing faculty at a prospective graduate program will
be difficult if you are physically ill (the travel and performance
anxiety are usually stressful enough).

H. End of First Term of Senior Year: December and Winter Holiday Break

___1.   If possible, visit any campuses you have not already seen, but do
so before the application deadline (see chap. 15).

___2.   Compose your essay statements and get feedback from others be-
fore finalizing (see chap. 19).

___3.   Fill out any applications due in December, January, and early
February. Also, complete those that are due later, if you can (see
chap. 18).

___4.   Mail out applications, 2 to 4 weeks before the deadline if possi-
ble, but by each program's stated deadline at the very latest (see
chap. 20).

___5.   Order transcripts for courses you have just now completed (if the
grades were not available in time to be sent with your earlier
transcripts).

I. Immediate Post-Winter Break and Early Spring Term of Senior Year

___ 1.   Fill out any remaining applications with end-of-February or later due dates.

___ 2.   It is acceptable now to take elective courses that are mostly for interest, although, of course, you must finish any outstanding requirements or any courses that you (and your referees) assured graduate school selection committees you would take prior to graduation.

___ 3.   Make sure that your referees sent their letters before the deadlines (see chap. 17).

___ 4.   Follow up to ensure that each application arrived and is complete (see chap. 21).

___ 5.   You will begin hearing news about your applications in late March through April for doctoral programs, perhaps a little later for master's programs (because they tend to have later deadlines). You may have to apply for loans at this point, depending on your financial situation and the outcome of your applications (see chaps. 13 and 21).

___ 6.   Plan to send official transcripts for spring-term classes to the program you will attend if these are required.

Modifications to Fit Realities

If you are well along in your education when you first lay eyes on this ideal timetable, some of these items will simply have to be sacrificed, some will have to be done more hastily than desirable, some will be done later than desirable, and some will require a great sacrifice of time and energy because they simply must be done properly. To enhance your chances as much as possible, however, start from where you are, try to mop up what you can from previous steps you missed, and move forward with the model as best you can. Some of the components of the ideal timetable are desirable but not essential, such as attending conventions or joining professional groups. Others, such as some research or relevant field experience, are so highly desirable that without them you may be a substantially less attractive candidate than those who have had such experiences, at least for most competitive doctoral programs.

You may realize that you have cut things too closely with regard to time and that the possibility of doing a credible job with applications is virtually nil. If you are already well into your senior year and have not done any groundwork outlined in this timetable, taking an extra year to build experience and to consider choices carefully may be far preferable to frantic actions or settling for less desirable options. In this case, we suggest reading the rest of the book now and then reflecting on your situation. The best course for you will probably emerge.

CHAPTER 3

WHAT ABOUT MY PARTICULAR SITUATION?

This chapter is for students who are not stereotypical undergraduates or who are members of groups that require some special comment. If you changed majors late in your college career, or intend to shift to a different field for graduate study, or are currently enrolled in graduate school but hope to switch programs, or earned an advanced degree but wish to return to graduate school to specialize in another area, or are seeking part-time graduate training, portions of this chapter will be relevant to you. We also discuss selected student groups based on other criteria—namely, nontraditional students, women, ethnic minorities, homosexual and bisexual individuals, students with disabilities, and foreign-born and international students.

Before we delve into special circumstances, however, let us stress that graduate program selection committees will look, first and foremost, for evidence that the applicant can complete the program and has promise for contributing to the profession. All applicants, regardless of circumstance, must meet these criteria.

Late-Change Majors

You may be among the many students who did not decide on a particular major until their junior (or even senior) year. This need not necessarily prevent you from graduating as planned and entering graduate school the following fall. The main problem is that you may not be perceived of as "fully ripened" because you will take most of the courses in your major study area during your senior year, and the graduate program selection committees will evaluate applications before you have completed a number of the critical core courses. For example, for psychology majors the list of courses would include statistics, social psychology, abnormal psychology, and research methods.

Some majors complement graduate study in a related area. For example, if you were working toward a degree in biology or statistics but decided to change your major to psychology, and you are seeking a biopsychology or quantitative psychology program, evaluators may well view your applications competitively even though you have not completed many psychology courses by the time applications are due. Generally, those with strong science backgrounds will be competitive applicants to experimentally oriented graduate programs.

What about "late-change psychology majors" and clinical psychology programs?

Being a psychology major, per se, is apparently more important to evaluators in clinical and other applied psychology programs than to evaluators in experimentally oriented programs. This means that if you have completed very few psychology courses, you may not yet be a competitive candidate for clinical, counseling, and related psychology programs. The application materials frequently indicate the core courses that applicants are expected to have completed.

Should I even bother to apply to a clinical psychology program if I haven't completed many psychology courses yet?

We do not want to discourage anyone from trying. Late-change students, however, must prepare for the possibility of an unsuccessful application the first time around (i.e., for applications sent out during the winter of their senior year) unless they have taken some core courses and their records are very strong. However, if you do not get into a program and you are willing to try again the following year, you can erase the deficit and build up assets and experiences that can strengthen your position. By the time you apply the following year, you will have finished all of your course work in the major, but your typical competitors will still have some courses to take. You may also be able to use that extra time to accrue the kinds of additional experiences described throughout this book (especially see chaps. 4, 8, 9, and 10). We have known many late-change psychology majors who were not accepted into any graduate programs during their first eligible application period and then were accepted to most of them the following year!

Shifting From One's Major Into a Different Field for Graduate Study

Graduate program materials often explicitly indicate a preference for students who have completed undergraduate majors in that field. However, those same materials almost always express a willingness to consider students from other majors on an individual basis. What is important is that the undergraduate major provides sound preparation for the newly chosen field of study.

I'm interested in graduate programs in psychology. What kind of background in a nonpsychology major could qualify me for a psychology graduate program?

Nonpsychology majors with a chance of acceptance into psychology graduate programs have typically taken several of the core courses in psychology. These include the introductory course, a statistics and research design course, and some of the primary topic area courses such as physiological, abnormal, social, developmental, or cognitive psychology. It is best if a couple of these courses involve a laboratory experience. Some programs specifically mention the desirability of a course in history and systems of psychology.

The more popular or "softer" psychology courses, such as Personal Adjustment, Human Sexual Behavior, or Personality Evaluations of Great Characters in Literature, will not substitute for the basic course requirements, no matter how many of these electives you have taken or how well you did in them. As a nonpsychology major, you may have to undertake an extra postbaccalaureate period of study to remedy the major deficits in your academic background. Sometimes, however, a provisional acceptance is offered that will allow you to make up the missing undergraduate course work at the graduate institution.

Are there ever exceptions to the requirement of taking most of the core psychology courses first?

Such exceptions, though rare, do exist because each applicant is evaluated individually. For example, an applicant to a physiological psychology program with only a couple of psychology courses, but who majored in biology and earned an excellent record of academic achievements in that department, could be excused from the prerequisites or allowed to make them up while enrolled in the graduate program. In fact, one student we know entered a highly competitive experimental psychology graduate program having taken no psychology courses! His computer science background and experience, coupled with extraordinary GRE scores (including his near-perfect score on the psychology subject test), were obviously persuasive to evaluators.

Most of the material in this book will be informative and directly useful for nonpsychology majors who aspire to graduate training in psychology or a related field. We strongly suggest that you read the parts that appear, at first glance, to be irrelevant if only to learn about the more typical student with whom you will be competing. This may help you formulate strategies to show how similar you are to psychology majors. It may also help you illustrate how your contrasting background could enrich both yourself and the program you hope to enter.

Students With a Degree
in an Unrelated Field

Students who already have degrees in fields that are far removed from the graduate programs to which they are applying are in a similar position to the late-change and different major groups previously discussed. If your degree is in, say, music or English literature, and you took very few courses in areas relevant to your newly chosen field, you will probably have to prove your capabilities in that field. This usually involves taking some undergraduate prerequisite courses as a postbaccalaureate student. The closer your record is to the background competencies required by the program you wish to enter, the fewer additional courses you will have to take. Strong students whose work suggests an extremely strong probability of success in graduate school may not be required to make up any course work.

Students with master's or other advanced degrees in unrelated fields face the same dilemmas as the other groups previously discussed. However, you will often have additional questions about whether any of your previous graduate-level work will count toward the requirements for your next degree. If you have been away from school for a time, you may also face some of the dilemmas of the reentry student described later.

Students who have already earned advanced degrees in another field are looked at separately because they simply do not resemble the typical candidate. It is impossible, then, to predict how you and your record will be evaluated. Evidence of past success in graduate work is a reasonably good prediction of potential for success in graduate school, but be prepared to explain your reasons for changing your interests. You will need to allay evaluators' concerns that you are unclear about your goals or become easily dissatisfied.

Students Already in Graduate School
Who Are Seeking to Switch Programs

Some students who start a graduate program fully intending to complete it decide to leave midstream. Reasons range from a desire to relocate for the sake of a personal relationship, homesickness, the student's needs not being met by the program, or personality or other types of conflicts with faculty or other students.

Wanting to switch programs creates an awkward situation, regardless of the reason, because you are stuck in the middle of a pipeline. Sometimes students in the initial stages of a doctoral program can complete the requirements for a master's degree before moving on. If you are in this predicament, the best advice is to be honest about your situation with the new schools to which you are applying. Refrain from criticizing your current institution and its faculty, however, because that will make you appear potentially difficult or whiny. There are ways to indicate that your needs are not being met without being disparaging.

It is quite probable that the selection team members at the schools to which you are applying will contact someone in your current program, even if you do not list any of them as references. It is probably more difficult for you to switch programs if there was some sort of trouble in the previous setting than if your emerging needs would be better fulfilled by another program or by relocation. If your current program presents problematic issues, you may wish to offer the name of a faculty member sympathetic to your position.

Students Seeking Part-Time Graduate Study

Although most doctoral programs do not accept part-time students (sometimes referred to as limited-load students), a substantial minority of students enrolled in graduate psychology departments are part-timers. An even greater proportion of master's students attend school part-time, most of whom are women and are students enrolled in practice-related programs.

Earning an advanced degree on a part-time basis certainly fills the needs of many people who might otherwise not have a chance to further their education. Drawbacks exist, however, and include the shortage of financial assistance available to part-time students and the lack of opportunity to connect fully with the graduate school experience. Most students who attend graduate school part-time do so for a specific reason, typically involving the need to work or care for a family.

What if I simply can't afford to be a full-time student?

Some part-time students would prefer to be full-time students but cannot because they need to work. If this is the case, consider taking out student loans so that you can attend school full-time. If, when you earn your degree, there are jobs available that pay twice as much as you are earning now, and if full-time study would cut your time-to-degree to less than half, you may lose money by going to school part-time! (See also chap. 13.)

Reentry Students

College classrooms today are no longer exclusively populated with shiny 18- to 22-year-old faces; the rate of reentry students continues to increase. The reentry student population is a varied one, which is especially enriching to those of us who teach. Some reentry students are seeking a career change, a phenomenon that is likely to increase as people feel able to admit job burnout or a poor original career choice. Some reentry students already have earned degrees in one field and seek additional advanced degrees. Others were not able, for whatever reason, to continue their educations earlier in their lives.

Common feelings that can plague returning students include a self-defeating sense of urgency and low self-confidence. Reentry students, many of whom have little interest in the social and other trappings of campus life, are typically more focused on the end product—their education and its associated degree—and would like to get there as soon as possible. They may load up with more courses than they can handle despite having heavy family or job responsibilities as well. Others may worry that they cannot compete with newly minted college graduates.

Sometimes reentry students buy into the old saying, "You can't teach an old dog new tricks." This is usually fallacious, as any of us who regularly teach reentry students can attest. Consider two former students we know: One completed a doctoral degree at a major university while she had six children at home, the youngest a toddler. Another student received her PhD at the age of 63. Keep these stories in mind!

Working with reentry students can be rewarding for faculty because the broader experience that comes with a longer time spent on this planet often allows these students to absorb and integrate information more easily and deeply. However, although reentry students may have an advantage over their younger counterparts when it comes to life experience and verbal and reading skills, they are often at a disadvantage in quantitative skills (perhaps because it has been longer since they were exposed to such course work as an undergraduate or high school student). The statistics courses required in many graduate programs can be intimidating, and the mere thought of surviving the Quantitative subtest of the GRE can be immobilizing (see chap. 10).

Reentry students who have been away from college for a while often face additional obstructions, such as course prerequisites that have only been offered in more recent years, limits placed on the age of accepted credits, and changes in graduation requirements. Finding appropriate persons to write letters of recommendation may be a problem, and it is unlikely that professors from the past, even if they are still alive and can be found, remember these students well enough to write effective letters. Grade inflation could make a 3.4 GPA appear unimpressive, although you may have been near the top of your graduating class in 1982. Finally, some selection committee members may be systematically biased against returning students.

Many returning students seek part-time training. Financial aid is usually restricted to full-time students, and the need to attend school part-time may preclude the option of entering a traditional or fully accredited program. Reentry students may be limited geographically, due to the occupation of an immediate family member or a commitment to maintain constancy in their children's lives, which narrows their choices even further. However, we know increasing numbers of families who carefully selected one spouse's program in a completely new locale that also offered the other spouse equal or better employment as well as a great place to resettle with kids. It is a notion worthy of a family discussion.

If you are a reentry student who is currently finishing your undergraduate work or making up prerequisites, virtually all of this book will be relevant as it stands. If you have been out of school for a while, you must first decide whether you want to attempt direct entry into a graduate program or whether you need to take a few courses to catch up. You may wish to consider graduate programs that will accept students provisionally until they make up prerequisites. If you are feeling very insecure (saying to yourself, "Psychology has changed so much since I went to college 18 years ago!"), remember that you can become far more comfortable on your own by reading a few recent textbooks. Even a good introductory psychology text—one of the harder-nosed ones written as an overview of the field as opposed to the flashier variety geared to attracting student interest—should bolster your self-confidence.

If you are geographically restricted, explore every option within driving distance, even if what little you know about a program seems uninteresting. When choosing a program, carefully review its time demands; do not forget fieldwork and internship hours. Families must often learn to accept an entirely new regime at home so that mom or dad can study. Relationships may have to be temporarily renegotiated in terms of scheduling and expectations.

What if the application requirements do not apply to me? Will I be discriminated against?

Some graduate programs—mostly at the master's level—actually cater to working students. In contrast, many other reentry students who were accepted into doctoral programs have reported that they had to try harder than their younger or more recently trained counterparts to convince selection committees they were sincere and worthy of consideration. Remember, however, that maturity is a valuable commodity in all fields.

Describe your situation completely to graduate program selection committees. They will want to know what you have done since leaving school and will be curious about your current situation. They will want to know if children or other responsibilities will interfere with your ability to participate effectively in their program. They will not likely ask you these kinds of questions directly because of a legitimate concern that they could later be accused of discrimination should you be denied admission. Their unspoken fears, however, may bias your application anyway unless you offer information that will alleviate their concerns. This is a double bind for sure, but you need to be aware of this reality.

Let the program representatives know that, despite some differences between you and the more typical applicant, you are a very serious student who is highly motivated and who has something valuable to offer. Any evidence that suggests you are stable and responsible—such as a long-held job or grown and successful children—will be helpful and deserves mention. Although letters from employers in jobs not related to your chosen graduate study area are not highly recommended for most applicants (see chap. 17), returning students who have enjoyed a lengthy and positive work history are exceptions. Such letters will describe who you are now, filling the gap between the present and any letters from faculty with whom you studied years earlier. You might also briefly mention any specialized skills, special recognitions, or honors that you have received, even though they are unrelated to the program to which you are applying. A record of achievement suggests that you will succeed as a student.

Respecialization Students

Sometimes those with master's degrees or doctorates in one field wish to train in another, closely allied discipline. The most frequent motivation is to make a career move into human services and, toward that goal, to seek additional training in a clinical, counseling, social work, or other applied psychology program.

Because respecialization applicants are processed very differently, we direct you to the training sites themselves (e.g., see http://www.apa.org/ed/respec.html for a list of APA-accredited doctoral programs in psychology offering respecialization opportunities). Respecialization is not often mentioned in the promotional and informational literature sent to prospective students, and this usually means that the program has no provision for—or interest in—taking on this type of advanced student. Sometimes programs will make exceptions on a case-by-case basis.

You may have to relocate geographically to gain competent retraining. Because many students have jobs, families, and community ties, this hurdle may be too high.

Applicant Categories Based on Nonacademic Characteristics

Cultural diversity is a much-discussed goal in higher education. Very simply speaking, this goal acknowledges that greater numbers of students who belong to certain groups—by virtue of their gender, age, ethnicity, sexual orientation, physical ability, country of origin, and so on—who have historically faced greater difficulties gaining entry into U.S. colleges and graduate programs should be better accommodated. Even though affirmative action has lost its previously powerful legal grounding, diversity appears to remain attractive.

This section provides a brief overview of some of the challenges that designated applicants should consider as they make their graduate school plans. By this point you probably have had several years of experience in higher educational institutions and have faced many special circumstances. Our presentation, then, focuses on issues more specific to graduate school.

Women

Much of the earlier writing about women and graduate school stressed how female socialization processes deflected women from academic accomplishment. Fortunately, the picture has changed dramatically in all fields. Currently, in the typical psychology graduate program, female students outnumber male students by a healthy margin.

The greater number of women enrolled in psychology graduate programs does not suggest, however, that female graduate school applicants finally "have it made." Indeed, women seeking entry into psychology graduate programs are currently placed in unusual dilemmas. For one, they are largely competing against each other, particularly for clinical and other practice-oriented programs, with the possibility that male applicants may be somewhat advantaged by being in the minority.

Furthermore, graduate faculties do not reflect the same gender composition of enrollments. The majority of graduate faculty members are men, and the female faculty members are usually at the lower ranks. Female graduate students may not always have sufficient access to mentors and influential role models.

Other more entrenched problems for women who aspire to graduate school persist. A major one is the conflict over how their personal and professional lives will be integrated. Women may set lower goals than they could actually achieve, or they might adopt what Lunneborg (1988) called the "until" orientation, which goes like this: "I will wait until I get married" or "I will work as a clinical social worker until I have kids." If you experience any of these dilemmas, and they are revealed to selection committees by you or your referees, your application may be downgraded. Graduate faculty members want to invest their energy in training people who will devote a significant amount of their time, over the course of a lifetime, to the field.

Assuming that you have every intention of establishing yourself firmly in the field, you may still face the burden of proving that you are a serious student who views your education and eventual career as priorities, especially if you are seeking entry into a competitive doctoral program. Although some lines of questioning legally cannot be asked (e.g., Are you going to get married and quit school? Will your young child take up too much of your time?), that does not mean, unfortunately, that such concerns do not cross anyone's mind. You may wish to address these stereotype-based fears.

If you visit the actual sites of the programs that interest you, try to ask current female graduate students about their experiences and the availability of mentors. Finally, we recommend a book titled *Educating the Majority: Women Challenge Tradition in Higher Education* (Pearson, Shavlik, & Touchton, 1989), which offers perspectives on many types of women students, such as those returning to school after a long delay, lesbians, and women of color. Also recommended is *Taking Women Seriously: Lessons and Legacies for Educating the Majority* (Tidball, Smith, Tidball, & Wolf-Wendel, 1998).

Ethnic Minority Members

There is a critical need for minority mental health service providers, school psychologists, and counselors. More ethnic minority professors are needed to provide role models for students, inspiring their entry into psychology and related fields. Accordingly, an applicant's ethnic minority status is often viewed by evaluators as a definite advantage. Most graduate programs express considerable interest in attracting minority students, and some programs make extensive recruitment efforts.

With all of this activity and interest, you would think that the numbers of minority graduate students in psychology and related fields would have escalated considerably over the last couple of decades. In fact, there has been only a small increase. Despite the seemingly sincere desire to recruit more ethnic minority applicants, the task is far more complicated than simply setting a welcome mat at the front door.

Ethnic minority students may be concerned about the effects of social isolation or identity maintenance once enrolled in a graduate program, whether they will be perceived as token minority students who were accepted because of their ethnic status, and whether racism—albeit, perhaps, subtly expressed—will cloud their paths. Not every ethnic minority group member is an expert on his or her own ethnic group, is similar to others with the same ethnic designation, is a civil rights activist, or aspires to specialize in research on, or service to, other ethnic minorities. Yet these stereotypes are too frequently assumed to be true.

If you are a member of an underrepresented ethnic group and a very strong student, you will likely be recruited and receive more than one good offer. You may want to check out the ethnic composition of the campus (e.g., What relevant chartered organizations exist? How many other graduate minority students are there? What is the minority student retention rate, and how does that compare to the nonminority retention rate?), the ethnic or cross-cultural relevance of the training program itself, and the number of minority faculty. A visit to the campus is strongly recommended so you can experience the ethos of the school and the surrounding community.

If you are currently an undergraduate student, we strongly encourage you to locate an advisor in your major department, if you have not already done so. This person does not have to be an ethnic minority group member but should be someone who is interested in students' career development and sensitive to ethnicity. Because undergraduate departments are encouraged to spur ethnic minorities to enter psychology and related fields, you will likely find someone willing to become involved with your educational planning.

You can obtain a list of ethnic minority faculty in psychology by contacting the APA Office of Ethnic Minority Affairs (American Psychological Association, Public Interest Directorate, 750 First St., NE, Washington, DC 20002-4242; telephone 202-336-5500). Applicants to psychology graduate programs may also contact the current Secretary of Division 45 of the APA (Psychological Study of Ethnic Minority Issues) as listed in the July issues of the *American Psychologist* (or see http://www.APA.org/about/division.html). If you are applying to clinical psychology or neuroscience programs, contact the Minority Fellowship Program, American Psychological Association, 750 First St., NE, Washington, DC 20002-4242 (telephone 202-336-6027).

Gay, Lesbian, and Bisexual Individuals

It is entirely reasonable for students to expect their graduate study environment to be socially and psychologically comfortable. Unfortunately, however, the prejudiced views of homosexuality within the public at large are frequently mirrored in the academic community. Gay, lesbian, and bisexual (GLB) applicants must make a difficult decision: "Do I assert who I am and risk nonacceptance, or do I indicate nothing now or in the future and risk living several years in the closet, possibly having to silently endure overtly expressed homophobic attitudes?"

Because GLB individuals are hardly a homogeneous group with regard to needs, circumstances, and the degree to which they have disclosed their sexual preferences, we offer you issues to contemplate rather than telling you what you should do. First, you may wish to see if the schools with programs of interest to you have a GLB Student Association or similar campus-chartered group. That would give you some inkling of the attitudinal climate. Programs in small communities, or very politically or religiously conservative communities, bear a closer look in terms of possible negative attitudes and limited social outlets.

Second, if any faculty members in your present department are openly lesbian, gay, or bisexual, and you would feel comfortable discussing the matter with them, you may gain some information about current programs known to be supportive as well as other helpful hints. After all, these people have already been where you want to go.

Fortunately, there are GLB faculty (Liddle, Kunkel, Kick, & Hauenstein, 1998) and graduate programs in psychology that provide a supportive learning environment. Contact the APA Public Interest Directorate to find out the latest information on such programs (American Psychological Association, Public Interest Directorate, 750 First St., NE, Washington, DC 20002-4242; telephone 202-336-5500). Applicants to psychology graduate programs may also be interested in contacting the current Secretary of Division 44 of the APA (The Society for the Psychological Study of Lesbian, Gay, and Bisexual Issues) as listed in the July issues of the *American Psychologist* (or see http://www.APA.org/about/division.html).

GLB applicants comprise the only minority group discussed here with an option to disclose—or not to disclose—their status on their applications or during interviews. For others, except those with certain types of physical disabilities that are not readily apparent, there is no feasible way or logical reason to conceal membership in a distinctive group. The status of invisible minority, however, places GLB graduate students in a number of dilemmas, often because the GLB culture remains unacknowledged (both in the curriculum as well as in their immediate social situation) by graduate training institutions.

One possibility to consider is that people are less discriminatory against someone they know personally before that person's sexuality is revealed than they are if they learn that someone is gay, lesbian, or bisexual but have not yet met him or her. Also be aware that if you had practicum or field experiences that were largely in agency placements serving GLB populations, or if you have conducted research that deals with homosexuality, members of the selection committee may make attributions about your sexual orientation (including incorrect ones for straight students interested in sexual orientation issues). Again, you must decide what you believe is right for you to reveal about yourself.

Students With Disabilities

The Rehabilitation Act of 1973, along with the subsequent Americans With Disabilities Act of 1990, mandated that postsecondary institutions receiving federal funds provide accommodations and services for a variety of persons with disabilities. These acts did not require affirmative action but specified that institutions shall remove both physical and attitudinal barriers that reduce the participation of students with disabilities in higher education programs and shall provide aids or make special accommodations to neutralize the effects of disabling conditions.

Graduate school applicants with a physical condition or disability are a difficult group about which to generalize because their needs vary widely in both level and type. Some will require only one form of accommodation, such as wheelchair access or extra time to take exams, to fully participate in graduate school. Others will have multiple needs or a need that requires highly specialized resources or personnel. Ignorance or lack of sensitivity among faculty and administrators may further compound the problems faced by students.

If you have a physical disability, contact the appropriate office at the schools that interest you about the available resources should you be admitted. Also peruse the schools' all-university graduate catalogs, which should describe special resources and programs for students with disabilities. The Office of Disabled Student Development (or some similar name) in your current college or university may also have resources as well as sound, specialized advice regarding graduate training ideas and issues. Contact the HEATH Resource Center for relevant information as well (HEATH Resource Center, American Council on Education, One Dupont Circle, NW, Suite 800, Washington, DC 20036-1193; telephone 800-544-3284). Applicants to psychology graduate programs may also contact the APA Public Interest Directorate (American Psychological Association, Public Interest Directorate, 750 First St., NE, Washington, DC 20002-4242; telephone 202-336-5500).

When you actually apply to graduate programs, state your specific study interest as clearly as you can. As we mentioned regarding ethnic minorities, people may simply assume that your goal is to specialize in research on, or service to, persons similar to yourself.

In our experience, the students with disabilities who have been accepted into competitive graduate programs often had relatively easy-to-manage disabilities that did not require complicated resources or large expenditures. The successful applicants whose conditions were more problematic tended to be among the top academic-performing group in their graduating classes. More effort needs to be directed toward creating options for talented students with disabling conditions that happen to require greater institutional accommodation.

Foreign-Born and International Students

The *foreign-born student*, for our purposes, is a U.S. citizen who grew up in another country and, therefore, has a different cultural and possibly linguistic background. *International students* are noncitizens who currently, or up until recently, resided in their homeland.

Foreign-born students, especially those who have been in this country for some time, will generally be evaluated similarly to applicants born and raised in the United States. The advantages of being foreign-born may include the ability to speak more than one language fluently and a unique background perspective to share in the statement of purpose. The main disadvantage, in our experience, may be trouble scoring competitively on the Verbal section of the GRE. Our advice is to clearly describe your language skills in the statement of purpose or cover letter. Mention the probable reasons for your less impressive GRE Verbal scores to your referees as well, because they are in an excellent position to attest to your current speaking and writing abilities.

One foreign-born student we knew spoke and wrote English extremely well. Even her research papers scored in the top range. However, her Verbal GRE was under 400. Her problem was the large words that people rarely use in conversation or general-purpose writing, although she was incorporating these words, slowly but surely, into her English vocabulary. She was, nevertheless, accepted into one of the nation's most competitive psychology doctoral programs.

International students infuse considerable richness into a program and, with the growing global consciousness and its implications for human behavior, psychology and related fields may begin to attract more international students. Graduate programs typically require students from non-English-speaking countries to take the Test of English as a Foreign Language (TOEFL, P.O. Box 6151, Princeton, NJ 08541-6151) or some similar measure of proficiency in English. Such applicants are typically not excused from taking the GRE, and, although selection criteria may be applied somewhat differently, one usually must meet competitive standards similar to those required of applicants from the United States.

Many international students are sponsored financially by their own governments. Financial support from conventional sources within the United States often stipulates that the recipient must be a U.S. citizen, must permanently reside in the state in which the program is located, or must meet other criteria that would exclude persons who are in the country temporarily. Many schools require international students to certify that financial support has been arranged for the duration of their graduate studies. Sources of financial assistance will often be in the form of a research or teaching assistantship paid from the graduate institution's own funds. In the case of teaching assistantships, the ability to speak

English well is important, because U.S.-born undergraduate students must be able to understand you.

The logistics of maneuvering through the U.S. Immigration Service and obtaining the proper student papers is beyond the scope of this book. However, it is important to start gathering information early. If you currently reside in your homeland, selection committees often must evaluate your application ahead of schedule because it can take many months to process you into the country.

Very early on, contact the office at each graduate school of interest to you that deals with international and exchange student programs. You may have many questions about the campus, available friendship or support groups or host families, the numbers of enrolled students from your geographical region, and so on. Also, many organizations, such as the National Association of Foreign Student Affairs (NAFSA, 1860 19th St., NW, Washington, DC 20009), offer substantial information and assistance, such as the *NAFSA Handbook*.

CHAPTER 4

WHAT ARE "THEY" LOOKING FOR?

What do graduate schools seek? The ideal student, seen through the eyes of graduate faculty, is gifted and creative, very bright and extremely motivated to learn, perfectly suited to the program, eager to actively pursue the lines of inquiry valued by the faculty, pleasant, responsible, and devoid of serious personal problems. Outstanding graduate students are visible in the department, work hard, have professional values compatible with those held in high esteem within the program, work closely with one or more faculty members, and validate the faculty's investment in training them. This perfect graduate student will complete the program on time and with distinction and then venture out into the world as a shining representative, bringing pride to the graduate training institution.

The truth is, of course, that most applicants are mere human beings rather than the stuff of which graduate faculties' fantasies are made. Still, selection committees attempt to attract the best students they possibly can. One problem is that the techniques used to identify promising students and to predict their success in the program and the profession are far from foolproof. Furthermore, not all programs can compete for the students they hope to attract.

The Primary Graduate Student Selection Criteria

Most graduate programs attract from 2 to 50 times more students than they can accept. Some programs are extremely competitive, meaning that they attract huge numbers of applicants with very strong records. Many others draw either fewer numbers or mostly students with more modest records. In any case, applicants who meet the minimum qualifications set by any program will almost always outnumber the slots reserved for first-year graduate students, especially in clinical psychology doctoral programs.

There is no one accepted method for sorting through the application materials to make initial decisions about the most promising applicants. Selection committees typically begin with some traditional criteria, usually grades (especially the last 2 years of undergraduate study) and test scores (usually the GRE). Letters of recommendation are the major sources of information used to supplement these numbers.

Some selection committees establish cutoff points, often based on some combination of GPA and GRE scores. This means that applicants who do not attain a certain minimum level are not considered further. Some programs rely heavily on statistical formulas and computer-generated predictions, each based on test scores, grades, and other numbers gleaned from ratings of the files, letters, and other information. Other selection committees believe that the numbers do not tell enough of the story and will consider applicants with lower test scores or mediocre grades if they have notable strengths in other areas. These programs often rely more heavily on human judgment, sometimes referred to in this context as clinical prediction.

The many difficulties with the definitions of the criteria, the validity and restricted range of the predictors used, the intricacies and foibles of human judgment generally and of individual selection committee members specifically, and methodological problems associated with pulling it all together are all well beyond the scope of this book. However, an overview of one dilemma—using GRE scores—will illustrate the problem.

It is easy to rank applicants according to GPA, but what does that really mean? We frequently hear students bemoan the apparent emphasis that graduate programs place on standardized test scores. Students commonly remark, "My standardized test scores aren't too hot, but I'm obviously a good student because I have a strong GPA." However, place yourself in the position of the members of a graduate selection committee faced with 100 applicants with high GPAs. These students came from a hundred different undergraduate institutions, taking thousands of courses of various sorts and levels of difficulty from hundreds of different professors who have different expectations and grading practices. How, then, can GPAs between applicants be compared?

How can I know the criteria before I apply?

Many program brochures, published directories, and Internet sites offer selection criteria in general terms, which we discuss more later. A wise strategy, however, is to apply the knowledge that we have accumulated—and that is presented throughout this book—and optimize your record in ways that virtually all programs will find attractive.

Second Order Selection Criteria

What happens after I have passed the initial evaluation?

Once the pool of applicants has been narrowed to those who meet the program's basic criteria, things become even less clear. Such ambiguity occurs whenever a group of human beings begin to deliberate under conditions where specific rules do not exist. It has been suggested that the process now becomes idiosyncratic. Those applicants who most strike the interest of one or more of the selection committee members may be invited to enroll in the program, the remaining applicants who seem especially good may be put on an alternate list (see chap. 24), and the rest will receive letters of regret.

This doesn't give me much to go on. Are there any hints as to how I can stand out in this process?

A few applicants will have such stellar credentials that it will be diffi-cult to pass them by. The majority of applicants who survive any cutoff procedure, however, require the application of some additional criteria to sort them out because they all look relatively similar and generally ac-ceptable. So, what do the selection committees do next to discriminate among applicants? Although committees will vary considerably, the fol-lowing list indicates the importance generally placed on various criteria. These rankings are based on previous surveys of faculty members in-volved in graduate selection (Bonifazi, Crespy, & Rieker, 1997; Keith-Spiegel, Tabachnick, & Spiegel, 1994). (The criteria are not presented in any particular order within each category.)

Very Important Criteria

- Degree to which the applicant's skills and interests match the pro-gram goals.
- Research experience resulting in a publication credit in a scholarly journal.
- Research experience resulting in a paper presentation at a profes-sional conference.
- Degree of interest expressed by one or more members of the selec-tion committee in working with a particular applicant.
- Clarity and focus of applicant's statement of purpose.

Generally Important Criteria

- Experience as a research assistant.
- Writing skills as revealed in the applicant's statement of purpose.

- Status and reputation of the applicant's referees (the people who wrote letters of recommendation).
- A strong, supportive mentor who actively advocates an applicant's candidacy.
- Degree to which the applicant is knowledgeable about and interested in the program.
- Underrepresented ethnic minority membership of applicant.
- Number of statistics/research methodology courses taken as an undergraduate.
- Number of harder science (e.g., biology, chemistry) courses taken as an undergraduate.
- Prestige and status of psychology faculty in applicant's undergraduate department.
- Prestige of applicant's undergraduate institution.
- Potential for success as judged by a preselection interview or some other personal contact.
- Honors or merit scholarships awarded to the applicant by the undergraduate institution.

Somewhat Important Criteria

- Area of undergraduate major (e.g., being a psychology major when applying to a graduate program in psychology).
- Field or volunteer experience relevant to the program.
- Social and personality style as revealed through preselection interview or other personal contact.
- Paid work experience relevant to the program.
- Neatness and professional look of application materials.
- Experience as a teaching assistant.
- Level of active participation in departmental activities (e.g., chair of the student colloquium committee).

Minimally Important or Not Important Criteria

- Student affiliate status in a relevant professional organization (e.g., APA, APS).
- Degree to which an applicant would help balance the gender ratio within a program or department.
- Membership in a student professional organization or honor society (e.g., Psi Chi).
- Multilingual capabilities (i.e., degree to which applicant is fluent in English as well as another language).
- Contribution to geographical diversity (i.e., degree to which an applicant from out of state has an advantage).

Although we caution against overemphasizing or misinterpreting these lists, there is much to learn from them. First, there are a number of criteria that virtually any applicant can successfully meet with a little planning and effort. These include choosing programs carefully to maximize the degree of fit between you and the programs to which you apply, taking the statement of purpose and other application essays very seriously, and submitting a professional-looking application package.

Second, for those with some time left before applying to graduate school, ideas for setting priorities most certainly emerge from the lists. Research experience jumps to the forefront. Also, the types of course work that are considered impressive should be seriously considered.

Finally, you have little or no control over some criteria. These include the prestige of your undergraduate institution and its faculty, your ethnicity, and your ability to speak another language. Do not dwell on what you cannot change. You can still succeed.

What do you mean about overemphasizing or misinterpreting these lists?

Don't become discouraged simply because you do not have a published article, because most other applicants do not have one either, even among those who are accepted to the top programs. Similarly, just because your undergraduate institution is not considered prestigious does not automatically mean that you will not be accepted to a top graduate program. Students enrolled in even the top graduate programs are not exclusively those who scored at the top in all criteria.

Generally, students in solid graduate programs are all talented, but such talent is revealed in different ways. Some students have very high GPAs and GRE scores. Others, some of whom had less impressive grades and test scores, have considerable research or field experience. A few have been involved in interesting or unusual projects as undergraduates. Selection committees, then, look for individuals who shine in some way, but no single applicant will be exemplary in every area.

You should also consider some of the lower ranked items carefully before deciding that pursuing them would not be worthwhile. For example, "active participation in departmental activities" and "teaching assistant experience" are not highly ranked, yet involvement in both activities is a great way to get to know professors, which, in turn, is the only way to get effective letters of recommendation. Some of the criteria may not have received high ranks, not because they are unimportant, but because they are common among applicants and therefore not useful in making final decisions. So not having some of these activities on your record could actually be somewhat of a liability.

Finally, a few of the rankings appear to contradict advice we give in other parts of this book. For example, we later encourage you to apply to schools away from your local area or state and to join a student organization such as Psi Chi, even though the data we just presented appear not to support these recommendations. This is because respondents to the survey upon which the preceding lists were based were asked to rate these items for a very narrow purpose. We imagine that virtually all the survey respondents would welcome out-of-state applicants and respect involvement in student organizations such as Psi Chi. However, these factors in and of themselves are not major ones in making final discriminations among qualified applicants.

Are there any differences in the final selection criteria for those applying to research-oriented as compared to clinical or other applied programs?

There are generally far more similarities than differences between research and applied graduate programs with regard to the qualities each seeks in prospective students. Differences that do exist are not large enough to be of much practical significance. However, as you would expect, research-oriented programs generally place more weight than do clinical or counseling programs on the prestige and status of the faculty at the applicant's undergraduate institution and on the number of science and statistics and methodology courses taken as an undergraduate. Clinical and counseling program representatives tend to place more weight on the applicant's active participation in departmental activities, relevant field and volunteer experience, and potential for success and personality and social style as judged by a preselection interview or some other personal contact with the applicant. No big surprises so far.

Perhaps less readily predictable is that clinical and counseling selection committee members also place more value on recruiting underrepresented minority group applicants, achieving gender balance, and gaining geographical diversity among students compared to nonclinical, research-oriented programs. Both types of programs, however, place high value on research experience, presentations at professional meetings, and publication credits in scholarly journals.

Less Tangible (But Significant) Criteria

Motivation and Commitment

If selection committees perceive that an applicant is not highly motivated to pursue graduate studies, he or she will probably be rejected in favor of other similarly qualified students who demonstrate a commitment to advanced training. Applicants who demonstrate their sincere motivation to work hard and achieve are greatly advantaged. As Williams (1989) related,

A friend of mine who used to read applications always said that he was relentless in his quest for passion, some evidence in the folder that there was a real, vital person with experiences and ideas and a commitment to learning. That's a good way to get accepted and, I may add, not a bad way to live either. (p. 63)

Similarly, Rosovsky (1990) said,

Who should be encouraged to seek a PhD? Talent to complete a particular curriculum is an obvious necessity, and only rarely a problem. Talent is no longer sufficient under present circumstances. We should also look for passion, preferably even an obsession with the proposed subject. We should be looking for young men and women who find it difficult to distinguish between work and pleasure when it comes to academic tasks. (pp. 150–151)

Passion is not usually the first word that comes to mind when you think of graduate school. Yet based on our survey of successful graduate students' answers to the question, "What was the major influence on your decision to pursue advanced work in your field?" passion is indeed apparent:

"I love school and the school environment. I love teaching."

"The puzzle-solving fun of research is powerful."

"I envisioned for myself a career in which I could empower people with knowledge about themselves."

"It's the only career that I am really fascinated by. I never seriously considered not going to graduate school."

The Concealed Agenda You Need to Understand

You may not yet realize, because you are so focused on your own needs for your future, that a large measure of your chances for acceptance into a competitive graduate program will be based on whether you appear capable of fulfilling the needs of others! Bloom and Bell (1979) described the ideal graduate student as one who "listened, learned, grew, and produced, which in turn made the faculty member feel worthwhile and rewarded for his/her investment and chosen occupation" (p. 231).

Because graduate faculties must be diverse enough to represent the breadth of the discipline within the department, any given faculty member may not have a single colleague in the department who is knowledgeable about, or interested in, his or her area of expertise. The remedy for such isolation and frustration is, of course, to attract students who will share an appetite for the professor's area. Much of the sharing is done in the form of collaborative research or scholarship, an activity that for many professors is a form of mental renewal.

In addition, research dissemination and scholarly productivity are the primary criteria by which faculty are evaluated and rewarded. Faculty members are retained, advanced, and given pay raises on the basis of their contributions to the field, most commonly in the form of publication in scholarly journals. Their status and feelings of personal worth are also heavily invested in their scholarly output and the resulting impact it has on their peers. You have probably heard of this phenomenon in the simplistic phrase, "publish or perish." Thus, for faculty, finding students who seem right for the program means much more than most applicants realize. It is not a matter of simply finding students who are intelligent enough to master the material; it is a matter of finding students who can work shoulder-to-shoulder to enhance the faculty's own productivity, reputation, and livelihood. As Rosovsky (1990) wrote,

> Faculty members consider the teaching and training of new generations of graduate students as their highest calling. They believe that working with graduate students maintains and develops their [own] professional skills more effectively than any other activity. It may be the main reason for the great attraction to academic jobs. (p. 137)

In the most competitive graduate programs, faculty members may themselves be judged largely by the size and quality of their graduate student followings. Thus, working with compatible students becomes even more essential to a professor's status and recognition. The faculty in less competitive programs and master's programs also want students who are inspiring to teach, who are eager to collaborate on research projects, and who will bring respect to their alma mater, even if these programs cannot always compete for the most impressive applicants.

If you were not previously aware of the needs and types of reinforcements that characterize a great many graduate-level faculty members, you now can better understand why a good match—the degree to which the graduate program and the student fit well together and serve each other's needs—is so important to graduate selection committees. Because the graduate faculty do not come to you, it is up to you to present yourself effectively to them. This is why it is vital to know a great deal about each program—and the makeup of each faculty—to which you are applying. In upcoming chapters we teach you how to obtain this information.

Ironically, the best way to ensure that you will be what "they" want is to know what you want. That way, you will apply to the programs most appropriate for you. In the next chapter we address your needs and how to clarify them.

CHAPTER 5

WHAT DO I WANT?

We concluded the previous chapter by suggesting that being aware of your agenda is indispensable to reaching your educational goals. Knowing what you want is every bit as important as making yourself attractive to graduate program selection committees. So, before you go any further with your graduate school plans, consider whether what you think you want is, in fact, what will best suit your educational needs and long-term goals. Taking time to ponder why you are willing to spend more years engaged in rigorous study and to clarify your eventual goal is well worth the effort now for two reasons. First, you are at a major crossroad. You are making a choice that will substantially affect what you do with most of your waking hours for most of the rest of your life. Second, graduate school evaluators also are interested in your answers to these questions and will look for them in your statement of purpose. How your life vision fits with what a program has to offer is an important component of the decision to be made about you.

Psychology and related fields are confusing. I sometimes feel like just pulling something out of a hat and keeping my fingers crossed.

We empathize with such feelings, so let's try to sort things out. If you are interested in studying behavior or working therapeutically with people, there are several options. Psychology and its kin are made up of a colorful array of topics and career options that seem to expand every year, resulting in confusion and frequent territorial disputes among the various related professions. Even within psychology, there is considerable internal conflict over how to present the various aspects of the field and how to best train people to represent each. All of these conditions affect you right now, in one way or another, though you may not be aware of it. We turn first to the different training orientations offered to those who wish to become doctoral-level psychologists. Afterward, we discuss other training options at the doctoral and then the master's level.

Training Models in Psychology

Professional psychology offers three basic training models: the *research scientist model*, the *scientist–practitioner model*, and the *professional (or practitioner, or scholar–practitioner) model*. Your knowledge of these terms and their relevance to graduate training could be extremely influential in determining which schools and programs you should consider. Unfortunately, the large majority of graduate-school-bound senior psychology majors do not understand the differences among the training models well enough to use them effectively in making graduate school decisions.

The *research scientist model*, historically the first to emerge, characterizes programs in the academic core areas such as experimental, social/personality, quantitative, physiological, and developmental psychology. As the name suggests, the focus is on training scholars who will contribute new knowledge to their specialty areas. These programs focus on the content of the specialty area as well as the development of research skills. These programs are typically described as area specializations (e.g., experimental or social) rather than as programs training you to perform a specific job function. Many graduates go into teaching at colleges and universities, consulting, or research for governmental agencies and corporations.

Some programs in clinical psychology also follow a research scientist model with an emphasis on training future researchers rather than mental health services providers. However, the more common training models in clinical psychology are the scientist–practitioner and professional models, which we describe next.

The *scientist–practitioner model*, affirmed in 1949 at the historic Training of Clinical Psychologists Conference in Boulder, Colorado, holds that clinical psychologists should be trained both as scientists qualified to do basic research and as practitioners competent to deliver psychological services. Scientist–practitioner training is often referred to as the "Boulder model."

Although this dual-track model was reconfirmed at other conferences, discontent began to surface. Practicing clinicians, on average, do little or no research. Increasingly, concern was expressed that the reservoir of knowledge was becoming so vast that students were not being trained thoroughly in either realm (research or practice) and that the research-oriented academics who were teaching the courses had little actual desire to train practitioners. Accordingly, some clinical psychology programs are dedicated to producing what we might refer to as *clinician scholars*, people who will conduct research rather than deliver human services directly.

If your goal is to become a practicing clinical psychologist, read the graduate program literature very carefully to avoid applying to clinical psychology programs that have little investment in training practitioners.

make sure to express an interest in research & teaching in your PS

Clinical-scholar programs tend to be very competitive, so if you indicate that your goal is to "help people" or "have a private practice," you will have wasted your time and application fees regardless of the strength of your record.

Another historic conference, held in 1973 in Vail, Colorado, determined that explicitly professional training programs could be justified, and that the PsyD (Doctor of Psychology) would be the proper degree to confer on graduates of such programs. Thus was born the *professional training model* (or "Vail model," as it is sometimes called). Although a few doctoral-level professional training programs had been established prior to the Vail conference, the concept was now officially validated and such programs began to proliferate. With an emphasis on training students to become direct providers of psychological services, the role of scientific training was modified to educate students to be consumers of research rather than producers of it. The faculty in schools adhering to the professional model of training became largely composed of practicing clinicians rather than clinician–scholars or scientist–practitioners, offering a different type of role model for students.

Professional training programs are currently located mostly in free-standing professional schools or in professional schools affiliated with universities, similar to the way that professional schools of dentistry, medicine, and law are affiliated with universities. Some professional training programs are in university psychology departments, and a few others are in medical schools, hospitals, consortiums, or theological seminaries. Although there are fewer professional model training sites than scientist–practitioner training sites, they produce a relatively larger share of practicing psychologists.

As you might imagine, these major training model shifts have not emerged without lively debate and considerable controversy, and they are far more complex than this brief summary suggests. Frequently, questions concerning quality control, particularly among free-standing professional schools (i.e., those unaffiliated with a university), arise because such autonomy invites the creation of "exotic fringe" institutions that threaten the credibility of the professional school movement. (We talk more about incompetent training programs this later in the chapter.)

Some applied psychology programs, such as industrial–organizational psychology, educational psychology, or other programs that train students to deliver mental health services directly to consumers, do not fit comfortably into any of the three models developed to address clinical training. To complicate things even more, a variety of interdisciplinary graduate programs combine two or more study areas or models, such as business psychology, forensic psychology, and health psychology. Finally, a few traditional psychology research areas have expanded such that some institutions offer applied programs, such as "law and psychology" and "applied social psychology," that emphasize both traditional research training and application of psychological principles to real-world problems.

Because the breadth and variety of service and applied programs are so wide, you need to ensure that programs of interest to you offer training that you can later use. Academic institutions are not necessarily responsible for making you marketable. Learn what kinds of jobs graduates from the program hold and what proportion of them have found degree-related employment. If you want to practice independently, does the degree lead to license eligibility? If so, what kind of license does it lead to, and is that license available in the state where you will live? The program staff should be able to respond to such inquiries to your satisfaction before you decide to apply to a particular program. (See chaps. 11, 15, and 22 for details on the search and interrogation phases of your graduate study pursuit.)

Most of my friends want to get into clinical psychology doctoral programs in well-known universities. The competition must be incredible!

Yes, it is. However, competition is most keen for scientist–practitioner programs in traditional university clinical psychology programs, some of which accept fewer than 1 of every 100 students who apply. Although this book aspires to help you become among those who stand out from the crowd, it is also important to explore whether another kind of program might be better for you. Let's take a closer look at what you are up against.

The vast majority of students who want to go to graduate school want to do clinical work, creating what has been called the "clinical bias" (Korn & Lewandowski, 1981). As a result, and given the competition, many good students are turned away. Feeling discouraged and rejected, they may drop their goals of working in the mental health system altogether. Had these students been properly guided, however, they might well have made valuable contributions to human welfare after earning graduate degrees through other types of programs.

Many students undervalue or are unaware of training opportunities in areas related to clinical psychology that will lead to vocations involving work similar to that of clinical psychologists. Typically these other types of training programs have more modest or service-oriented selection criteria and much higher acceptance rates. Furthermore, most students who want to practice psychology have little or no interest in conducting research, and this hurts their chances of acceptance into scientist–practitioner programs. Why, then, do so many students even consider subjecting themselves to several years of heavy and advanced involvement in an endeavor they find difficult, dull, or even dreadful? If you find yourself in this unpleasant situation, we strongly urge you to look into other options.

What are some other routes for those who want to provide human services but who are not interested in research?

You might want to consider professional psychology programs (as already described), school psychology, clinical social work, counseling psychology, marriage and family therapy, and even psychiatry. In addition, a number of other professional programs exist in various departments other than psychology (e.g., music therapy, art therapy, occupational therapy, vocational rehabilitation, substance abuse counseling). Next, we address many of these options according to the degree they require.

Doctorate Degrees

The most commonly awarded academic doctoral degree is the PhD (Doctor of Philosophy). The PhD has a long tradition in Western civilization and is awarded in many parts of the world as the mark of highest achievement in preparation for active scholarship and research. In contrast, the PsyD (Doctor of Psychology) is a professional degree. Professional degrees are awarded by programs that train students to perform specific applied techniques or job functions such as practicing psychotherapy. (These degrees compare roughly with a physician's MD, a dentist's DDS, or an attorney's JD.) The EdD (Doctor of Education) is another professional degree awarded by some educational or counseling psychology programs. Regardless of the type, doctoral degrees typically require 4 to 6 years of full-time study.

This PhD and PsyD distinction is puzzling. What is the difference?

First, do not assume that the PhD is less preferred because it is more about philosophy than psychology. The PhD is conferred in most academic disciplines. Most of your undergraduate professors, regardless of what department they are in, earned a PhD.

So, if I'm interested in becoming a practicing clinical psychologist, is my best choice a professional school program?

There are reports that, in the service-delivery job market, PsyDs are not disadvantaged compared to PhDs (Scheirer, 1983). Many believe that the PsyD will eventually establish itself as the appropriate credential for the practicing psychologist.

Psychology doctoral programs in professional schools typically enroll more students than do scientist–practitioner programs, and the chances of acceptance for qualified students are much higher (Mayne, Norcross, & Sayette, 1994). Practice-oriented students usually find the curriculum in these programs far more aligned with their goals than those of the traditional scientist–practitioner programs. Professional schools value applicants who have substantial backgrounds in psychology, including research experience, because such graduate programs expect their graduates to be highly knowledgeable consumers of the research literature. They also emphasize, however, the applicant's personal characteristics (such as maturity) and fieldwork training or professional experience. Because there is less emphasis on generating new research, students in professional school programs generally earn their degrees somewhat more quickly than their peers in traditional PhD programs. Also professional schools may not require a doctoral dissertation. All of this may be good news for students who want to become practicing psychologists.

Most of the professional schools affiliated with universities award the PsyD to their graduates. The freestanding professional schools, however, are more likely to award the PhD even though they are not affiliated with universities. Reasons why they appear to shy away from the PsyD are complicated and include a concern that because the PhD is a known entity, the introduction of yet another doctoral designation will confuse the public. Another concern is that the PsyD will be classified as a second-class degree or a watered-down version of a "real" doctorate. There are also potentially negative consequences to having a PsyD rather than a traditional PhD. Professional school graduates are at a distinct disadvantage should they apply for positions in research or academic settings. Whether this constitutes a detriment for you depends, of course, on your career goals. If you think you want a teaching career at the university level, we strongly recommend that you seek entry into a research scientist, clinical scholar, or scientist–practitioner program.

The flip side to the higher admission rates among PsyD and professional school programs compared to PhD programs is that the students, once enrolled, typically get less one to one attention from the faculty. Assistantships (which typically include tuition waiver and a stipend; see chap. 13) and other forms of aid in PsyD and professional school programs are the rare exception rather than the rule (Mayne et al., 1994). In contrast, traditional PhD programs in clinical and counseling psychology often have small enough class sizes to ensure such financial support for most of their students. In summary, you may have an easier time getting into a PsyD program but are liable to have much larger classes and be responsible for paying the tuition and living expenses for 4 years.

How do counseling psychology programs differ from clinical psychology programs?

Historically, counseling psychology and clinical psychology differ on the basis of training students to work with those who have everyday living adjustment problems as opposed to those exhibiting more serious psychopathology, respectively. More recently, however, the distinction between the two fields has blurred. If a particular counseling psychology doctoral program and a particular clinical psychology doctoral program are both accredited by the APA, then each must contain certain core courses and training experiences. The degree of overlap between the two programs would be considerable.

Counseling programs are sometimes offered in departments other than psychology (e.g., education). In the end, however, the curricula and rigor may vary substantially among individual programs (whether clinical or counseling psychology), and you need to check each carefully to ensure that they offer competent training and qualify you to enter the career you desire.

What if I want to work clinically with children, adolescents, and their families?

Child clinical psychology programs are relatively rare and exceptionally competitive. School psychology or school counseling may, however, be viable career options for those who want to work with children (Minke & Brown, 1996). School psychologists typically work in school systems, focusing on learning and mental health problems among children and adolescents in that school system. As such, school psychologists consult with parents and teachers, in addition to individually testing and counseling children. The potential downside is that the setting in which school psychologists and school counselors work is typically limited to the school system. (Some states do allow for independent licensure that allows school psychologists to provide services independent of the school system.) If this is not a major concern for you, we encourage you to explore school psychology and school counseling as training options.

You mentioned psychiatry, but I don't see myself having what it takes to become a physician.

It may seem outlandish to suggest psychiatry as an alternative to traditional clinical psychology training, because many students view medical school as completely out of reach, requiring some specialized undergraduate premed preparation. Yet for those who have an interest and strength in the basic sciences, and who are willing to perhaps spend an extra year taking more undergraduate biology and chemistry courses, medical school deserves serious consideration. In fact, the odds of being admitted to medical school are greater than the odds of being admitted to competitive scientist–practitioner clinical psychology programs, and an undergraduate degree in psychology is acceptable for applying to medical school.

Psychiatry is simply one specialization within medicine, so psychiatrists earn a general medical degree (MD) before specializing in psychiatry. This specialization takes the form of a residency (a type of internship) that lasts 3 or 4 years after earning the MD. Students must typically take out loans to pay for medical school, but one's earnings as a psychiatrist are typically much higher than those of a psychologist. Other potential advantages of psychiatry include the ability to prescribe medications (although psychologists may achieve limited prescription privileges in the future) and perform inpatient treatment. Potential disadvantages include the emphasis on biomedical treatment at the possible neglect of psychotherapy.

Most of the options you've discussed so far have to do with mental health services. What about an academic or research career?

There are many options for teaching or conducting research in the psychological and social sciences. Examples include general *experimental psychology*, which emphasizes empirical research skills in general and application of those skills to a particular area of interest to the student. *Biopsychology* and *behavioral neuroscience* focus on the functioning of the brain and hormonal systems and may include laboratory work with humans or animals to investigate such topics as memory, learning, motivation, and neurological impairment. Specific emphasis on thought processes, including memory, language, perception, attention, and problem solving, describes *cognitive psychology*. Examining human experience within the context of the life span falls under the purview of *developmental psychology*. Those most interested in personality, attitude change, social and environmental influences on behavior, and dynamics within dyads and groups should investigate *social psychology* as a career option. *Industrial and organizational psychology* addresses the myriad issues surrounding individuals in the workplace. As mentioned earlier, clinician–scholar programs in *clinical psychology* prepare students to pursue careers in the empirical study of psychopathology and treatment.

In addition to these traditional disciplines within psychology, many relatively newer ones have emerged. These include *health psychology* and *behavioral medicine*, which emphasize the interface of psychology and physical health. Those working in *neuropsychology* are concerned with the functioning of the brain from a clinical perspective and often study individuals who have had brain injury or other sources of cognitive impairment. *Community psychology* involves consideration of environmental factors as they impact mental health, whereas *forensic psychology* focuses on human behavior and the law, including criminal behavior as well as factors influencing juror behavior. *Sport psychology* is, as the name implies, concerned with using psychological principles to achieve optimal performance during athletic activity and competition.

Although there are multiple facets of scientific psychology, the field by no means holds a monopoly on research concerning human behavior and experience. Scholars in sociology, family and consumer sciences, criminal justice, social work, and medicine also seek to better understand social and psychological phenomena. Although becoming a university professor and researcher in these areas almost invariably requires a doctoral degree, working in applied settings in these fields often requires only a master's degree, which we talk about next.

Master's Degrees

Master's degrees, which typically require 2 years of full-time study, generally indicate that the graduate has mastered a program in a particular field sufficiently to pursue quality projects in that field. Recently, the number of master's degrees awarded has increased at an even faster rate than the number of bachelor's degrees. The variety of master's degrees has proliferated so extensively that it is difficult to generalize about the level of achievement that students reach in them.

At the master's level, the two academic degrees are the MA (Master of Arts) and the MS (Master of Science). In addition, there are also professional degrees such as the MSW (Master of Social Work) and the MFT (Master of Family Therapy). Because there are numerous designations for professional master's degrees in fields related to psychology, no attempt will be made to sort through this alphabet soup. Rather, we stick primarily with the academic master's degrees because they are the types most commonly awarded by departments of psychology and allied fields (with the exception of the MSW).

My friend had a choice of going to either an MS program or an MA program. She chose the MS program because she says an MS has a higher status than an MA. Is that true?

Your friend chose her program for entirely the wrong reason! Whether to designate an academic master's degree an MS or MA is decided by the program or university. The early distinctions—separating engineering, agriculture, and sciences students from other disciplines—have largely disappeared on many campuses. Some MS programs in psychology or related fields are not scientifically oriented, and MA programs in psychology and related areas have nothing to do with the arts as we typically define the term. Many MA programs in psychology and related fields, on the other hand, are heavily quantitative or research oriented. In short, select your program based on what it has to offer you rather than on what the letters stand for.

What are the pros and cons of getting a master's degree?

There are advantages and disadvantages associated with choosing a terminal (or master's-only) degree program. You should consider all of these ramifications before deciding whether to apply to a master's program. Doctoral programs are not for everyone, and a master's degree for some purposes is a rational choice.

Master's degrees in psychology and related fields have a bad reputation in some quarters. Some even consider master's degrees to be consolation prizes for those who could not complete doctoral-level work or as half-step programs for those who could not qualify for doctoral programs. Some hold the concept of master's-level training in disfavor because the need for doctoral-level positions might be jeopardized and the image of psychology might be downgraded.

The belief that one who possesses a doctorate in psychology is the only true psychologist—a position supported by the APA, which asserts that the doctoral degree is the minimal requirement for the independent and unsupervised practice of psychology—has created a kind of second-class citizenship for those who terminated their advanced training at the master's level. These individuals are not offered full membership privileges in the APA or in most state psychological associations. Master's-level psychologists have been a politically controversial issue within the APA for years, resulting in curious historical cycles of fervent debate and activity followed by benign neglect; the result has been no significant or productive resolutions except for unspoken recognition that master's-level personnel are needed in some capacity.

Licensure qualifying individuals for independent practice as psychologists is not available to master's-only psychologists in most states. Master's-level psychologists have no well-established core identity within organized psychology. Therefore, many MA psychologists affiliate with other types of professional groups and some become licensed under other-than-psychology statutes, such as marriage and family counseling. As a group, master's-level psychologists earn less than do doctoral-level psychologists, and the salary ceiling is lower.

Having hit you first with the negative side of the master's level issue, we now offer you the more positive perspective. Most master's-level psychologists are gainfully employed in the field, are in increasing demand by mental health agencies, and perform many functions similar to those of their PhD counterparts. Many states have created licensing specifically for master's-level counselors, affording them a fair degree of autonomy in the mental health arena. In fact, some mental health centers only hire master's-level therapists because doing so is cost-effective.

Master's-level clinicians earn their degrees in a shorter amount of time, thus spending less for their education. Also, some are able to go to school part-time, which is a less viable option for doctoral students. Master's-level clinicians perform needed services, sometimes by taking jobs that doctoral-level psychologists would find unattractive. For some specialties, such as human factors and school psychology (as well as clinical social work), the entry-level positions are typically at the master's level.

Master's programs, then, are worth considering for students who do not have the time or interest to commit to a doctoral program, who have a focused career interest that is best satisfied by a master's program, or who have a strong motivation and flair for the field but do not have the academic strength to compete for doctoral programs.

What are my options with a master's degree in mental health fields?

Training in psychiatric or clinical social work (MSW degree) is an option many find particularly attractive. Compared to clinical or counseling psychology, odds of acceptance into programs are higher, time spent earning the degree is shorter (typically 2 years), training is applied in nature, and insurance reimbursement (a strong contribution to income) is available in more than two thirds of the states. Another advantage for many students is that GRE scores are not typically required for admission.

Finally, it is easy to locate a variety of graduate-level professional programs in departments with names such as Educational Psychology, Counselor Education, Child and Family Studies, Family and Consumer Science, Applied Human Ecology, Criminal Justice, Rehabilitation Counseling, Human Services, and so on. Each trains students to work in some aspect of counseling or the mental health system or with some particular client population.

Is it easy to get into a master's program?

Master's programs differ in competitiveness, just as doctoral programs do. However, most master's programs will only accept students who have attained sufficiently good grades (often a 3.0 GPA or higher) and who have demonstrated other strengths indicating that they are well-suited to the profession. Taking the GRE or other tests (see chap. 10) may be required or highly recommended. The application process for master's or doctoral programs is very similar.

The "Master's-First" Route
to the Doctoral Degree

What if I'm not sure about going on for a doctorate? Should I get a master's degree first and decide about the PhD or PsyD later?

Taking on a doctoral program is a major commitment. If you lack self-confidence, are unsure of your goals, feel you need a little more ripening time, or believe that your record can be significantly improved to make you a substantially more competitive doctoral program candidate, then getting a master's degree first might be right for you. Most master's programs, like doctoral programs, offer small classes and individualized instruction that allow students to mature both academically and personally. Such settings allow greater opportunity to stand out and earn stellar letters of recommendation. For those considering the PsyD, an additional advantage of earning a master's degree first is the potential cost savings. Because the typical student in a PsyD program is responsible for paying tuition, earning a master's degree in a program offering an assistantship and tuition waiver would save the student the cost of tuition had the student completed those same years of graduate work in a PsyD program.

Can I apply to a master's program at a school where I think I want to get a doctorate and then just transfer later?

That seemingly simple move is usually not possible. Many graduate programs offering the doctoral degree do not consider admitting students from their master's-only track. Even the boundaries within departments offering both terminal master's and doctoral degree programs are usually impenetrable. Students completing a master's degree in the program would still be required to apply to the doctoral program just as an outsider would.

Exceptions do occur, however, so check out the possibilities with the schools that interest you. We also know of a few students who entered terminal master's programs and eventually completed doctoral programs at that same institution, although sometimes in a different department. However, they needed to formally apply again and meet the qualifications set by the doctoral programs.

A related issue is being admitted to one program (e.g., social/personality psychology) within a department and then desiring to transfer to a different program (e.g., clinical psychology) within the same department. This attempted switch is typically frowned upon or expressly prohibited, no matter how sincere your attempt. Faculty in such cases are always leery that the student had such plans from the start and attempted to beat the system by applying to the less competitive program.

If I earned a master's degree at one university and was admitted to a doctoral program elsewhere, would any master's-level course credits transfer later so that I could earn a doctorate in a shorter amount of time than someone starting the doctoral program fresh from undergraduate school?

According to Hines' (1986) survey of directors from APA-accredited clinical psychology programs, some time can be saved in most programs, although 10% of the programs sampled allowed no course transfers. Some types of course credits, usually basic content requirements, were more likely to be transferred than others. Still, the doctoral program may require you to repeat particular clinical course work to ensure a comparable level of mastery with your new classmates who took all of their graduate work within the program. Whether your master's thesis project will fulfill an MA requirement in a doctoral program should be addressed with the head of the program. Your thesis completed elsewhere may be accepted without question, or a new committee at the PhD program may be convened to evaluate it.

Is there any prejudice against applicants to a doctoral program who have already earned a master's degree?

Typically, program directors today do not see the possession of a master's degree, per se, as affecting the individual's acceptance. Still, some programs may hold a negative bias against students who received the first half of their graduate training elsewhere. This may be less of an issue in PsyD programs because about one half of the students admitted have earned a master's degree previously (Mayne et al., 1994).

Earning a master's degree does not automatically make an applicant more or less attractive to doctoral programs. An applicant with a master's degree is still competing against very bright applicants with bachelor's degrees. If the applicant with a master's degree did not have the credentials to gain admittance to a doctoral program the first time around, that applicant will have to stand out with his or her master's work to be competitive as a doctoral applicant.

What could I do while in a master's program to increase my attractiveness to a doctoral program selection committee?

One might think that earning good grades in a master's program would be a sure ticket to admission into a doctoral program. However, the range in grades at the graduate level is usually quite narrow—virtually everyone gets As and Bs—making it difficult to discriminate among master's-degree holders on the basis of grades. So, your undergraduate grades are still considered important.

The mere possession of a master's degree is not what will make you an attractive doctoral program candidate. Rather, what you do with the time you are in a master's program will determine your acceptance in a doctoral program. At the same time, clinical practicum experience does not seem to be a heavily weighed factor for gaining admission to clinical psychology doctoral programs. Doctoral program evaluators appear more interested in getting a solid, academically trained master's student than one who is already versed in clinical techniques. Doctoral program faculty apparently prefer to take on that function themselves.

What, then, is important to focus on? The primary activity a master's student can undertake to be more attractive to doctoral selection committees is research and other forms of scholarly activity. Ideally, this involvement would culminate in presentations at professional conferences and publication in scholarly journals (see chaps. 4 and 8). Such research accomplishments are more important in gaining admission to a PhD program in clinical and counseling psychology than a PsyD program in clinical psychology. At the very least, however, such involvement allows you to strengthen research skills, demonstrate an interest in research, and develop working relationships with faculty who can then write strong letters of recommendation on your behalf (see chap. 17). Finally, keep the GRE requirements in mind and maximize opportunities to help you fare better on these tests the next time around (see chap. 10).

What is the best kind of master's program to select if my ultimate goal is to earn a doctoral degree?

Be sure that the master's program you choose will be an asset to your doctoral program application. Avoid master's-only programs that train you in how to practice a specific application (e.g., art therapy, marriage and family, or rehabilitation counseling), because their curricula do not provide an array of core subject and research courses. General experimental or clinical options with a research emphasis are your best bets. Even these programs differ with regard to the research productivity of the faculty. Because you will fare better with your doctoral-level application if you have research experience, make sure that some faculty in the master's program you choose are active researchers. Seek them out as soon as you arrive on campus.

Competent Training—No Matter What!

Regardless of what degree or training model you ultimately seek, you want to receive competent training by a recognized academic institution that offers a legitimate degree certificate. Professionals in mental health fields often have responsibilities that impact heavily on the lives of others, many of whom are exceptionally vulnerable. Shoddy or inept training could cause you, even inadvertently, to harm people.

Unfortunately, the United States is glutted with bogus "institutions" of higher learning that issue master's and doctoral "degrees" that are not worth the paper they are printed on and that can even get you into legal trouble if you attempt to use them as legitimate credentials. These outfits, often referred to as diploma mills (Bear & Bear, 1998; Stewart & Spille, 1988), are unconcerned with ethical standards or whom they might hurt and simply prey on people who are looking for shortcuts. Avoid these rip-offs as you would the plague.

How can I tell if an institution is bogus?

Watch for signs that you are dealing with a diploma mill rather than a legitimate graduate school. Bogus institutions typically offer no actual (or very little) classroom experiences. (This causes confusion when attempting to differentiate them from legitimate distance education programs.) The time between start and finish, as compared to similar programs in legitimate universities, is usually very short. "Backdating" of degrees is sometimes allowed, something a legitimate school would never offer. A rendition or photograph of the fancy diploma you will receive may appear in the promotional materials.

Many of these so-called schools have been in existence for only a short time because they have a way of changing names and locations, sometimes with legal authorities in close pursuit. Often there is a P.O. box but no physical facility. Some have names that are very similar to those of legitimate schools. Bogus institutions often try to come off as legitimate—or as in the process of achieving legitimacy—by using such phrases as "pursuing accreditation" or "licensed" or "state approved." The latter two phrases may merely refer to business licenses. As for pursuing accreditation, intentions can be announced indefinitely without ever actually applying to a legitimate accreditation agency, which, in the case of a bogus institution, would be an exercise in futility.

What signs should I look for instead?

The Council on Post-secondary Accreditation (COPA) publishes an annual directory entitled *Accredited Institutions in Post-secondary Education*. Although no institution in the United States is required to seek accreditation, most eligible institutions do so because of the many benefits associated with the status. Look up any institution that interests you if you are unsure of its accreditation status. If it does not appear in this book, do some independent checking before proceeding further. Ask questions and beware if the answers are evasive.

There are six recognized nongovernmental regional accreditation agencies (Middle States Association of Colleges and Schools, New England Association of Schools and Colleges, North Central Association of Colleges and Schools, Northwest Association of Schools and Colleges, Southern Association of Colleges and Schools, and Western Association of Schools and Colleges). Representatives of these agencies make on-site evaluations of applicant institutions to ensure that they meet minimum established quality standards and promote self-examination by requiring institutions to demonstrate their standards of excellence and quality. There are a few other recognized national accrediting agencies. Watch out, however, for the so-called accrediting agencies that bogus institutions have created for the purpose of accrediting themselves to further delude and confuse the public.

Some legitimate but nontraditional graduate training may have a couple of features in common with bogus institutions, such as no-contact classes. However, legitimate nontraditional programs should have quality control and evaluation procedures and require considerable effort from students.

What is APA accreditation?

The recognized regional and national accrediting agencies evaluate the quality of entire institutions. The APA is a recognized national professional agency empowered to evaluate practice-oriented psychology programs to ensure that the educational criteria meet society's needs. APA is a private professional organization, and its accreditation is sought voluntarily. APA accredits graduate doctoral programs in clinical, counseling, school, and combined professional–scientific psychology.

To receive APA accreditation, certain criteria must be met, a site visit must confirm that the program meets APA standards, and quality must be maintained over time. The three levels of APA accreditation are *full*, *provisional* (criteria not all met currently but it appears they will be in the foreseeable future), and *probation* (when a previously accredited program appears not to be in current compliance with the accreditation criteria).

Programs in non-practice-related areas, such as experimental or social/personality psychology, are not part of the APA accreditation program. Notice that programs rather than departments are accredited. Therefore, it is possible for one practice-oriented program to receive APA accreditation and another practice-oriented program in the same department to be denied accreditation.

Graduation from an APA-accredited program generally carries more status, and some internship training sites and employers require or strongly prefer graduation from APA-accredited programs. Accordingly, admission to APA-accredited programs is more competitive than to non-APA-accredited programs.

Are there no APA-accredited master's programs?

APA does not accredit master's programs. Whether APA should accredit practice-oriented master's-only programs has generated some discussion, but no action has been taken.

Is APA accreditation the same as licensing?

No. Licensing is a state-by-state regulatory procedure, determining entry standards and definitions of practice required of psychologists engaged in unsupervised practice. Licensing involves certain degree and experience requirements, such as postdegree supervised hours and passing a written (and often an oral) exam. If you want to work as a psychologist, be very concerned if the word *psychology* is not in the title of your prospective graduate program, because graduation from such a program may not qualify you for licensure as a psychologist.

In all states it is illegal to offer services to the public under the title of *psychologist* unless you are licensed. States vary with regard to whether other mental health professionals are licensed, including master's-level clinicians or counselors. Before you apply to a particular program, find out if the career to which you aspire requires licensure and, if so, make sure that whatever program you enter will allow you to be eligible for licensure. The mere possession of a graduate degree does not mean that you can qualify for licensure.

Licensing laws specify certain educational requirements. We, therefore, recommend that you send a request to the appropriate state examining boards for the laws regulating the license that interests you in the states where you think you might eventually work. You may have to contact more than one state government office because related professionals, such as school or educational psychologists, social workers, and family counselors, may be overseen by different regulatory agencies. What you need might be found on the Internet on the state government agency's web page.

Can I get licensed or get a job if I enter a program that is not APA-accredited?

If your educational institution and program of study meet the state's licensing criteria, you can become licensed to work in the field. Graduating from an APA-accredited program, however, practically guarantees that you meet the educational requirements for state licensure as a psychologist and greatly simplifies the application process.

What if I decide I want to be a professor or maybe do research. Do these careers require a license from the state?

No. Licensure is primarily aimed toward those who will autonomously offer direct mental health services to the public. Many doctoral-level psychologists, particularly those working in academic or research institutions, do not have to be licensed, nor is there necessarily any mechanism for them to become licensed in their specialty area.

If I want to be licensed, do I need to attend graduate school in the state in which I eventually wish to practice?

No, not if you want to be a clinical psychologist or a professional in most traditionally recognized professions related to psychology. You will need to get a license in each new state in which you practice, but you will usually qualify without going through any retraining. Once you have earned a license in one state, obtaining a license in a new location often involves completing the required paperwork. However, not all states offer reciprocity, especially if the educational requirements in the new state are more stringent.

Master's-level licensure is more ambiguous, and you will have to be much more careful here. If you are very unsure of where you will want to live for the rest of your working life, check out as thoroughly as you can now the potential uses of the degree you seek to pursue at this time. Speak with your academic advisor and other professionals. Although the degree you earn may be legitimate and highly respected, and you are counting on it to set you up in a private practice or a job that requires applicants to be either licensed or qualified for licensure in the state, you may learn that there is no relevant license for which you qualify. You may ask the staff of the master's programs to which you are applying about licensure requirements and careers that graduates can reasonably expect to enter upon completion of the degree. Asking the right questions early on can prevent disappointments later.

I heard about a graduate program in psychology that is conducted mostly over the Internet. What do you think of that?

Distance education of various sorts is becoming increasingly popular and will likely burgeon alongside the stunning innovation in technology. Although we believe that some types of subject matter can be adequately taught on-line, we are not convinced that the benefits of the close interactions and supervision that characterize live course work (not to mention the considerable professional socialization that takes place in less formal contexts) can be effectively duplicated. Whether degrees (or even individual courses) will even be acceptable to licensing boards or employers has yet to be proven. Thus, we urge considerable caution here.

Part II

Enhancing Your Chances—
For Those With Some Time

CHAPTER 6

HOW DO I GET HELP
FROM FACULTY?

It is important to find appropriate supporters to put in your corner, people who take a personal interest in your educational and career development. Although help can come from many sources, we focus on your instructors because they are usually the most effective advocates for graduate school applicants.

What kinds of students do undergraduate professors admire and encourage? In contrast, what kinds of student behavior do they dislike and discourage? Unfortunately, many of the negatively viewed behaviors are common and simple acts that students commit without even thinking. Be assured, however, that professors do see and remember them.

If you have some time left before applying to graduate school, and you do not already have a special relationship with a professor, advisor, or supervisor, you would be very wise to seek out one. Although students can and do get into good graduate programs without having mentors, those who have are substantially advantaged.

It seems to me that the main thing a professor can do to help students is to give good grades. So, if you study hard, isn't that all there is to it?

One of the biggest mistakes that students make is to see their educators solely as grade-dispensing devices. For graduate school aspirants, that grade you earn is not the most important potential benefit a professor may bestow upon you. Even the best performing student in the class may not always be a student whose graduate school application the professor would support.

What else can professors do to help?

Graduate school applicants must seek out people ("referees") who will submit letters of recommendation in favor of their application. Selection committees assume that professors are especially well-positioned to judge the applicant's suitability for graduate-level work.

Academic performance is certainly an important factor in assessing applicants, but so are a number of other considerations including social style, personality, motivation, responsibility, level of maturity, and ability to make sound judgments, to name only a few. Therefore, when professors agree to support your application, these letters will speak to much more than the number of points earned on tests and grades on assignments. After all, your letter grade in a particular course can be easily gleaned from your transcript.

Professors can also involve valued students in research activities, and such experiences greatly enhance the attractiveness of graduate school applicants to all types of programs, especially doctoral programs. Sometimes professors introduce students they value to others who can facilitate the students' goals. Or they may go out of their way to arrange some special opportunity such as a trip to a conference or relevant summer work. They also hire their best students as teaching assistants. Finally, professors can serve as priceless sources of information and encouragement. Most students we know who successfully applied to graduate programs credit at least one professor or an advisor with having given firm but gentle support, providing special learning activities, bolstering their confidence, discussing graduate program options, reading application essays, and being there whenever any question or snag arose.

Having a supportive relationship with a professor sounds great. What are some things students do that enhance or reduce their chances of gaining such support?

Before launching into some generalities about admired and disliked student characteristics, we note that professors evaluate students holistically. Their overall view of the student may offset a few irritating or unattractive behaviors or characteristics. Evaluations are also made in a context of previously established expectations that individual professors have of students in general. Evaluations of students are quite subjective, even though it has been assumed that professors can accurately integrate information from their numerous encounters with students.

Individual professors also vary widely in their tolerance for different behaviors. For example, based on discussions with our own colleagues, the issue of students bringing food or drink to class elicited opinions ranging from, "So long as they don't splash it all over the floor, it's okay with me" to "This is an academic setting, not a night club act, and I have no use for students who cannot tell the difference." We can, however, offer some fairly sturdy generalizations to students who would like to maximize their chances of attracting support.

Positive In-Class Behavior

What kinds of students do professors want to help get into graduate school?

Naturally, an intellectually gifted student will be supported, even one with some personality or other quirks as long as these are not too overbearing. Students with more modest abilities, however, can receive support from professors if they possess a number of other highly admired traits such as enthusiasm, motivation, industriousness, and commitment to academic and professional goals.

Professors admire or appreciate and, therefore, support students with the following behaviors, listed in descending order of their attractiveness ratings by the survey respondents: displaying interest in the course, offering good answers to the professors' questions during class discussions, remaining attentive during lecture, asking well-reasoned and well-formulated questions during class, rarely missing a class, helping other students by sharing lecture notes, and giving occasional compliments on a good lecture. These traits obviously form a portrait of an involved, motivated, appreciative, and dedicated student.

Students who disagree with a professor's opinion or lecture points are also somewhat advantaged if it is done respectfully and reveals that the student is thinking critically about the topic. Compare this to the low rating, cited subsequently, of the student who disagrees arrogantly or abrasively. Many professors apparently enjoy being taken on by students, just as long as it is done respectfully.

Is there anything else I can do to make a good impression in class?

Students who want to attract a professor's support should sit near the front of the class, as close to where the professor stands as possible. This way professors get very used to seeing you, and you become easier to remember. You also benefit by being able to hear clearly, being less distracted by other students, and thereby learning more. (Of course, because you are so visible, you want to ensure that your classroom demeanor is attentive, your dress appropriate, and your attendance consistent! Students often underestimate the extent to which faculty notice students' yawns and other signs of lack of interest.)

Serious students should never sit in the back of the class, because professors often hold a negative back-row bias. Many students seem to think that faculty cannot see what is going on back there, when, in fact, the majority can. The back row is often either in motion or dozing, and it seems as though students who are least interested and least capable in the class retreat to the rear.

Positive Out-of-Class Behavior

Students who elicit very high ratings are those who show up frequently to departmental colloquia (presentations) or other programs sponsored by the department, those who can always be counted on to help with departmental events, and those who are active in departmental clubs or honor societies (e.g., Psi Chi or a psychology club). Notice that these characteristics all involve visibility in the academic department. To be familiar to faculty, and to be seen as a student who gets involved with and is linked to the academic department, may pay off in more ways than most students realize.

Faculty like students who display enthusiasm, smile, and say "Hi" when they pass in the hall. Another admired out-of-class student behavior includes dropping by during office hours on occasion to discuss something from class that sparked an interest or seeking assistance with class material.

Positive Personal Characteristics

Highly admired or appreciated personal characteristics in students include a motivation to achieve, responsibility and dependability, professional and mature manners and attitudes, and likeability. Generally admired or appreciated personal traits include respectfulness toward faculty and cheeriness.

Remember not to discount your professors' teaching assistants as you ponder the findings we have presented. Positive as well as unflattering commentary often is passed from the teaching assistant to the supervising professor, and such input is not likely to be ignored.

Do you think that a student's grooming or fashion style influences professors' opinions?

Personal appearance is a powerful factor when it comes to making attributions about people, and professors are not completely exempt from this influence. Even if a professor agrees to write a supportive letter for a student who habitually wears extremely unusual attire or displays inadequate grooming, the graduate selection committee members will make their own assessment of the student's appearance. A friend of ours wrote a positive letter for a brilliant student who also had numerous piercings in her ears and on her face. Our colleague, however, did not mention the applicant's adornments in her letter. When a colleague from the school to which the young woman had been invited for an interview ran into our friend at a professional meeting, the colleague said, "You sent us a pin cushion! Why didn't you give us some warning?" The young woman was not accepted into that program.

Negative In-Class Behavior

Passing notes, talking to your neighbor, off-task behavior, and daydreaming are common in-class behaviors that weary high school teachers in public education systems may learn to tolerate, if only barely and not always gracefully. College instructors have different expectations, however, and such behaviors are not only annoying but are personally insulting, especially because no student is required to be enrolled in college. Professors have trained for years not just to be teachers but to be experts in a specialty area. A great deal of pride is invested in the information they impart. Thus, distracting or disruptive behaviors are interpreted as not only rude and immature but also as a message that prized knowledge is of little importance or so uninteresting that this student cannot even politely endure it for an hour.

Students sometimes say and do things that are almost amusing—although they have no intention of being funny—but that also ease them away from any future favor. Our personal favorite is, "I've been absent for 2 weeks; did I miss anything?" We always want to say, "No, I just stood up in front of class and ruffled my lips with my fingers waiting for you to come back." Fowler's (1985) collection of negative student behaviors includes placing blank sheets of paper after the title page, abstract, table of contents, and reference page to make a term paper look longer than it actually is; visiting the professor's office for the first time at the end of the semester, after receiving poor marks on exams, to ask for an opportunity to do extra credit; and asking, after an hour-long presentation on a topic not included in the required reading, "Is this going to be on the test?"

Are there data to show what professors don't like about students?

Our survey of undergraduate faculty revealed several extremely disliked in-class behaviors that would greatly reduce a student's chances of receiving future support. These included sleeping in class, lack of attention, talking to neighbors, sneering, eye-rolling, and reading a book or engaging in other off-task behaviors.

Coming to class late and frequently missing classes were also disliked behaviors. Some students seem not to realize that entering a classroom late diverts everyone's attention and may disrupt the professor's train of thought. The habitually late student, then, runs the risk of being resented.

Students who miss class frequently convey the message that they see the course as unimportant and, by implication, the professor as well. So, why should this student later become important to the professor? Other disliked in-class behaviors include leaving class early (without apparent reason), disagreeing with professors' opinions or points arrogantly and abrasively, making off-target or rambling points during class discussions, taking more than one makeup exam, handing in assignments late without a good reason, and never participating in class discussions.

Students who take an incomplete in a course for nonemergency reasons are also disadvantaged when it comes to attracting later support. In fact, students who ask for any short-term special consideration usually do not realize the potential long-term costs. Every professor knows that educational demands can put students under enormous pressure. They certainly understand why a stressed-out student would request an extension on an assignment date, ask to be excused from a quiz because of a fight with a close friend, or request putting off an exam because another one was scheduled on the same day. Many professors even comply with such requests without any academic penalty. However, students who ask for special favors more than once may reduce their chances for support later, because any pattern raises concerns that the student may not be able to cope with the demands and level of responsibility expected of graduate students.

Negative Out-of-Class Behavior

Other behaviors to definitely avoid include openly hostile or critical behavior toward the professor, giving compliments that the professor perceives to be manipulative, repeatedly dominating office-hour time with discussions of personal needs and problems, "nit-picking" over test questions after every exam, and unsolicited disclosure of personal problems. Other behaviors that professors slightly dislike include complaining about the fairness of tests and stopping professors in the hall for an extended discussion. (Remember, professors are usually in the hall because they are on their way to somewhere they need to be.)

Negative Personal Characteristics

The lowest rated personal characteristic in the survey of faculty was arrogance. Other student characteristics with low ratings were silliness and chronic depression. A student who requires considerable and structured direction to handle course material is also rated as less likely to receive future support, probably because such a student would not be expected to be capable of the independent thinking required of graduate work.

Our survey revealed very similar responses between male and female professors, except for one instance. Respondents were asked to rate how they viewed the "flirtatious and seductive" student. Although female professors rated such behavior as generally undesirable and disliked, male professors rated such behavior as extremely undesirable and disliked. We hear so much about the lecherous professor engaging in sexual harassment—almost always described as behavior perpetrated by male professors against their female students—we may forget that most male professors neither commit such acts nor are impressed when sexual harassment is directed toward them by students. One of the survey respondents revealed a slightly different spin on this finding when he wrote the following in the margin of our survey form:

> As a man I cannot tell you that such behavior does not pleasantly ignite my fantasy life just a little bit, but as a professional in the role of selecting serious students to recommend for jobs or graduate training, I do not view such behavior at all positively. And I certainly don't want to be known as the guy who recommends bimbos!

Thus, a sexualized approach to getting support from others is highly discouraged for a number of reasons, one being that it is very unlikely to work!

Mentors

One of the most important factors that could enhance an applicant's candidacy is a strong letter from a supportive mentor. The vast majority of successful applicants to the most competitive doctoral programs have at least one professor in their undergraduate institution who took a special interest in them. Conversely, those who are unsuccessful frequently lack a mentor.

What do you mean by mentor?

The term *mentor* is used here loosely to refer to an established professional in the student's general study area who facilitates the student's undergraduate accomplishments and the path to graduate school. Learning, advisement, and moral support are the main gifts bestowed by a mentor, although the mentor may also become a primary role model. The mentoring relationship is self-limiting because the student who is successfully mentored will leave upon completing the transition to another level. However, these relationships may persist and mature. Well-mentored undergraduate students often stay in touch with their professors.

Mentors come in different forms: They can be professors, advisors, or job, practicum, or research supervisors. The intensity of the relationship between student and mentor can range from structured and frequent meetings to infrequent or casual contacts. The more frequent the contact, the more active the relationship in terms of ongoing projects or shared interests. And, the more one-to-one time spent together, the more likely the mentor's influence will positively impact the student's graduate application process and outcome.

How should I find a mentor?

Motivated students who are visible in their academic departments, and who actively seek opportunities to work with professors, will usually find someone who is interested in a student–professor working relationship. Smaller, closer departments afford worthy undergraduate students more opportunities because outstanding students are easier to spot. Large, research-oriented departments with active graduate programs offer exceptional potential, but the undergraduate student must take the initiative to seek opportunities, because most faculty at research universities focus almost exclusively on their own graduate students. Large teaching universities are probably the most challenging of the mentor hunting grounds, especially if undergraduate classes are huge or a large percentage of undergraduate classes are taught by part-time (adjunct) faculty, most of whom usually do not get very involved with students outside of the classroom. Potential mentors will often have to be sought out, office by office. No matter what your situation, it is all right to take the initiative. This is viewed as a positive, can-do attitude.

If you present yourself around the department as wanting to get involved, committed to the field, and creatively competent, you may actually be approached by faculty members who want to be your mentor. If you have experience processing data, performing statistical analyses, or using certain computer software, you will be especially appealing to particular professors. Tell professors whom you know already that you are looking for opportunities to work closely with someone on a research project. If you are perceived as having good potential, the word will get around.

Think twice about soliciting the most congenial and popular professors in your department. Even though they may be easily approached, they may have more students flocking to them than they can possibly mentor effectively. Also, volunteer to work with a professor only if you have the time to commit. Being enthusiastic early on only to fall behind or drop out of a project prematurely will reflect more negatively on you than if you had not become involved at all.

Consider those faculty members—whomever they might be, and whether you are acquainted with them—whose interests at least roughly parallel yours and who are active researchers. Some professors are not well-known by students or may have a reputation of being difficult or un-approachable because they spend so much time in their laboratories or off-campus. Some professors may just be shy. However, such professors could be exactly the people who would be interested in collaborating with you and who could help you the most.

Show up during the office hours of a professor who might be a good mentor for you to ask a question or two about graduate school or your career interests. If the professor seems interested in discussing these matters, state your desire to gain some research or teaching assistant experience and inquire as to whether he or she has any openings or knows of anyone who might. Even if no pay is involved (it rarely is for under-graduates), carefully consider any encouraging response because the long-term payoff could be worth far more than the hourly undergraduate research assistant wage. (See chap. 8 for more information about research experience, how to obtain it, and the personal responsibilities such experiences require.)

I'm not sure if I'm the kind of student that would be of interest to professors. How can I know?

Our hunch is that students who are truly motivated to succeed usually gather the courage to hunt for someone who can help them. These students also have long-term vision and, therefore, do not get hung up with immediate gratification.

As an example, one of us (PKS) was once looking for a student to assist on a part-time and flexible basis with a small project over the summer. The requirements were stringent, but the available pay was minimum wage. The job did offer intangible rewards, such as research experience and a publication credit. Unstated but implicit in the arrangement was a letter of recommendation should all go extremely well. All 11 students who enthusiastically responded to a note on the bulletin board seemed to fully understand what was more valuable than money at that point in their lives. The ones who mentioned that they saw the note but did not apply were also the ones who would probably be passed by later. Comments from these students included, "I was thinking about applying, but the pay was too low" and "I would have applied if the job was during the school year, but I like my summers for recreation." Had they applied they would not have gotten the job because they would not have demonstrated the commitment and spirit necessary to do it well.

Think of your undergraduate experience not only as developing your intellectual capital but also as building relationships and an image of who you are that will, in turn, shape your future options. This will help to keep you connected and on track and sustain you through those times when you would rather put off an assignment or miss a class.

CHAPTER 7

WHAT CAN I DO ACADEMICALLY?

This chapter explores questions about the standing of your undergraduate institution in the eyes of graduate school selection committees and the importance placed on academic competence indicators such as your GPA, the quality of your performance on academic assignments, and specialized skills you have mastered. In addition, we look at the courses you should consider taking if you still have time and whether you should have a minor study area.

The Status of Your Undergraduate Training Institution

I guess that graduates from places like Stanford, Harvard, and Yale have a built-in edge when it comes to impressing graduate school evaluators.

They do attract attention and, if their academic records are also strong, they earn a very close look. Students who have studied in well-known and highly regarded departments (and this correlates positively with, but is not synonymous with, a prestigious campus) also have advantages.

The way a department stands out as special is almost always due to the visibility and respect accorded its faculty. Such status is achieved in academia largely through conducting research and disseminating it through well-regarded scholarly publications. Students in this kind of setting, then, have an opportunity to become involved with such people and their activities. As we suggested in the previous chapter, to work with and to be mentored by a respected, research-oriented faculty member are among the best predictors of gaining acceptance into a doctoral program (and that includes most traditional clinical and counseling psychology programs).

However, a degree from a prestigious college or university, in and of itself, does not automatically mean acceptance. If you are not in such an environment, don't become discouraged, because students who do have such opportunities may not necessarily use them effectively. Well-known faculty are often more interested in working with their current graduate students than in taking time to coach a less knowledgeable undergraduate or to risk the chance of errors that an inexperienced student is more likely to make. Only very skillful, dedicated, and persistent undergraduates are likely to exercise their advantaged situation fully. In addition, in chapter 8 we present ways to get quality research experiences that do not depend on having top-notch researchers at your school.

I'm at a small college that is not well known. Am I doomed when it comes to getting into graduate school?

You may have a dreadful image of the selection committee members asking each other, "Where's Maryhill College?" This concern largely can be eliminated by informing and educating them up front. In your personal statement (if it fits with what is asked, otherwise in a cover letter) you can share a little about Maryhill College and why it is special.

Help the reader evaluate what your transcript means. Your undergraduate experience may have involved small classes, allowing for considerable individual attention by caring and invested faculty. Or, your school may have a unique type of program that emphasized individual research projects or some other positive feature that would explain why you chose this school (and department) or benefited from it. Give the evaluators a mental picture of the place, enough to make them feel comfortable that your degree is indeed valuable. You may even send them a copy of your department's program from the catalog, even though this information is almost never requested.

Small religious schools may pose even more of a dilemma, because, in addition to the possible drawback of being relatively unknown, graduate selection committee members may be concerned that the course work was not scientifically rigorous. When an applicant we knew, despite her high grades and excellent GRE scores, was rejected from a doctoral program, the graduate program chair agreed to share the reason with her: "It's most likely because of that little place you come from. Do they teach any real psychology there?" She decided to work for a year (at a job unrelated to her academic field) and reapply. Her application and credentials were the same as for the previous year except for one thing: Her statement of purpose described the academic climate of her "little religious school" and the types of solid academic experiences she had there. She was accepted into the same program that had rejected her a year earlier and went on to earn her PhD with distinction.

Not all unknown schools are small. What about applicants from bigger but lesser known or less prestigious schools?

Applicants from larger colleges or universities that are not well-known or prestigious—a description that would fit many universities in state-funded systems not offering the doctorate—may face similar disadvantages, especially if applying to programs in another state. The same pains should be taken to inform evaluators about your university and department.

Lesser known undergraduate training institutions often have features that compensate for their obscurity among graduate program evaluators. Often the focus is on teaching undergraduates and on giving them an enriched, involved mode of training. Point this out, if applicable, because it can give you an advantage over applicants from prestigious schools with faculty who are not much interested in undergraduate training or undergraduate students.

If you are from smaller or lesser known schools, make your referees aware of the possible disadvantage you face during evaluation. Faculty who write letters of recommendation can add a few statements characterizing the department or the program (e.g., nature of the facilities, number of faculty and majors) to assure the reader that the applicant is coming from a legitimate, even if little-known, training setting.

My friend went to a 2-year community college. What effect will that have?

There may be a slight negative bias, according to our survey data, toward applicants who took their first 2 years at a community college. Fortunately, however, the effect appears to be quite small. In the end, what you have done rather than where you come from will make the greatest difference.

Getting Good Grades

In chapter 4 we noted that one's record of academic performance, as indicated by grades earned, is a major criterion used by graduate program selection committees. Therefore, a primary way to enhance your chances of acceptance into a graduate program is to do your best academic work. Not only will your GPA be higher, but other opportunities are likely to be made available if you do well academically. For example, professors typically invite only their best undergraduate students to become teaching or research assistants, and the effect of having that experience on your application is quite positive. If you can minimize the amount of time that you need to work at an outside job, particularly during your junior year and the first term of your senior year, you can devote more time and energy to your courses when the need is the greatest.

But that would mean I would have to live at home or have several roommates. I've been looking forward to getting my own apartment, even though I would have to work to pay the rent.

Reconsider your priorities. If you have nice enough parents (so they are a little overprotective) or roommates (so they aren't quite as neat as you are) and a quiet place to study, this will help your grades, and there will be plenty of time to live on your own a little later in life. Furthermore, many students who live alone find it relatively lonely.

My grades are only average, and I have only two more semesters before I have to apply. Am I in trouble?

Chapter 14 deals exclusively with strategies to consider if your grades are only fair. For now, do not give up. Use the time you have to show that you can do better. Even those graduating with a modest GPA are often rated favorably if their grades show a marked upward swing during the last 2 years.

I find it difficult to concentrate on my studies.

Any problem with undergraduate academic studies should be resolved now or you probably will not be successful in graduate school. Sometimes such problems just involve poor habits. Your campus counseling center or learning center may have programs to help with such academic difficulties as poor concentration, slow reading, procrastination, test performance anxiety, low self-image as a student, and lousy time management. Now is the time to take advantage of them.

What other deficits might I have that should be remedied?

Several other more common problems may apply to you. You should know how to use a computer, at the very least for word processing. You should be skilled at finding resources in the library and using computerized information sources (such as *Psychlit*). If you are a poor speller, you should make a considerable effort to improve. Finally, and this is the most difficult change to make, we have found that a number of bright students make basic grammatical errors in their writing and everyday speech. These are deeply rooted habits that will take some doing to alter, but the effort will be well worth it. A top student will lose many points if she says during an interview, "I had went there, but she don't know either."

What Courses to Take as an Undergraduate

Students often do not realize that to impress graduate school selection committees, it is important to take the right courses. Or, what students believe is the best selection is way off base.

Isn't my GPA more important than what courses I take?

The strategy of taking easier courses to beef up one's GPA is a big mistake. It is similar to crashing a party, only to be recognized quickly as someone who does not really belong there. Once graduate school evaluators have selected a candidate to review more closely, any attempts to elevate one's record with many lower division or "soft" elective classes will quickly be unmasked. The applicant with a lower GPA but who attempted more challenging courses will have a big advantage.

Easy courses get their reputation because they are elementary for almost everyone, thus precluding your chance to demonstrate that you are a serious scholar. This does not mean that you have to avoid every course that lacks rigor or interesting electives that you would enjoy. Just be sure that they are relatively infrequent entries on your transcript, or consider saving them until the last semester of your senior year.

I have already taken a number of courses that would probably be seen as "fluff." What can I do?

If you have time, be sure that your remaining courses are of the right sort. Consider summer school. If you must submit your applications within a couple of months, you have no remedy for this particular feature of your record. Focus on making a good impression in every other way over which you still have control. (If your graduate school applications should prove unsuccessful, and it appears that your inadequate course selection was a major factor, consider reapplying the following year after taking—and excelling in—a few harder nosed undergraduate courses as a postbaccalaureate student.)

What kinds of courses are considered impressive to selection committees?

Courses that cover a substantial body of knowledge and appear to have challenged you to think will be viewed more positively than courses that appear to have provided little more than an interesting experience or a general introduction to a topic. Evaluators favor scientific and mathematical/statistical courses, even for most clinical or applied programs. Professional schools also prefer students with solid content and methods courses.

Graduate program evaluators are impressed with no-nonsense psychology courses that teach students the fundamentals of theory and the science of behavior. Courses in statistics, cognition, learning, perception, physiological mechanisms regulating behavior, genetics, and research methodology are usually very highly regarded. For psychology applicants, basic survey courses in some of the more traditional specialty areas—such as social psychology, personality theory, and child development—as well as a course in history and systems in psychology are also advantageous. Laboratory course work experience is highly desirable, as is some field experience for those interested in applied or human service careers. (See chap. 8 for more detail on the value of field and practicum experiences.)

Should I take every single course that is offered in my department?

Selection committee members are not as impressed as you might think with students who took far more courses in their major than were required. These students may be seen as too narrowly focused. For example, the student who wants to be a counseling psychologist and attempts to prove his or her sincerity by taking every course related to how to counsel people may be disappointed by the minimal, or even counterproductive, impact of this strategy. For programs offering human service training, evaluators see the graduate level as the proper place to learn specific skills and techniques.

The primary goal of the undergraduate experience is to become educated in a general and well-rounded sense. Taking solid courses—ones in which you think you can perform reasonably well—from other departments is encouraged and often is preferable to simply stacking up more credits in your major. However, select courses that you are committed to completing. More than one or two *withdrawal* or *incomplete* designations on your transcript may detract from your candidacy, perhaps because leaving or not finishing courses on time may be interpreted to mean that you are not up to the program's intellectual demands, you are irresponsible, or you quit easily. You might find it useful to briefly explain any extraordinary circumstances in your application statement, such as a family death, that forced an incomplete or withdrawal.

What about waiting until my senior year to take the really difficult courses in my major? Is there any problem with that?

It seems to make sense to work up to the more difficult courses in an orderly fashion, saving the most challenging courses until the very end. Unfortunately, two realities interfere with this reasoning.

First, you will take the GRE during the first term of your senior year. If you are a psychology applicant, and unless you do considerable outside studying for the subject test, you may miss many questions because you have not yet taken the courses that cover this material. Also, you do not want to crunch your most difficult courses into the first term of your senior year, if you can avoid doing so, because you will need that time to prepare your applications. As one student suggested, "Think of filling out applications as a three-credit class or a part-time job."

Second, the selection committees will view transcripts listing courses you have already taken and will be interested both in your grades and in the courses you have chosen. That means that they will make their decisions before you have completed the last term of your senior year. (In fact, you may not have even completed the first term of your senior year, because some schools have application deadlines in early December!) How well you perform in any substantial courses you saved for your last semester will be an unknown variable for the graduate selection committee members, which will work against you.

Our advice (to those who still have time to follow it) is to take the bulk of your solid and the most difficult courses in your major during your junior year. Avoid taking more than two core courses for the first term of your senior year.

Should I have a minor, and if so, what minor should I choose?

Many students believe that taking one or more minor study sequences is a great way to enhance their chances of getting into graduate school. Sometimes earning a minor makes sense in terms of career goals. For example, an individual who wants to perform research for private industry might envision earning a master's degree in experimental psychology. Therefore, as an undergraduate, majoring in psychology with a minor in computer science or business would make sense. However, taking a minor just to have one on your record is not the most worthwhile use of your valuable time and resources. Having a minor that closely resembles your major makes very little sense (e.g., psychology major and counseling psychology minor). Our survey data do not indicate that completing a minor is particularly helpful. You would be better off using your electives to round out your education, perhaps taking solid courses in several departments outside your major.

Honors, Scholarships, and Awards

Take advantage of any opportunities available, and for which you can realistically compete, to receive honors, merit scholarships, or other awards. Aside from having something to put on an application line and aside from the inherent value in receiving recognition, honors and merit-based scholarships attained during your undergraduate years are quite attractive to selection committees. Even prominent high school achievements, such as a science fair prize, may at least slightly enhance your application to graduate school.

Awards are sometimes given without the recipients actively applying for them. Usually, however, one must apply for scholarships or other academic prizes. Many of these go unawarded each year simply because no one bothered to apply. For example, one year in our department only three students applied for a distinguished award that also carried a financial prize of $500. Although the three applicants were worthy enough candidates, there were many more of our students with even greater accomplishments who did not, for whatever reason, apply. Another student was the only applicant, and therefore the winner, of a monetary prize offered by a local family. Keep an eye out for these opportunities and apply if you think you have any chance of qualifying. You may be far more likely to win than you think! (See chap. 13 for more information about scholarships and other financial awards.)

Honors Programs

My university offers an honors sequence. I didn't think I was interested because I figured it just meant more work.

Many academic departments offer some sort of honors program, frequently involving a project to be carried out during the senior year or an honors course. The formats vary from small seminars to individual honors thesis projects. Involvement is typically by invitation or application, based on criteria developed by your department or your college or university. Sometimes a departmental honors program is linked to an all-school program.

If such a program is available to you, learn exactly what it takes to qualify. Should you receive an invitation, accept it. If you must apply, do so. Such involvement greatly enhances your attractiveness to graduate selection committees. Any project completed as part of the requirements for the honors program may also strengthen your graduate school application.

The Assigned Term Project: A Hidden Gold Mine

Unfortunately, many students react to required project assignments with indifference, at best, and execute them with uninspired resolve. The chore becomes one of finding enough material to meet the minimum length requirements. (If we had $100 for every time we were asked, "How long does this paper have to be?" we could retire.) Those who are willing to put in effort that exceeds expectations for an undergraduate student, however, can use that project as a valuable opportunity.

Doesn't a good project just help me get a good grade in the course?

The grade assigned to a project may be the least important benefit for the student with hopes of entering a competitive graduate program. A project or paper provides an unparalleled chance to demonstrate to the professor that you can think, integrate information, write, and create. Among the most highly prized skills an applicant can demonstrate is the ability to write well.

Projects also offer a chance to prove that you take pride in your work and that you stand out with regard to thoughtfulness, dedication, and enthusiasm. These are also among the most important positive attributes that referees include in describing an applicant, and the term paper is likely to be the only evidence a professor has of these qualities. This will be especially true if the class is large or if the course exams consist primarily of multiple-choice, true–false, or fill-in-the-blank items.

Most letters of recommendation are fairly brief and general, often spattered with adjectives such as *bright* and *pleasant*. Evaluators are far less impressed with undocumented characterizations, even when they are positive, than with descriptions of the criteria upon which these judgments are based (see chap. 17). An excellent term paper assignment provides the professor with evidence on which to base a substantive statement about you. A recommendation letter that speaks directly to what you have actually done will help you the most.

Another benefit of taking special care with course projects becomes evident as you fill out graduate program application forms. Most programs to which you apply will request that you discuss your academic interests and experiences (see chap. 19). Although it would be inappropriate to inflate their significance, you will nevertheless find that your outstanding term papers and projects provide a basis for this challenging portion of your application. Good work also demonstrates that you are a person who can follow through with your ideas and interests.

Still other benefits may present themselves. An excellent paper will come in handy if an example of your writing or research is requested by a graduate program. Less likely, but certainly not unheard of, is the possibility that an outstanding paper may turn into something more, such as a presentation at an undergraduate conference or other professional meeting, or even a publication in a scholarly journal.

Including an extremely well-done research paper in an application packet (even if not requested) may enhance your chances of acceptance if the topic is relevant to your proposed study area. One student sent her research paper, which earned an *A+* and included the instructor's many and very flattering comments, to a prominent professor who was conducting research in exactly the same area. That student went on to enroll in the professor's graduate program and to conduct research with him. Lucky break? Hardly. The student was genuinely interested in the area, did her homework to learn where the experts could be found, and offered concrete proof of her sincere commitment and ability.

Finally, save all of your term projects (or a copy of them for professors who do not return the originals). Those who agree to write reference letters for you may wish to review your old assignments from their classes, or they may have forgotten your fine work.

Special Skills to Enhance

Applicants can stand out because they have some special, admired, or useful skills that would be a welcome addition to the graduate environment. It is probably too late for you to acquire such skills from scratch, but you can improve on one or more skills that you have already begun to develop.

If you have demonstrable talents that are the least bit relevant to your graduate program interest area, share them somewhere in your application materials. Encourage your referees to mention skills that you can't logically include in your application. We have known a number of applicants who never mentioned something that we knew was very special about them. Once, for example, a student who had won top prizes for his computer graphics neglected to note this talent anywhere in his application package. Another student forgot to mention that she was graduating with honors in writing. Oddly, students sometimes discount their strengths and special skills.

What skills may be impressive?

Computer skills and familiarity with a variety of software applications are rapidly becoming staples of the modern person's repertoire of abilities. Mention computer-related competencies you have developed, because they are viewed positively by graduate program evaluators. If you have advanced skills, give some examples of what you can do or have done (e.g., constructed web pages for several friends).

Data entry and analysis are prized by graduate school evaluators, particularly those in research-oriented programs. The ability to operate specialized equipment used in behavioral science research, to perform particular assessments or other complicated experimental procedures, and to record systematic observations may also be impressive, especially if one or more of the graduate faculty members personally value such skills. Students with these types of abilities almost always learned them from their professors in the course of doing research together, thus providing another valuable reason for undergraduate research experience.

Applicants who are outstanding speakers or teachers are also rated positively by graduate school evaluators. Therefore, if you have excellent speaking ability, verbal skills, or teaching ability (especially if it can be corroborated by at least one of your referees), by all means mention it.

Fluency in a foreign language can be a plus if you apply to programs that train students to work in certain settings. In southern California, for example, Spanish-speaking applicants are especially attractive to evaluators for school psychology, social work, and mental health programs. Do not overstate your linguistic abilities, however. One student we know, raised in a roaming military family, received a call from a graduate faculty member who conducted the entire inquiry in Korean! She wanted to assure herself that someone with a name like Bobby Brown really could speak Korean. (Fortunately for him, he actually could.)

What about other abilities? I play the piano very well, and I can type almost 100 words a minute.

Although these are unrelated to your area of study, you may be wise to briefly mention such special skills somewhere on your application, if only to suggest that you are a competent, interesting, and well-rounded person or as further evidence that you are creative (e.g., musical or artistic abilities) or well-disciplined (e.g., karate). Some applications actually ask specifically about your hobbies, talents, and extracurricular activities. Certain interests or abilities may lead to or evolve from research or practicum experience, which we discuss in the next chapter.

CHAPTER 8

WHAT ABOUT RESEARCH AND PRACTICUM EXPERIENCE?

Most graduate school applicants have solid grades and acceptable test scores, but everyone knows that these accomplishments, while surely significant, provide only a partial picture of the candidates. Other things that applicants have done with their time—especially activities that indicate fitness for, interest in, and commitment to the discipline—become decisive criteria in choosing graduate students. Two of the most important activities considered by selection committees are research and practical experience. Useful practical experience takes several forms but most often involves supervised volunteer work with people in a community agency, school, or hospital. Both research and practical experience indicate that socialization into the profession has already started.

Which is more important: research or practical experience?

The general answer is research. Experience as a research assistant, or, even more important, involvement in a project that resulted in an authorship credit on a presentation or an article published in a scholarly journal, is extremely impressive for applicants to both scientific and traditional clinical programs (Bonifazi et al., 1997; Keith-Spiegel et al., 1994). One reason for this is that many undergraduates do not have impressive research experience, so those who do stand out. Thus, you should gain some research experience if at all possible, but you are not doomed without it.

Research is also highly valued because most of your professors in graduate school will be very actively involved in it. In addition, research experience indicates that you carefully worked through a process that likely involved thinking, organization, problem solving, and commitment. Furthermore, research experience, especially if you presented a completed project at a research conference or in a scholarly publication, is likely to be a reasonably accurate predictor of your ability to contribute to the field.

With fieldwork and other practical experience, the situation is quite different. With so many opportunities available to volunteer in the community, and given the ease with which students can earn academic credit through such activities, it is very common for applicants to psychology programs (as well as to programs in related disciplines) to have this type of experience. Activity along these lines, then, is usually expected of applicants to clinical and counseling psychology programs and other programs training mental health service providers. Applicants to experimental psychology or other research-oriented programs typically need not have any fieldwork or practicum experience. However, except for certain professionally oriented programs that place minimal emphasis on research, applicants to clinical or applied programs are highly advantaged if they have research experience.

Research Experience

How do I get this important experience?

If you start looking early enough, you will likely find a way to become involved in interesting research. The most frequent and accessible route is to assist a faculty member in your academic department with his or her ongoing research projects. Faculty are often on the lookout for bright, committed students eager for a research opportunity, thus creating a complementary relationship. Students can often earn academic credit for this type of collaborative work as well.

This sounds like a good way to get a few easy credits and some experience as a bonus.

Yikes! This is the kind of response that makes professors shudder. Once a student enters into a collaborative relationship, the faculty member relies on the student to provide careful, diligent work and to follow a schedule that often leaves little room for compromise. Faculty cannot afford unreliable or careless assistants. The student looking for a few filler credits or an easy *A* is not likely to devote the quality and amount of labor required to do good research. Faculty members seek students whose primary goal is research experience, who have a proven record of doing careful and quality work, and who are only incidentally concerned about other benefits.

How do I find out who is doing research in an area that interests me?

Perhaps your academic department has a roster indicating which faculty members are doing what kinds of research. If not, start asking around and knocking on office doors for leads as to who might be looking for undergraduate research assistants.

You may not find anyone working in an area that you find fascinating, but keep an open mind to new areas. What intrigues you now might change (perhaps several times before you complete your studies), and your undergraduate or graduate faculty members will play a significant role in defining those interests. This is not to say, however, that you should agree to assist someone with a research project that seems very boring or that you have great difficulty understanding. The work you would perform under such circumstances could be shoddy to the point of compromising the integrity of the research, thus hurting everyone involved.

When you find someone with whom you might like to work, describe very carefully and honestly what you can offer (skills, number of hours per week you can spend on the project, etc.). Such research activity must never be considered as something you do after you have taken care of your other obligations. Even if you receive no pay or academic credit, treat your research duties as you would your other primary responsibilities.

Why assign a high priority to your research activity? A positive payoff will ensue only if you perform competent and reliable work. Most of us have had awful experiences with undergraduate students who appeared initially to be sincere in their interests, only to fade away shortly thereafter. Our projects were disrupted and the student earned neither credit nor any other benefit, such as a letter of recommendation. Furthermore, if the poorly performing student lists the research activity on her application anyway, and a selection committee member calls the supervisor to confirm the experience, the student will have little hope of surviving the selection process following the feedback the supervisor is bound to offer!

On the other hand, the loyal student who works side-by-side with the researcher on a project through its various phases is in line for a significant payoff. The faculty member should credit the student's assistance in some way, perhaps joint authorship if the contribution was substantial, or a footnote of appreciation in the published paper for routine help. An appreciative faculty member will also likely reward the assistant with a positive letter of recommendation. If the project itself is impressive, the impact on the selection committee could be significant.

Another word of caution: If a faculty member selects you as a research assistant, you will likely be assigned the tasks that require the least professional skills, commensurate with your training and experience. You may well have to learn and demonstrate a certain tolerance for drudgery. Someone has to duplicate surveys, count pencils, clean laboratory equipment, feed the mice, and the like. That someone may well be you! This is not to say that you should be confined to these sorts of tasks. But the excitement of discovery also involves a lot of tedious and exacting work.

What about doing my own research? That way I can do something that really interests me.

Most undergraduate departments offer an independent study option that allows students to pursue their own lines of inquiry. Typically, a faculty member must agree to serve as your sponsor or supervisor. The only way to maximize this opportunity, however, is to find a supervisor who views your topic as interesting or who is devoted to helping students with their professional development. Otherwise, you will receive insufficient attention, the project may not succeed, and the connection between you and the faculty member will be weak. Undergraduate students typically do not have the background or experience necessary to successfully negotiate presentation or publication opportunities, so it is also less likely that the project will gain recognition beyond the status of an independent study project if the faculty sponsor is not actively involved with and interested in the project. A student's project of any consequence may require space or other resources that are already in huge demand. Finally, a project that would draw positive attention from others is likely to take a larger commitment than a single semester's work. Students attempting independent projects should be very realistic about what they can do on their own.

This is not to say that an independent study project is a bad idea, even if you have no supervisor who is heavily invested in your project. You simply need to accept that you will be largely on your own and that you will be less likely to accrue the complete array of rewards. You can, however, still benefit from an independent study in an area that fascinates you because it counts as experience, and you will learn much more about your interest area in the process. A full description of your interest areas is almost always requested on graduate program application forms, at which point an independent study project could come in handy (see chap. 19).

Could I work with a faculty member in another department if no one in mine is available or interested in what I am doing?

Sometimes this is exactly the way to go. You may have to search more diligently for the right person, but he or she might be close by. Some colleges and universities have "research in action" or "research institutes" and other innovative programs for students that involve cooperative arrangements between the campus and outside agencies or corporations. Check out these possibilities, too: They may offer exciting opportunities.

What about research opportunities off-campus?

This is another viable option available in most urban settings. A larger university, medical school, or institute close by may place a heavy emphasis on research. Also, nearby hospitals, community agencies, and clinics often welcome unpaid volunteers who help collect data for project evaluation or for clinical research projects. Government agencies and occasionally private industry offer other possibilities. If you start calling around, however, make it clear that you are not seeking to do your own research nor are you seeking a paid research assistant position. Those opportunities are not available often, yet the staff who answer the telephones often assume that inquirers are asking for one or both and may abruptly cut you off.

If you have a strong interest in pursuing a graduate degree at a university that is within a reasonable drive from your home, becoming involved in research with a faculty member at that university (ideally in the department of your interest) is a wise tactic. There are no guarantees, but if you are a loyal and highly competent volunteer, you may well earn a letter of recommendation and have a persuasive insider in your corner.

This plan will work only if you prove yourself to be exactly the kind of person that the faculty wants to recruit. Your edge is not based on appreciation for your generous donation of services; that is, the faculty member will not owe you a spot in the program. Rather, your admittance in such a case rests on your record as a competitive applicant in your own right and that you are known to at least one faculty member. If you do not get into the program, you have not wasted your time. Your research experience will still help your application to other programs.

I have some extra time over the summer. Are there any summer opportunities?

This could work! Whereas some faculty members disappear during the summer, others use that time to focus on their research projects. It is likely that some of them would be delighted to be offered competent help. You may not get paid, but weigh the advantages of earning a little extra money at a summer job and gaining experience that might make a difference in your life. Also, see if there are summer research institutes for students at your institution or in your geographical area.

Are any paid research assistant positions available?

Such positions are typically offered to graduate students. Only occasionally do such opportunities open up for undergraduates, so ask around. Sometimes a faculty member has a research grant that provides a modest payment for assistants. These may be trusted undergraduates who are paid an hourly wage.

How much of my time would be involved as a research assistant?

Time commitments vary tremendously, and you should not enter into any agreement without first making sure that both you and your supervisor very clearly understand each other's expectations for both the hours you will work and the duties you will perform. Most supervisors realize that bright undergraduate students have heavy schedules, and they may ask for only 3 or 4 hours of your time per week. But they will fully expect that you be there for those hours. Sometimes, however, due to the nature of the research, many more hours are required, or more hours are required during concentrated data collection periods. Honestly assess your schedule and politely decline the opportunity if it would jeopardize your own commitments or put the research project at risk. Do not accept any opportunity, regardless of its merits, if what is required of you is more than you have to give.

Does a project have to be data-based research? What about a theoretical paper or an innovative literature review?

We stress research because it is very impressive to selection committee members and is the type of experience that students, especially undergraduate students, are more likely to have available. Certainly other kinds of collaborative or independent work may be pursued and, depending on the quality, may be useful. Papers in which you critically review the published literature on a particular topic, describe the development of or a new use for a piece of equipment, or explain a novel application of theory to a particular area are among the alternative possibilities.

What if I write a very good data-based or review paper for one of my classes? Could I use it for a presentation or publication?

Maybe, especially if you have a supportive professor willing to help you expand on it. Turning an undergraduate class project into a publication in a refereed professional journal is rare, but a number of other opportunities are available for students to present their own work, such as undergraduate research conferences. Let's look at some possibilities.

Research Outlets

Research credit is admired by selection committees even if the applicant's paper was not presented at a prestigious professional conference or published in a highly competitive scholarly journal. Nor does the student have to be the senior (first-listed) or sole author. Indeed, a sole-authored article by an undergraduate student in a top journal is so rare that it may be looked at with doubt and disbelief!

What outlets are available?

Hundreds of scholarly journals and scores of professional organizations provide forums for the dissemination of research findings and other types of scholarly work. Browsing the periodicals section (a good habit in any event) of a major university library will show you how many professional journals exist. If you have collaborated with a professor on a solid piece of work, the project may go as far as the professor's skills can take it. Enjoy the ride. This is why we noted earlier that you want to work with a faculty member who is familiar and successful with the publication process.

What about more modest work, like that generally initiated by a typical student?

Student work, especially if there is no faculty or other professional-level collaborator, can most easily find a forum at annual meetings of professional organizations, undergraduate research conferences and journals, and university- or department-sponsored student paper or poster sessions. Professional meetings are held in state, regional, national, and international sites.

Students are allowed to submit their work to professional meetings or conferences, although they are usually required to obtain sponsorship of their paper from a full member of the organization. This work must compete with that of the many scholars and professionals who also will submit papers and posters for presentation at the meeting. Student projects, however, are accepted often enough at such meetings to make submission of your best work worthwhile.

A route with a higher probability of acceptance, however, is to submit the paper to a student competition. You may vie with graduate students as well as other undergraduates, but the selection criteria are less stringent than for professional conferences. As one example of this type of student outlet, Psi Chi, the national honor society in psychology, sponsors a student paper competition at regional professional conferences. Many of the presentations come from class projects and independent study efforts. Some college and university departments have their own undergraduate journals that are published once or twice a year. Papers from students outside of the department are often welcomed. Because these are small operations, you will need to keep an eye and ear out for submission calls.

Another possibility is undergraduate research conferences, which were designed expressly to give undergraduate students a chance to present their work. Such conferences are usually confined to small regions (covering a few states at most) and range from quite small (e.g., 15 presentations altogether) to very large (e.g., 250 presentations). Virtually all require that a faculty member sponsor the student paper. Most conferences are competitive; that is, a panel of judges rates the submissions on a variety of criteria and selects the best ones for the final program.

If you decide to submit a project for presentation at such a conference, remember two items of advice. First, follow all directions very carefully when submitting a presentation, and honor the due date. Sloppy, incomplete, or late submissions can very easily cost you an acceptance. Second, if your project is selected for presentation, be sure to show up to present it. Failure to follow through reflects very poorly on you (and your sponsor) unless you have a very legitimate excuse (plus you cannot list on your application what you never presented).

Finally, your own college or university, or academic department, may provide local meetings to showcase meritorious student work. If your department does not offer such a research forum, you might want to spark interest in establishing such a tradition. It is not a difficult or expensive project to implement, requiring only some interest from key individuals. With regard to graduate school, these types of presentations are not as impressive as those at professional conferences, but they do enhance one's application.

The Value of Community Service and Clinical Experience

If you aspire to provide mental health services to others, we strongly advise you to seek practice opportunities as an undergraduate, if only to validate to yourself that working with clients is what you want to do during most of your waking hours for most of the rest of your life. As you might expect, applicants who have clinical or community service experience typically have an advantage among evaluators in clinical, counseling, and mental health graduate training programs.

For those applying to nonclinical, research-oriented programs, such service experience provides little advantage. It probably would not hurt an applicant, and may even help in a few relatively rare instances, but other types of experiences should be far more dominant in the applicant's record. One potential concern is that extensive client-service experience may raise questions about the applicant's career choices: If the applicant enjoyed or valued client contact so much, why is he or she now applying to a research-oriented program? And, if the applicant had so much available time, why didn't he or she do more research?

Are some types of service experience better than others?

It might help to distinguish between community service and clinical experience. *Community service* refers to social action or "helping hand" kinds of work, such as socializing with chronically mentally ill patients at a VA hospital, assisting with a feeding program for the homeless, tutoring children who have behavioral problems or are at risk for school failure, being a "big brother" or "big sister," and so on. Community service experiences are often personally satisfying and they expose students, in a naturalistic setting, to the kinds of populations with which they may ultimately work. We typically advise students to do community service as their initial volunteer experience.

Clinical experience, for our purposes here, is carefully supervised work with a fully trained mental health professional. The work involves learning the techniques that professionals use and becoming increasingly independent (though never fully independent) in their use. Examples of this kind of experience include crisis-line counseling, cofacilitating groups with substance-abusing teens, and helping evaluate clients who may have eating disorders.

In most instances, impressive clinical experience, perhaps best indicated by the recommendation letter that the supervisor provides, is probably more persuasive to graduate school evaluators than is community service. However, you must carefully assess your clinical experience options, because some may be clearly inappropriate. Occasionally professionals are all too eager to take in undergraduate student volunteers whom they then expect to do work that no one else wants to do or to provide services for which they are not yet qualified. Sometimes it is difficult for students to object, partly because the student may not realize how inappropriate the assignment is and partly because it may be flattering to be given professional-level responsibilities. (On the flip side, don't waste your time with low-level work that does not teach you anything of value.)

If you think you are being asked to do work that should only be performed by trained professionals, look for another opportunity. Graduate faculty members plan to be the ones to teach you clinical and counseling skills. They may not look as positively as you might think on early professional training. If, as an undergraduate volunteer, you are given a title such as *intern* or *psychological assistant*, do not use it on your application. Such titles have specific meaning to psychologists and other mental health professionals, implying advanced training, thus they may be put off by someone who prematurely lays claim to such status.

There is a nursery school program about a mile away from my house, which would fit perfectly with my schedule.

The ease and convenience of a fieldwork site are certainly understandable criteria for the busy student. However, avoid using these criteria exclusively. A program associated with a large hospital or university is typically far preferable, given your present objective, than is the nursery school down the street. A supervisor who is a licensed mental health care provider at the doctoral level is the most desirable although not always available in community service settings.

An excellent type of experience, if at all feasible, is involvement in a university-sponsored or community agency *service research* project. Although students must usually commit up to 8 hours a week for up to a year, this double-duty opportunity is viewed with high regard by evaluators.

How about volunteering to help someone in private practice?

We do not recommend this setting, even if it is available, and also believe that it may raise concern among selection committee members. A private practice involves licensed professionals accepting pay for their confidential services. What is an undergraduate student going to do there? Serving as a receptionist is all that comes to mind, and that is unlikely to be a useful learning experience. Even current master's-level graduate students seeking doctoral training should be cautious about gaining clinical experiences in private practice settings.

If I want to apply to a clinical or service-oriented program, how much field experience should I have?

"The more the better" is not necessarily the best advice. Our selection committee survey revealed that 500 hours of volunteer field experience was not rated much higher than 100 hours. As we noted earlier, almost all applicants to clinical and related programs have had some clinically related work, so it is clearly beneficial for you to have done such work. But this experience is less useful than research experience when it comes time to discriminate among applicants. Achieving a balance between service-oriented and research experiences therefore is in your best interest.

What about professional schools or service-training programs that place far less emphasis on research backgrounds?

The less the research orientation of the program, the less important are research interests and experiences. This comes as a pleasant surprise to many students who want to be practitioners but who thought, perhaps based on advice or impressions gleaned from their more traditionally trained undergraduate professors, that natural ability in statistics and some level of passion for research were prerequisites for any sort of graduate training.

Although we cannot make sweeping generalizations about professional schools or other predominantly service-oriented university programs, these will typically expect successful applicants to have a considerable amount of clinical, applied, or practical experience. For these types of programs, a student who has never ventured out of the academic environment will be at a distinct disadvantage in the evaluation process. On the other hand, the applicant who has a record of sustained, successful, satisfying service that was well-regarded by supervisors may compensate for a more modest GPA or less impressive test scores.

Is it better to get a little experience from many different sites or lump all my time into one placement?

There is no answer to this question that is right for everyone. If you have an opportunity to do some specialized work with an outstanding supervisor at an impressive site working with the kind of population that you hope to serve during your career, it would be foolish to leave after a few months just for the sake of variety. However, if you are unsure of the population with whom you might want to work, if you feel you have exhausted what you can learn in one setting, or if you find an experience unrewarding, then you should move to a new site. However, the minimum time for any single experience should be several hours a week for no less than one academic term or one summer to ensure that you benefit from the experience and demonstrate that you are not prone to prematurely terminating commitments.

What if I find, after doing a lot of volunteer work, that I don't like working with people?

It would be disappointing to learn that a line of work you decided to enter, or a certain client population with whom you were sure you wanted to work, turned out to be unsatisfying. However, consider yourself lucky to have some important information that you can use when making your graduate school selection. It is better to find out as early as possible what you don't want to do!

A Word of Caution

In this chapter we stress the practical value of having a supervisor who can involve you in research or fieldwork activities. However, we must mention the unpleasant side of the story. Everything we have said rests on the assumption that your research or practicum supervisor is heavily invested in promoting your welfare beyond whatever benefits he or she may receive from your involvement in his or her work.

Occasionally a student runs into a sponsor or supervisor who ignores a student's needs. Horror stories circulate about researchers who give their hard-working helpers nothing in return, not even a footnote or a letter of recommendation. Worse yet are stories of professionals who claim student-initiated projects or contributions as their own work. Equally abhorrent tales involve supervisors in agencies or private practice settings using students to perform inappropriate duties, sometimes charging their clients for the students' work (money that the supervisor then pockets).

Fortunately, we believe that exploitation of this sort is rare. However, if you feel uneasy about a work situation or suspect that your trust is being abused, seek consultation, perhaps from a professor in whom you can confide.

CHAPTER 9

WHAT ABOUT PROFESSIONAL ORGANIZATIONS AND MEETINGS?

Psychology and related disciplines have numerous student organizations and honor societies, as well as their own professional organizations. Undergraduate and graduate students should seriously consider joining one or more organizations that will bring them in contact with people who can provide connections and support.

What do I get out of joining student or professional organizations?

An active student organization or chapter of an honor society allows students within a particular major to socialize and work together. Such groups often provide opportunities to become closely involved with faculty and departmental activities. Additionally, the informal networking that automatically connects members of active chapters—such as learning about practicum and research opportunities or graduate programs—provides a tremendous source of support and encouragement.

Although frequently allowed to join professional organizations, student members or affiliates typically do not have the advantages of full membership, such as voting rights and the opportunity to hold office. But associating with legitimate professional organizations is a good way to introduce yourself to your chosen career. Many of these organizations hold annual meetings or conventions. The newsletters and journals you receive, and any meetings you are able to attend, familiarize you with contemporary trends and issues, foster a sense of professional identity, and can even bring you face-to-face with the top people in your field.

A very practical reason for affiliating with these organizations is that many graduate school applications will request you to list relevant professional organization memberships. If you have not joined any, you will have to leave that line on your application form blank.

Groups to Join

What is the best group for me to join?

The answer depends on your major and the type of program to which you might apply for graduate school. We will not attempt to provide a comprehensive list of the possibilities, but we will discuss many under four headings: national honor societies, national professional organizations, regional professional associations, and community groups.

National Honor Societies

Psi Chi is the national honor society for psychology students. For students in social work, Phi Alpha is the national honor society. If your department has a chapter of a national honor society in your field, apply as soon as you qualify for membership.

Being psychologists, we are most familiar with Psi Chi. At the national level, Psi Chi promotes a number of activities helpful to graduate school aspirants in psychology. Certificates are awarded to students who present papers at annual professional meetings. Psi Chi's presence is strongly felt at the annual convention of the APA and at the regional associations as well. (These groups are discussed later.) Psi Chi brings in top speakers and provides workshops and other activities focused on the needs of student members. The organization also offers several awards and research grants for student members. In addition to providing prestige, these awards also include a financial component, ranging from monetary prizes for excellence in research already completed to small research grants to carry out a promising, proposed research project (see http://www.psichi.org/ for details). Consult directly with a Psi Chi member or faculty sponsor in your department about membership requirements. That way, you can get introduced to the people you will be involved with once you join. Psi Beta (see http://www.ivc.cc.us/psibeta), the honorary psychology society for students in community and junior colleges, offers services and activities similar to those of Psi Chi.

The vitality of Psi Chi at the local level (i.e., the chapter within your own college or university) will depend largely on the time and energy that its faculty and students are willing to devote. Some chapters are extremely active, involving themselves in multiple programs, whereas others are less active. Either way, it's good to join.

Some other disciplines have national organizations for their students, such as the Student Social Work Association. Some academic departments have their own clubs or other relevant organizations for their majors. Review the benefits of membership and, if a group brings you in contact with other students or faculty and with opportunities for en-

riched learning or special activities, strongly consider joining. Other national, prestigious scholarship groups, such as Phi Beta Kappa or Alpha
Chi, may have chapters on your campus and are worthwhile. Consult
your college or university catalog or contact your student activities office
for information.

National Professional Organizations

Professional organizations are major political and unifying forces within
all professions. Many such groups exist for psychologists and members
of closely related disciplines. Although some of these organizations allow
only graduate students to join (e.g., the American Association of Marriage and Family Therapists and the National Association of School Psychologists), others encourage undergraduate students to become members or affiliates. Most of these groups charge students a fee that is not
more than (and is sometimes less than) what it costs to supply the tangi-
ble benefits that students receive as members. Although low student
rates are a service, it is to the organization's benefit to attract students
early in anticipation of their eventually becoming full and sustaining
members.

What are some possibilities?

The American Psychological Association (APA), representing virtually
every facet of psychology, is the largest (86,000 members) and oldest of
the psychological associations. APA offers many benefits to its undergraduate and graduate student affiliates. Regular benefits include the
APA Monitor (a hefty and very informative monthly newspaper), the
American Psychologist (the flagship journal of the association and one we
strongly recommend that advanced undergraduate psychology students
peruse regularly), special membership rates for subscriptions to other
APA journals, and a reduced fee to attend the annual convention. The
APA Monitor also publishes many advertisements for position openings
in the field, which allows you to see what kinds of jobs are available in
the field.

You can print an application to become a student affiliate from the relevant Internet site (http://www.apa.org/students/) or contact the membership office (APA, 750 First St., NW, Washington DC 20002-4242; telephone 202-336-5500). As of 1999, the annual membership fee was $27 for
undergraduate students and $35 for graduate students.

The American Psychological Society (APS), founded in 1988, offers an
impressive array of student activities and services. APS has about 15,000
members and focuses on the scientific aspects of psychology. Undergraduate and graduate students may join as affiliates, which entitles
them to receive the *APS Observer* (a monthly newsletter), *Psychological
Science* (the flagship journal), and *Current Directions in Psychological*

Science (a journal containing brief reviews of research on particular topics). The *Observer* regularly includes a feature called "The Student Notebook" as well as articles of interest to students.

You can download an application to become a student affiliate from the APS Internet site (http://www.hanover.edu/psych/APS/aps.html) or contact APS at P.O. Box 90457, Washington, DC 20090-0457 (telephone 202-783-2077). As of 1999, the membership fee was $48 for students.

The National Association of Social Workers (NASW) has more than 150,000 members and publishes a newsletter (*NASW News*) and a scholarly journal (*Social Work*). For an application, see http://www.naswdc.org/ or contact NASW at 750 First St., NE, Suite 700, Washington, DC 20002-4241 (telephone 800-638-8799). As of 1999, the annual student membership fee was $40.

For more than 60 years, the National Council on Family Relations (NCFR) has provided a forum for family researchers, educators, and practitioners to share information concerning families and family functioning. NCFR publishes a quarterly newsletter and two scholarly journals (*Family Relations* and *Journal of Marriage and the Family*). There are 10 special interest groups within the larger organization. For an application, see http://www.ncfr.com/ or contact NCFR at 3989 Central Ave., NE, Suite 550, Minneapolis, MN 55421 (telephone 888-781-9331). Student members have the choice of receiving one or both of the journals; the annual student membership fee is adjusted accordingly (as of 1999, the fees were $50 or $75).

What about professional groups focused on particular interests?

A number of other national groups representing specialty areas in psychology or closely allied fields offer undergraduate students an affiliate status. Examples include the Society for Neuroscience, the Human Factors Society, the Association for Women in Psychology, the Cognitive Science Society, Psychologists for Social Responsibility, the Society for Personality and Social Psychology, the Society for the Scientific Study of Sexuality, the Society for the Psychological Study of Social Issues, the Society for Personality Assessment, the Gerontological Society of America, the Association for Applied Psychophysiology and Biofeedback, and the National Association of School Psychologists. Some groups, such as the National Mental Health Association (http://www.NMHA.org/), do not have a specific student membership category, but undergraduates may join.

Ask professors who specialize in your area of interest for ideas about specific nationally based professional groups with student affiliate opportunities. You can obtain contact information for those groups listed in the previous paragraph by asking professors or searching the Internet. For example, the APS web site offers a long list of links to web sites for various professional organizations in the social sciences and helping professions (click on Psychology Links).

Will joining a professional group help me get into graduate school?

Affiliating with a legitimate professional organization will cast a positive light on your application. Because the topic appears on some application forms, one could reasonably assume that this type of activity is of interest to those programs' selection teams. Evaluators may interpret such memberships as evidence that you are aware of life outside your own academic department, that you have begun to identify with the field, and that you have concretely demonstrated some interest in pursuing a particular profession.

Should I join as many professional groups as possible just to be on the safe side?

Signing up for groups just to do it is silly and expensive. Carefully select one or two legitimate organizations that represent your interests and offer membership benefits that you can actually use. Beware of organizations looking for people who want to boost their egos by connecting with any group that sounds impressive. Alignment with such groups will detract from your credibility.

You mentioned the term legitimate *when describing the types of groups I should investigate. What do you mean?*

Some bogus organizations have professional-sounding names and offer an impressive-looking certificate suitable for framing. Beyond requiring dues, most have no membership requirements whatsoever. Some cost so little to join that they are difficult to resist by those who need a shortcut to feeling important. On the other hand, most provide absolutely no benefits to members or anyone else. Most have no leaders or board members who are on the faculty of accredited universities. If you have any question about a professional organization, consult faculty members in the specialty area supposedly represented by the group. If none of the faculty in your department are familiar with a particular group, it probably will not be useful to you.

Regional Professional Associations

With regard to psychology, the United States is divided into seven large geographical chunks, each with a regional psychological association. Each regional group tends to focus on one activity: putting on a large annual professional meeting. In some regions, the locations change from year to year, so what may be too long a trip one year could be a short one in another year. The meetings are often great fun as well as providing considerable opportunities for students (described later in this chapter).

Regional groups differ with respect to student affiliate opportunities and membership costs, and we hesitate to list them here because policies change from time to time. However, you can consult any recent edition of the *American Psychologist* (look in the back under "Calendar") or view the relevant Psi Chi web page (http://www.psichi.org/content/) to learn the date, location, and other information regarding the next meeting in your region. Students can attend the meetings regardless of whether they are members.

Community Groups

Legitimate charitable, political, and social action groups are abundant. Although you may well support one or more such groups, whether you report your membership status on graduate school applications requires some consideration. A few applications ask explicitly about any involvement in local community group activities. You should list your membership if you have been active in the group beyond paying your annual dues. Any activities that involve responsibility and self-discipline will look good on your application.

If you simply have been a dues-paying member, consider noting such memberships only if they are closely aligned with your chosen study areas. For example, indicating membership in your local zoo society is advisable if you are applying to programs in animal behavior or comparative psychology but irrelevant for applications submitted to social work or clinical psychology programs. We advise against listing memberships in extreme activist groups or those that might be considered on the fringe by older, more conservative faculty.

Will involvement in a Greek fraternity or sorority, or leadership in a club not related to my academics, impact my application to graduate school?

Involvement in social clubs, including the "Greeks," will probably not detract from your application but will not enhance it either. Some evaluators rate this type of activity negatively, perhaps perceiving it as an indication that the applicant is not a serious student or places social activity above scholarly pursuits. Other club memberships, especially if you were elected to higher level leadership positions, may give the impression that you have people skills and that you are a well-rounded person.

Attending Professional Meetings

Professional meetings can be extremely informative and productive for anyone who wants to take advantage of them, and that definitely includes graduate school aspirants. Many students describe their first professional meeting as a rite of passage, an experience that gave them their first taste of professional life. As one student said,

> Standing there in that ornate room, chatting for no more than a minute with someone whose research and theory I had read about in books, was an awesome experience. He answered my questions and he asked where I was going in the field. I crossed over into some other realm in the way I looked at my studies and my future.

Professional meetings also provide the best way for students to learn what is going on in their interest area and in the departments of the graduate programs that interest them. The bonus is that the people delivering the speeches are graduate faculty members themselves. Their current (and former) graduate students may also be around, who are superior sources of information about particular graduate programs.

Could I just walk up to a person at a convention and say, "I'm interested in your graduate program" or "I admire your work"? What would they think if I did that?

The respondents to our evaluators' survey generally rated such an act positively. Only 3 of the 158 respondents said that they would view such behavior negatively, and even those few rated it as only slightly negative. Good manners dictate that you would not interrupt anyone who is actively engaged in a conversation or obviously hurrying to get somewhere. However, if a person of interest is alone or taking questions from a small group (as often happens right after presentations), or is chatting during a social hour, introduce yourself. You will get an immediate reading of the person's reaction, and you should not feel bad if the conversation does not go anywhere. Convention attendants often make many appointments to meet with people and, therefore, may be in a rush. Many times, however, you may enjoy a productive interaction.

How do I find these people in the first place?

Because most participants wear name badges that also list their affiliation, you can stumble across a person of interest almost anywhere. The elevator, book display area, poster sessions, or lunch and dinner lines are common grounds for striking up conversations with strangers wearing the same type of badge as you. Don't be shy about striking up a conversation. Such spontaneous conversations are expected to occur at conventions.

Study the printed program and attend presentations by people of interest, or by people from the graduate program that interests you, or where people from the kinds of programs that interest you are likely to be. You may not get to meet presenters immediately, but you will at least know what they look like. Perhaps the best opener for these conversations is to ask a question about the talk that the person has just given, especially if it can be prefaced with a compliment (e.g., "I enjoyed your presentation, and I was wondering . . ."). Sometimes people will ask about you, once they have answered your question.

The social hours (usually in a large hotel banquet room with a cash bar at both ends) are good turf for making contacts, because the purpose of the social hour is to bring people together who may not know each other. You may recognize a face of interest or spot a name badge attached to someone you would like to meet. Do not bolster your courage by having a few drinks beforehand. Otherwise, your introduction and demeanor may be memorable but not flattering! Remember that meeting people is serious business. Circulate, shake hands, and talk to the people you want to meet.

Check the program for any student-oriented events. As noted in the last section, the annual meetings of the APA (held in the late summer), the APS (early summer), and the large regional psychological associations (usually held in the spring) often have Psi Chi–sponsored programs to bring students and outstanding scholars together in relaxed settings. Similarly, Psi Chi frequently sponsors talks on applying to graduate school as well as graduate school information exchanges that allow students to meet with faculty representatives from various graduate programs.

Some of your current professors will likely be at the larger annual meetings, and they may be able to give you useful introductions. Many are happy to let you tag along as they make their rounds to presentation sessions. If your interests and those of your professor are similar, you could make some very helpful contacts. And if you have future opportunities to meet the same people again, you can always break the ice by saying, "We met at the APA meetings in 2000." (Incidentally, you often get to know your own professors better and in a somewhat different way at professional meetings. Behave as a responsible student, however, if your goal is to be viewed as someone whose professional plans are worthy of support.)

Scores of other organizations, including state associations and regional associations for behavioral science and mental health, hold annual professional meetings. Upcoming meetings are listed in every month's issue of the *American Psychologist* under the Calendar section or in the *APA Monitor* under Notes and News. Neither list, however, is comprehensive. A professor in your interest area may know of meetings that would be right for you. (Also see the Internet sites provided previously for each of the national professional organizations.)

Most professional meetings require steep registration fees for professionals but offer much more modest rates to students. Students typically cannot afford to be housed in the expensive hotels in which these meetings are often held, but more reasonable lodging (especially if you can go in small groups and share rooms) is usually not too far from the meeting site.

There is a difference between professional meetings and workshops sponsored by professional organizations. Workshops are usually geared toward the continuing educational needs of people already functioning as professionals and are much more expensive, although students sometimes can attend at a reduced fee. Some students who have attended professional workshops report learning a great deal and meeting some interesting people, but many others have found that the needs of students are not catered to and the material is too focused or advanced. Furthermore, such meetings do not necessarily cater to networking opportunities. Often there are brief coffee breaks and a lunch hour, and then everyone goes home for dinner.

Conclusion

Joining groups probably will not make a large difference in the competitiveness of your application to a graduate program. However, common sense tells us that an application containing evidence of involvement and commitment to the field of interest—and appropriate group involvement would be one indicator—would be viewed more positively than one without such evidence.

Simply attending a professional meeting or an undergraduate research conference, in and of itself, will not bolster an application. However, what you can learn and who you can meet are invaluable. Sometimes, while attending a professional meeting in their junior year, students see that delivering a paper might be something they could do. They subsequently submit a paper for the next meeting. What better way to learn the ropes than to observe professionals presenting their work to colleagues? And, as we saw in chapter 8, presenting a paper at a professional meeting is of great benefit to your candidacy.

CHAPTER 10

HOW CAN I IMPROVE MY PERFORMANCE ON STANDARDIZED ADMITTANCE TESTS?

Most graduate programs in the social sciences require applicants to take the Graduate Record Exam (GRE) General Test, and many programs in psychology require the corresponding Subject Test as well (Mayne et al., 1994; Steinpreis, Queen, & Tennen, 1992). Some programs in other areas may recommend rather than require the submission of GRE scores. In addition to influencing admission decisions, these test scores are sometimes used as a criterion for financial aid awards.

Brief Description of the Tests

GRE General Test

The GRE General Test yields three component scores: *Verbal Abilities* (analogies, antonyms, sentence completion, and reading comprehension items), *Quantitative Abilities* (arithmetic, algebra, and geometry problems, quantitative comparisons, and data interpretation), and *Analytical Abilities* (analytical reasoning and logic problems). Each component test has a maximum standardized score of 800. Most selection committees consider most carefully the performance on the Quantitative and Verbal components. (The Analytical Abilities test is newer and has not achieved a place as a standard evaluation criterion.) Accordingly, total GRE score usually refers to the sum of the Verbal and Quantitative scores, for a maximum of 1,600 possible points.

As of October 1999, the Educational Testing Service (ETS), the organization that develops and administers the GRE, added an optional GRE

Writing Assessment. This new test is being promoted as a way to demonstrate your ability to analyze written information and articulate your analysis through written expression. ETS plans to further add a Mathematical Reasoning Abilities test sometime between the years 2001 and 2003. Currently it is unclear to what extent, and in what way, scores on these new tests will be used in admission decisions in psychology and related fields.

GRE Subject Test in Psychology

The GRE Subject Test in psychology contains about 220 multiple-choice questions drawn from the basic core courses typically offered to undergraduate psychology majors. The questions are divided into three categories. The experimental or natural science questions (accounting for about 40% of the items) include learning, language, memory, thinking, perception, ethology, sensation, and comparative and physiological psychology. The social and social science questions (about another 40% of the items) cover clinical, abnormal, developmental, personality, and social psychology. The remainder of the questions, considered general psychology, include the history of psychology, applied psychology, measurement, research design, and statistics.

Subtest scores are computed separately for the experimental and social sets of items. Subject test scores can exceed 800, and the appropriate interpretation for the score you receive will be included in your GRE Report of Scores.

The Miller Analogies Test (MAT)

The MAT consists of 100 analogies (e.g., "Plane is to Air as Boat is to _?_" with four terms, including the correct answer, *Water*, to choose from). You have 50 minutes to complete the analogies. Your score is simply the number you answer correctly. Only about 10% of doctoral programs in psychology require the MAT, and most of these also require GRE scores (Sayette, Mayne, & Norcross, 1998), but more master's programs require the MAT scores. (See Sternberg, 1994, for information and hints about the MAT.)

Getting Test Information

In this chapter, we look more closely at general strategy information and testing issues rather than at the tests themselves. ETS (GRE/ETS, P.O. Box 6000, Princeton, NJ 08541-6000; telephone 800-537-3160) and the Psychological Corporation (MAT Coordinator, The Psychological Corporation, 555 Academic Court, San Antonio, TX 78204-3956; telephone 800-622-3231) publish very detailed and informative booklets each year that describe their products, related services, and how to register to take their exams. Additionally, each maintains web sites (http://www.gre.org/ for the GRE and http://www.hbtpc.com/mat/index.htm for the MAT). Another reason we do not focus on the tests themselves is because numerous study guides, practice tests, test-taking strategy books, and courses are available that offer far more than can be summarized in a single book chapter.

In registering for any standardized test, follow exactly the numerous directives, deadlines, and rules. Always go to the horse's mouth (the test companies themselves) for details about test offerings rather than relying on anyone else's printed or spoken word. Things change, perhaps only slightly, from year to year. You have to do everything exactly as required.

We highly recommend checking out the *GRE Information and Registration Bulletin* (issued annually by ETS and likely to be available somewhere on campus at no charge) or the web site (http://www.gre.org/ grepub.html) early in your academic career. Even sophomores, and certainly juniors, should read these resources to become familiar with the process and, perhaps, take advantage of learning and preparation opportunities that can maximize actual test performance.

How much does it cost to take these tests?

There is a fee for each test administration, for each additional report that is sent out to graduate programs, and for other miscellaneous services that may not apply to you (late registration fee, test date transfer fee, etc.). As of 1999, the GRE costs were $96 for the General Test and $96 for a Subject Test if taken in the United States or Puerto Rico ($120 each in U.S. funds if taken elsewhere). For the MAT, the fees are collected locally and vary from center to center.

The test fees include up to four test reports if, at the time you take the tests, you supply complete information as to where you want the scores sent. You should prepare this information in advance of test-taking day by identifying a few schools to which you are likely to apply. Additional GRE test reports are $13 each. Score request forms can be downloaded from the Internet (http://www.gre.org/code1st.html) or are probably available at your college or university testing office. Verify all of these details by reviewing the current versions of the free booklets provided by the test companies.

How Test Scores Are Used by Graduate School Selection Committees

Why do I have to take these tests? Don't my grades indicate my capabilities?

Without the use of a single measure required of all applicants, selection committees have no standardized way of comparing applicants to each other. Even if we could control for the types and levels of difficulty inferred from the titles of the courses applicants have taken, is the applicant with a 3.6 GPA from Bumpers State University really a stronger student than the applicant with a 3.4 GPA from Tumbolt College? Perhaps Tumbolt's courses generally are far more difficult, or the Tumbolt faculty grade their students more strictly. Selection committees cannot know the answers to these questions because they are dealing with applicants from hundreds of colleges and universities. How well standardized tests make meaningful discriminations among applicants, however, is a matter of endless debate.

Even the testing companies who create and administer standardized tests do not suggest that test scores should replace or even take priority over GPA and other factors. ETS, especially, clearly warns users against giving too much weight to GRE score when evaluating the worthiness of applicants.

Despite these cautions, strong evidence substantiates the major influence evaluators take from GRE scores in discriminating among graduate school applicants. Grade point average, particularly for the last 60 credits, and letters of recommendation are also significant sources of information. Successful applicants typically must show strength in at least one of these categories, and those with impressive showings in the other two as well are at a great advantage. As GPA and GRE scores rise, so do the chances of acceptance.

How do selection committees actually use an applicant's GRE scores?

Selection committee or program policies differ in the importance they attach to one or more of the GRE tests or the way these scores are used. Some programs establish cutoff GRE scores to eliminate candidates early in the screening process, even though the ETS recommends against this, or they use GRE scores to categorize applicants into a few major categories, such as *likely reject*, *possibly accept*, and *likely accept*. Other programs may use a statistical formula, weighing GRE scores with GPA and other factors to derive an overall score used to make some initial distinctions among applicants. Still other programs have minimum standards with regard to acceptable GRE scores, after which applicants' files are evaluated more subjectively (while still considering the strength of the GRE performance). In the end there is no uniform GRE policy to which most programs subscribe.

What scores do I need to get into graduate school?

There is no one answer for this question due to the variety of programs, the multitude of ways the scores are used, and your own strengths in other areas. However, to give you some idea of the expectations for doctoral programs in clinical psychology, the minimum preferred GRE scores on each subtest are around 540 for PsyD programs, 580 for scientist–practitioner PhD programs, and 600 for research-oriented PhD programs (Mayne et al., 1994). In general, more competitive programs command higher average test scores, although students accepted by many other good programs have lower scores than we list here.

When you gather information on the programs that interest you (see chap. 11), many of them will present their own statistics on accepted students from previous years. The more helpful tables also include the ranges. Carefully consider this information when estimating your chances of acceptance to a particular program.

Do these tests really predict success in graduate school?

That question has often been asked, and no fully satisfactory answer may ever be possible. A substantial research literature reports conflicting results, although at least a small correlation appears between GRE scores and grades in graduate school when one considers all disciplines in which such research has been conducted (Morrison & Morrison, 1995). From this research it is easy to conclude that, even though there are sometimes statistically significant correlations between GRE scores and graduate GPA, GRE scores account for so little variance in GPA that they are not useful as predictors of successful performance in graduate school. Critics argue that selection committees use the GRE, despite its unknown value as a predictor of success, as a quick and convenient way to do an otherwise difficult job.

It is almost impossible to determine the predictive validity of the GRE. A major reason why GRE scores may not be powerful predictors of success in graduate school is because those who are accepted into graduate school provide a rather narrow range of scores, most of which are on the high side. Because of the highly restricted variance, substantial correlations are less likely.

Huitema and Stein (1993) examined the issue among applicants to the experimental psychology program at Western Michigan University over several years. This graduate program did not use GRE scores in admission decisions, and indeed the range of GRE scores among those who entered the program and those who applied but were rejected was the same. Among those who were accepted to the program, GRE scores and grades in graduate courses were moderately correlated, whereas undergraduate GPA was not related to graduate school grades.

These authors calculated the same correlations among students who had GRE scores of 600 or greater on each subtest. Among this select group with restricted range in GRE scores, the correlation between GRE scores and graduate grades was small and similar to correlations found in previous research. Again, it may be that the relatively small relationship between GRE scores and grades in graduate school is due to the restricted variance that results from selecting students with the highest GRE scores.

[handwritten marginal note:] + B addendum: I hope I can demonstrate that test scores do not necessarily predict success rate in grad school. My scores may be low but I hope you can appreciate the accomplishments I've proven in grad school, despite these low scores.

Complicating the matter further yet is that those who are admitted with less than stellar GRE scores usually have compensating factors on some other criterion, such as considerable research experience, or a high GPA, or another attribute that would enhance the probability of success in graduate school. As Ingram (1983) wryly concluded, "We end up relying on a selection instrument whose validity for selection cannot be evaluated because we rely on it to do the selecting" (p. 712).

When to Take the Tests

The GRE used to be administered in mass testing sessions several times per year. However, the last such paper-and-pencil administration was in April 1999. Since that date, all administrations of the General Test have been done by computer. The new arrangement allows for much greater flexibility regarding when you take the exam. Nevertheless, if you choose a time that is popular with other applicants (near application deadlines), you could find yourself competing fiercely for limited testing space. Note that you must register in advance! Consult the current GRE Information Bulletin for details.

The MAT is given at hundreds of designated testing centers across the country. Exams are often scheduled by mutually agreeable appointment. Your local college or university may well be a designated test site; if not, you can contact The Psychological Corporation for information.

I figure I should take the GRE in December because my applications are not due until January or February, which gives me a chance to learn as much as I possibly can before taking them. Right?

Probably not. There are potentially serious problems with waiting until December to take the GRE if you are applying to programs with application deadlines early in the year. You do get your scores instantly, which may be factored in as you make your final selections, but they appear only on a screen and cannot be downloaded or printed. It takes approximately 2 to 5 weeks before your scores are mailed to the programs, assuming everything goes well. With thousands of scores to process, and the huge burden of holiday mail, your scores can get held up at many points along the line.

Won't a selection committee wait for my scores to arrive since they will know that I took the test in December?

Not necessarily. The selection committee members have lots of other responsibilities. They want to issue acceptance letters to the most attractive candidates and finish their job as soon as they possibly can.

Given the high probability that they already have a sufficient number of attractive applicants whose files are complete, why should they wait around for your test scores? The obvious way to avoid this most unfortunate possibility is to take the exams well in advance of application deadlines. That way, if your test scores are delayed or misdirected, there is plenty of time to track them down before selection committees begin (or finish) their job.

Another reason not to wait until December is that most applicants who are still in school are under extreme pressure at that time. Term paper deadlines are looming, and final exams are fast approaching. This is no time to put yourself under additional stress, especially because both your test and academic performance will determine the course of your academic future. Also your scores may not be as high as you think they could be. If you take the exam in December, you will not have time to schedule a retake if you believe you can improve your scores.

What if the programs I will be applying to have March or later deadlines?

In that case, December or January testing should be safe. Many master's program deadlines are in March or later; however, the deadlines for most doctoral programs come well before then.

What about scheduling the GRE Subject Test?

As of 1999, the Subject Tests were still only offered in paper-and-pencil format. Three mass testing sessions were scheduled per year (April, November, and December). Our advice is to take the Subject Test in November rather than December for the same reasons described previously.

Retaking Tests

Should I take the tests again if I don't do well?

With the computer administration of the GRE, you can only take the test once per calendar month. For those who take the GRE early enough to take it again, there is no one right answer for everyone. Keep in mind, as you assess whether to retake the GRE or MAT, that the selection committees will be provided with your previous scores (for the period spanning the past 5 years) as well as your retake scores.

If you retake the exams and score about the same (or even lower, as happens in a small percentage of cases), you will solidify rather than improve the selection committee's impression of you. If your scores improve, but only slightly, that may be perceived as a mere function of random fluctuation or familiarity with the tests and their formats. We advise retaking tests only if you are confident that your scores can be improved markedly, by at least 15%.

How do I know if my scores will improve dramatically?

It is impossible to know for sure. However, considerations might include the following:

1. You were ill the day you took the tests the first time.
2. You experienced immobilizing anxiety the first time you took the exam, but now you believe that you could be more focused and calm (perhaps with the assistance of a stress-management course or counselor).
3. Your GRE Quantitative score dramatically underestimates your actual ability to apply basic mathematical problem-solving strategies and formulas.
4. Your SAT scores were much higher than your GRE scores.
5. You had sporadic or no preparation for the tests and have since studied (or will study) for them.
6. You knew little about the tests themselves, what was being tested, what the formats were like, and so on, before taking the tests the first time. In short, you walked in ice cold.

If you were very familiar with the type of items on the tests, studied long and hard, and have no solid reason for believing that you could do better or work faster the second time around, retaking a test is probably not be a good idea.

Another approach is to take the tests one or more times—sort of—before taking the real thing; that is, simulate the actual testing conditions using the practice tests available. ETS sells software that simulates the computer administration of the GRE. One of the most valuable aspects of the simulated testing is getting a feel for the timing of the test and the level of difficulty of the questions. Afterwards, ask yourself several questions: Where are my weak spots? How did I feel and what would have minimized any distractions or negative parts of my experience? Try again, focusing more on picking up skill and speed rather than on improving the score.

Test Preparation

The tests cover general and quantitative knowledge, and in a sense you have been preparing for these tests since kindergarten. You cannot make up entirely for any deficiencies in your lifelong learning; nor, as in the case of your area exam, can you make up for what you did not learn in your major. However, you can maximize the score you are capable of achieving.

Your campus or local bookstore will likely offer an array of study guides for the General Test of the GRE, the GRE Subject Test in Psychology, and the MAT. These will contain test-taking strategies, ideas for additional study, and sample items. The test companies themselves also sell preparation books and software for their own tests. We strongly suggest that you borrow or purchase some of these resources, provided you have time to use them. The summer between your junior and senior year is a good time to commit, on average, at least an hour or two per day to test preparation.

One caution: Students have reported that these huge books can seem overwhelming and that some contain items that are more difficult than those in the actual tests. You may prefer the study guides available on CD-ROM, which are set up as games, making them less daunting. Pick away at it one day at a time, and try not to get discouraged. Students commonly plan to study over the summer, yet they put off the onerous task, week by week, until it is nearly test time. This adds regret to anxiety.

Can I raise my score by studying for these tests?

Most people seem to think so, although their reasons differ. Some say familiarity with the test formats and types of items reduces anxiety, boosts self-confidence, and saves considerable time, with a better score resulting for these reasons alone. Others say that only motivated and committed students put in considerable study time, so they have an edge from the beginning because of the kind of people they are. Many argue that much of the information one needs to know can also be learned over a relatively short period of concentrated study. The fact that the test companies themselves sell study aids seems to indicate that preparation can be effective.

Reviewing vocabulary-building books and a basic mathematics refresher book (e.g., *Cliff's Math Review for Standardized Tests*) would be wise. For the psychology Subject Test, reading over one or two high-powered, recent introductory psychology textbooks is highly recommended. Avoid the flashier ones geared mostly toward stirring readers' interest in psychology. Pick ones that summarize classic and important recent research and present the basic concepts in each subfield of psychology. Ask professors in your department what they recommend. They might even be willing to loan or give you a textbook. Also, check your college or university library for materials you can borrow.

To what extent can studying make a difference? One student we know took the exams twice, the first time cold and the second time, a year later, after considerable preparation. His scores went from the 50th percentile on all tests to the 90th percentile on all tests! He reported that he was always a good student but, as he put it, "had grown rusty in the basics, especially mathematics."

It sounds like preparing for these tests could take a lot of time.

Serious study for the tests does involve considerable time and effort. One has to keep at it, regularly, for quite a while rather than leaving it for later, for when the feeling hits, or for a fleeting session here and there. Studying for these tests is not fun, but if spread out over small chunks of time, it is not as burdensome as it sounds (it gets easier and less anxiety-provoking). Also, be sure to reward yourself immediately after each GRE study session. Remind yourself often that you are working toward an important career goal, something you are committed to achieving. And, like any worthy goal, this one will take serious, steady, and long-term effort.

What about those courses that promise to boost test scores?

Coaching sessions to improve your GRE scores are offered by several private companies, independent private tutors, and universities. The costs vary considerably, and many of them are quite expensive. The courses vary in length and in the type of experience offered. Some focus largely on test-taking strategies and "gimmicks" claimed to outsmart the test makers, whereas others include considerable content training and encouragement of outside study as well. One advantage of the formal courses is that they force you to spend that chunk of time preparing for the tests.

Do they work? Reports conflict, as you might imagine. That coaching could have a marked effect on scores is disconcerting to the test companies for several reasons. First, because coaching is often expensive, an inequity is created that discriminates against those who cannot afford coaching. Second, if the tests primarily measure test-taking strategy or facts that are memorized for short-term use, then the tests' validity is questionable. The test companies attempt to render useless as many gimmick approaches for scoring higher as possible and have even removed Analytical GRE test items proven to be susceptible to formal coaching. However, information that you can recall may well help. Our recommendation is to put some time and effort into studying for these exams.

The Night Before and Test Day

A few preparations will help make you comfortable during the exam. They take only minutes and are well worth the effort.

Lay out your clothes in advance. Banish any urge to make a fashion statement. Comfort is the sole criterion! Because you cannot know for sure the temperature of the testing room, create options through layering. The first layer should be a T-shirt or something just as light in case the room is too hot. The middle layer should be a somewhat heavier garment such as a sweatshirt or sweater, and jeans or sweatpants. Just in case, however, cart along a third warm item such as a heavy sweater or a jacket. Try on the outfit, one layer at a time, to ensure that nothing scratches or binds, that your arms can move freely, and that your body feels comfortable.

Lay out the items you need to take with you: required identification, admissions ticket, the address and room number of where you are to report, and a reliable watch (with any chime or alarm feature switched off). Also include a list of the exact information about four programs to which you want your test scores reported.

Do not cram for the exams the night before the test. Your dream state will likely be an agonizing swirl of words and mathematical symbols, and you may wake up exhausted. Eat a moderate-sized dinner consisting of foods that you know will not cause you any gastric distress, and relax at some "no-brain" activity that you find pleasurable but not overstimulating. A walk or watching a benign television program is the kind of thing we have in mind. Go to bed early, and get a good night's sleep.

On test day you want no aggravations or surprises. Eat a healthy breakfast of foods that are easy on your stomach. Leave plenty of time for getting to the testing site and finding the correct room. (If you are unfamiliar with the test site, and it is within driving distance, consider visiting it a week or more before the actual test date. If you traveled to the test-taking area the day before, consider going to the specific site as your early evening pretest activity. Some students report that this exercise contributed to calmness on test day because they knew exactly where to go and where to park.) If you live reasonably close to the test site but getting there will involve driving for 20 or more minutes in heavy traffic, consider asking someone to drive you there.

In the end, taking the GRE and other standardized tests is something you must do on your own. Still, we wish you best of luck. Remember that, after it is over, you join the ranks of students who can commiserate about this academic rite of passage.

Part III

Making Your Choices

CHAPTER 11

HOW DO I GET INFORMATION ABOUT PROGRAMS?

We have discussed what graduate program officials look for in applicants and what you might want in a prospective program. Here we discuss how you actually identify and obtain information about specific programs. This process involves two stages: identifying programs that may interest you (including how to contact them), and actually contacting the program to request specific information and an application.

Identifying Viable Programs

The resource listings that follow are recommended for a single purpose: to acquaint you with the possibilities that are out there. You should not rely on any single source of information about potential programs but rather should use as many sources as you can.

Purchasing resources that are not available on loan can strain a student's budget, but because the information you gain may affect your entire professional career, the money spent is a good investment. Still, you may save money by checking whether your academic department, an advisement office, or your local campus library has copies of these resources. It is likely that some of these resources are already available.

Sometimes we refer to resources on the World Wide Web. If you are not familiar with searching the web or accessing a specific web site, be assured that these skills are very easy to learn. Simply ask a friend or a campus computer lab monitor to spend a few minutes to show you the ropes. Make bookmarks for programs of great interest. We suggest downloading and printing information of great interest because you can highlight and mark critical information. Following is a review of the primary resources.

Peterson's Guides annually publishes a set of educational guidebooks (see http://petersons.com/). The volume of most interest here is titled

115

Graduate Studies in Social Sciences & Social Work. The volume includes a CD-ROM and provides basic information on institutions providing nearly 5,000 programs in the social sciences and social work. As of 1998, the book/CD-ROM combination listed for $24.95.

The Graduate Record Examinations/Council of Graduate Schools (GRE/CGS) also publishes a set of resource manuals each year. Although most of the programs of interest to our readers (psychology, sociology, student counseling) are in *Volume C: Social Sciences and Education*, social work is included in *Volume D: Arts, Humanities, and Other Fields*.

The GRE/CGS manuals consist mainly of massive tables that can be mastered with a little practice. Basic information is included (degrees offered, number of students, etc.) as well as prerequisites (required tests, preferred undergraduate major, and reference letter specifications). One section lists special and interdisciplinary programs that include combined or more unusual advanced degree programs such as East–West psychology, engineering psychology, and cognitive and linguistic studies. Schools offering "individualized" graduate degrees (specially designed to fit your unique needs) are also listed. There are brief sketches of each institution, organized by state, and a section of addresses for applications, financial aid, and housing information for each institution. Order forms for this series appear in the *GRE Information Bulletin*, usually available on all college campuses, or you could contact the organization directly at http://www.gre.org/ or 800-537-3160. As of 1999, the cost was $20 per volume.

For those interested in doctoral programs in clinical or counseling psychology, the *Insider's Guide to Graduate Programs in Clinical & Counseling Psychology* is published every 2 years by Guilford Press (http://www.guilford.com/ or 72 Spring St., New York, NY 10012; telephone 800-365-7006). This volume includes general information about applying to graduate school, selecting programs, and so forth. In addition, APA-accredited doctoral programs are listed, along with contact information and a profile of each, including the number of applicants and acceptances during the previous year, the proportion of students who are ethnic minorities or women, the theoretical orientation of the program, the relative emphasis the program places on research versus clinical training, and the required, preferred, or typical GPA and GRE scores. The 1998 edition cost $21.95.

For those interested in some form of graduate study in psychology, either at the master's or doctoral level, the APA publishes *Graduate Study in Psychology* (updated every 2 years with an addendum made available in the off-years). This is a helpful and lengthy guide (nearly 700 pages) offering relatively detailed descriptions of graduate programs in the United States and Canada. The book does not, however, include every possible option. Participation is voluntary, and not every program chooses to be included. Most interdisciplinary programs and master's programs related to psychology in departments other than psychology are excluded. However, the selection is wide, especially for programs housed within departments of psychology. (For a guide to master's programs, see Buskist and Mixon's *Guide to Master's Programs in Psychology and Counseling Psychology*, 1998, published by Allyn & Bacon. It has basic, useful information about a great many master's programs, but is not complete. For example, the three master's programs in our department are not included!)

This APA guide can be ordered directly from APA (http://www.apa.org/ or APA Order Department, P.O. Box 2710, Hyattsville, MD 20784; telephone 800-374-2721) or through a bookstore. The 1998 edition cost $21.95, well worth the investment if you intend to cast a wide net in your search for graduate training in psychology. Similar guides for sociology and anthropology are published by the American Sociological Association (http://www.asanet.org/) and the American Anthropological Association (http://www.ameranthassn.org/), respectively, and may be available to view in the appropriate departments at your local university.

What information can I get from the APA Guide?

You will learn the mailing address of each department, the year the department was established, the name of the department chairperson, the number of full-time and part-time faculty, and the types of programs and degrees offered (including how many of each type of degree have been awarded recently). A Student Information section provides data on enrollments in the various programs within a department and, sometimes, statistics on the number of women and ethnic minorities enrolled in the program.

A section on admission requirements offers a variety of figures such as minimum test scores considered, course work you should already have completed, and minimum GPA. Two designations are often provided: One is a P, which indicates the preferred GPA, course background, or test score, and the other is an R, which indicates the required minimum test scores, background courses, and GPA. Criteria for applicants to master's and doctoral programs are often presented separately because they are typically different.

Does that mean that I shouldn't apply to a program if I don't meet their R criteria?

If your grades, test scores, or completed courses fall well below the R levels listed, that is a reasonable conclusion. The very competitive programs typically attract plenty of applicants who reach their P levels. If you fall only a little below the R level in a particular area but have strong compensating components on your record (e.g., considerable research experience), you could be considered on other merits. Some very competitive programs list only their P levels, perhaps to leave the door open for the unusual student who does not have all the right courses or numbers on his or her record but who would be an attractive candidate based on other factors.

The information in the APA guide (and the others we describe) is usually at least 2 years old by the time it appears in print. In addition, such a huge and complicated publishing achievement may contain some editing and printing errors. Other authors have questioned whether some of the information supplied by the program representatives themselves is entirely accurate. Because you cannot know where the errors lie, we suggest that you write down the information for any program that seems a good match for you, even though the data seem strange (e.g., numbers that do not quite "add up," or information that deviates markedly from what you have learned about that program from another source). Seek out more information; current materials that you receive or find should resolve most ambiguities.

What about the Internet as a resource for finding programs?

The Internet offers a wealth of free information. For example, one site provides contact information for programs in numerous disciplines (http://www.gradschools.com/). A current list of APA-accredited doctoral programs in clinical, counseling, and school psychology is also available on the Internet, along with contact information for each program (http://www.APA.org/ed/doctoral.html). Particular web sites list information on, or links to, graduate programs in school psychology (http:www. education.indiana.edu/cep/spprog_contents.html), neuroscience (http:// www.andp.org/training/USindex.htm), and social work (http://www.web-com.com/nfscsw.schools.html).

Similarly, such information is available on the Internet for a variety of master's programs that are accredited by appropriate professional organizations, including the American Art Therapy Association (http://www. arttherapy.org/subpages/facilities/programs.html or 1202 Allanson Road, Mundelein, IL 60060; telephone 847-949-6064); the American Association of Marriage and Family Therapists (http://www.AAMFT.org/ or 1133 15th St., NW, Suite 300, Washington, DC 20005-2710; telephone 202-452-0109); the Council on Social Work Education (http://www.CSWE.org/ directory.htm or 1600 Duke St., Suite 300, Alexandria, VA 22314; telephone 703-683-8080); and the Council for Accreditation of Counseling and Related Educational Programs (http://www.counseling.org/cacrep/ directory.htm or 5999 Stevenson Ave., Alexandria, VA 22304; telephone 703-823-9800). This last organization accredits master's programs in school, marriage and family, mental health, and community counseling.

The publishers of Peterson's Guides also maintain a web site (http://petersons.com/graduate/) containing names of institutions offering graduate degrees in particular fields. Specifically, one can search within the social sciences (http://petersons.com/graduate/select/soci.html), social work (http://petersons.com/graduate/select/socw.html), or, for those interested in rehabilitation sciences and occupational therapy, the health sciences (http://petersons.com/graduate/select/heal.html). Although contact information is provided for some programs, for others the browser is referred to Peterson's print guides. Still, the web site provides names of programs that may be of interest, and one can typically find contact information elsewhere with a little investigation (as discussed next).

How might I find programs that offer specific training in a specialty area?

Some professional societies offer directories of graduate programs in a particular field. For example, the Society for Neuroscience (http: www.sfn.org/ or 11 Dupont Circle, NW, Suite 500, Washington, DC 20036; telephone 202-462-6688) issues a directory that describes relevant graduate programs and their contact information. Because advanced degrees with a biological bent are not always housed in psychology departments, students interested in physiological or biological psychology should definitely consult this resource.

The Human Factors and Ergonomics Society publishes the Directory of Human Factors Graduate Programs in the United States and Canada. This user-friendly guide details programs and is essential for students interested in this specialization. Best of all, the directory is free and can even be downloaded from the Internet (http://hfes.org/publications/grad-schools.html or Human Factors and Ergonomics Society, P.O. Box 1369, Santa Monica, CA 90406-1369; telephone 310-394-1811).

One of the attractive aspects of psychology is the diversity of the field. Accordingly, the APA is divided into 50 divisions, most of which represent a content specialty area. (Divisions are numbered 1 to 52; Divisions 4 and 11 no longer exist.) Each division, often referred to by its number, has its own governance, special projects, and focus, some of which may relate to student training and career planning. The APA divisions are as follows:

1. General Psychology
2. Teaching of Psychology
3. Experimental Psychology
5. Evaluation and Measurement
6. Behavioral Neuroscience and Comparative Psychology
7. Developmental Psychology
8. Personality and Social Psychology
9. Psychological Study of Social Issues
10. Psychology and the Arts
12. Clinical Psychology
13. Consulting Psychology

14. Industrial and Organizational Psychology
15. Educational Psychology
16. School Psychology
17. Counseling Psychology
18. Psychologists in Public Service
19. Military Psychology
20. Adult Development and Aging
21. Applied Experimental and Engineering Psychology
22. Rehabilitation Psychology
23. Consumer Psychology
24. Theoretical and Philosophical Psychology
25. Experimental Analysis of Behavior
26. History of Psychology
27. Community Psychology
28. Psychopharmacology and Substance Abuse
29. Psychotherapy
30. Psychological Hypnosis
31. State Psychological Association Affairs
32. Humanistic Psychology
33. Mental Retardation and Developmental Disabilities
34. Population and Environmental Psychology
35. Psychology of Women
36. Psychology of Religion
37. Child, Youth, and Family Services
38. Health Psychology
39. Psychoanalysis
40. Clinical Neuropsychology
41. The American Psychology–Law Society
42. Psychologists in Independent Practice
43. Family Psychology
44. Psychological Study of Lesbian, Gay, and Bisexual Issues
45. Psychological Study of Ethnic Minority Issues
46. Media Psychology
47. Exercise and Sport Psychology
48. Peace Psychology
49. Group Psychology and Group Psychotherapy
50. Addictions
51. Psychological Study of Men and Masculinity
52. International Psychology

Many of the APA divisions have relevant information available to students, such as listings of graduate programs offering training in that specialty area or short, helpful brochures describing careers or the kinds of expertise professionals in a specific interest area typically possess. Some divisions charge nominal fees for materials to cover printing and mailing costs.

Because APA divisions are active and changing, the best tactic—if there is an APA division that represents your specific interest area—is to send your request for information to the current secretary of the division. Include a self-addressed, stamped envelope to facilitate a speedy return. You can find the list of current division secretaries and their addresses on the Internet (http://www.apa.org/about/division.html) or in the most recent July issue of the *American Psychologist* (found in most university libraries).

It would be nice if relevant graduate programs sent me information without me having to contact them.

This is the idea behind the GRE Search Service. After you register with the service, basic information about you is sent to graduate programs which have requested that students matching a particular profile be identified for recruitment purposes. Programs seeking students like you will send you information about their program. Registration with the Search Service is free to the applicant and can be done regardless of whether one has taken, or even intends to take, the GRE (see http://www.gre.org/). Register early, because information about possible applicants is sent to graduate programs only three times per year (October, December, and April). Institutions taking part in the service represent a relatively small subset of the potential programs available to you, so do not depend on it alone. Very qualified students have told us that they were contacted by very few schools, or none at all, as a result of the search service.

Finally, faculty members at your local university or professionals in your community may give you some program ideas to consider. Try to assess how thorough and recent their information is. Sometimes our impressions of graduate programs are secondhand or simply reflect our own biases. Many of us cannot even accurately describe the current programs in the graduate schools we attended because so many changes have occurred since we were students there. So, although you should take advantage of the opinions that others are willing to share with you, temper them with second opinions and additional research of your own.

Obtaining Information
From Specific Programs

I have a list of programs in which I might be interested, but I don't have contact information for all of them. What should I do?

You definitely will need to contact each program to which you might want to apply. However, to do that, you have to have a postal address, telephone number, or e-mail address for a program representative. Also, there is no point in requesting applications from programs that clearly do not match your interests and abilities. For these reasons, we advise that you attempt to locate a web site for each program on your list, even if you already have contact information for that program. Sometimes it is even possible to print out an application from the program's web site.

You may learn enough about programs from their web sites to determine that you are no longer interested. For example, your goal may be to become a practicing clinical psychologist, but you may discover from a web site that a particular program is in the business of training clinical scientists.

To search for a departmental or program web site, you need only know the institution that houses that department or graduate program. Typing the name of the educational institution into a search engine should reveal a web site for that institution, if indeed it maintains one. More conveniently, there are at least two web sites that offer links to hundreds of institutions of higher education in the United States (http://www.clas.ufl.edu/CLAS/american-universities.html and http://www.isl-garnet.uah.edu/universities/).

From a particular institution's web site, you should be able to link to a site for the graduate program or academic department in which you are interested (if that program or department has its own web page). Regardless, the more general web site will provide contact information for the institution, and from there you can obtain contact information for the specific department or program.

Once I have contact information for all of the programs that are still of interest to me, then what?

Most schools will be ready to receive requests for applications and program information about 15 months prior to the time students will enter or start the program (which is only about 4 to 7 months before the applications are actually due). Programs with early annual deadlines (late December or early January for entry the following fall) almost always have materials ready by the late summer before the deadline. Programs with later deadlines may not have their materials ready until the previous fall, or about the time you start your senior year in college.

If you do not request information directly from a web site (or a program of interest does not offer that option), prepare short, typed letters on standard, plain white bond paper. Prepare a plain letter-sized envelope with the same care. If you absolutely must write the letters by hand, take the time required for your neatest penmanship. Do not use fancy or cute stationery or printed letterhead stationery of any kind for this task or any other correspondence with graduate schools. Do not use lined notebook paper, and do not save time by making photocopies of one generic request form. Do not fold your note several times and cram it into a tiny envelope.

***Why so many rules? Why do I have to be so proper at this point? I only
want some information.***

All of the "don'ts" listed previously say something about you that you
do not want said. This note is the first descriptor that the program evaluators have of you. You want to appear professional, not silly or immature. You want to appear to be sincerely interested in each program you
are exploring.

There is a good chance that the administrative assistant will not dis-
card this first note. Rather, an initial request for information is often put
in your application file. A messy, silly, or duplicated all-purpose inquiry
may become the first item evaluators see every time they open your folder! So, that first inquiry is the way you begin to assemble a persuasive
package of credentials. First impressions do count, and your folder is all
the evaluators will know about you. Make it as solid and impressive as
you can in content and appearance from the very beginning.

What should my letter say and where do I send it?

A letter should be quite short and to the point. This is not the time to
tell them much about yourself because you do not yet know what they
want to know. The content can read something like this:

Date

Department of Psychology [or Educational Psychology,
    or whatever the name of the department]
Graduate Program Office
ABC University
City, State, and Zip

To Whom It May Concern:
    I am interested in applying to your *X* [put appropriate degree, such as PhD
or MA] program in *Y* [put name of appropriate program here, such as social
psychology]. Please send me an application and any other information you
have available that describes this graduate program.
    Thank you in advance for your timely response to my request.

Sincerely,

[Your signature]

[Your full and correct mailing address printed or typed below your printed or
typed name.]

---

you can use this format ↓ for your addendums

Many programs offer the e-mail addresses of their secretarial staff on their web sites. A short message, adapted from the content of the previous note, may get your materials to you even faster.

If I'm interested in psychology, why can't I just ask for information about psychology in general. What do you mean by "appropriate program"?

The vast majority of academic departments that offer graduate work in psychology have one or more specific graduate programs (e.g., developmental, clinical, or social) within that department. The advantage of specifying the program in your note is that you will be sure to get any pamphlets or special information about that specific program. Otherwise you may receive only general information, because it is often considered too expensive to include materials for every program within a department as a response to a general inquiry letter.

It is acceptable to ask for information about two or more programs within a single department if more than one is of genuine interest to you. (If you later decide to submit an application to the department, however, you will virtually always be required to pick only one.) If two programs at the same university interest you but are housed in different departments, you will have to write two separate inquiries, one to each department. (Typically, there is no problem applying to two programs if they are housed in different departments.)

Be sure that the word *graduate* is in the address and that your note itself specifies clearly that your interest is in graduate study. Also, create a master list of the program names, addresses, and telephone numbers, so you can easily check off programs as they send information and can readily identify those who did not respond to your inquiry or about which you have more questions. You can then easily contact these programs again. Keep copies of all correspondence, and organize all of these materials to prevent losing crucial information.

Almost all graduate training institutions (with free-standing professional schools being the major exception) also have an all-university Graduate Admissions Office for all programs in every academic discipline, and their staff will probably send you materials as well. However, we have found that getting program information from the department first (because that is your focus) is usually best, and that the rest usually follows without further prompting by the applicant. (That is, either the program or department offices refer your specific inquiries to the main graduate administrative office, whose staff then forwards additional materials to you, or the departments have copies of the all-university materials already and include them in the departmental material sent to you.)

When I request information, how long does it usually take to get a response?

The time between requests for information and receipt of materials varies widely. With the cooperation of a number of students, we collected systematic information about request and receipt dates for over 250 graduate programs. If we generalize from our findings, the range of the time you will wait for responses after mailing your note will vary from 4 days to forever! The typical period was 10 to 25 days. Although about 15% of the schools responded almost immediately, another 15% did not respond with any information for 8 weeks. Requests made at least 2 months before the application deadline date were processed much faster than requests sent closer to the deadline. Some programs were very slow, taking more than 10 weeks to respond, even when the request was mailed 4 months before the deadline for receipt of applications. A few schools did not respond at all. Therefore, you should be prepared to follow up with a polite call or a second note if you do not receive anything within 4 to 6 weeks. (Here is one reason to keep copies of your correspondence: so you know when you sent requests.)

Some schools send program information out in one big chunk, whereas others dole their materials out over a period of time. Occasionally your request will get stuck in a computerized system and you will receive the same materials over and over again. You may even be kept on a mailing list and receive bulletins and other information for the next year or two!

You may find that the material you receive in the mail is not as bulky as you expected. Instead, you will often be referred to a web site. The cost saved by posting as much information as possible on the Internet is, of course, the reason behind this trend.

What should I do with all of this stuff that is arriving in the mail or that I downloaded?

It is important that you process very carefully the materials you receive as they arrive. Fight that overwhelmed voice inside of you that tells you to stick it all in the corner (unopened) until you are in the mood to get around it. We next discuss, step by step, what you need to do instead.

First, thoroughly read everything you get. If you get an initial, distinct impression that this program is not for you after all, or that it is very unlikely you will qualify for admission, omit that program from your list. If you are slightly below but close to meeting all of the stated requirements, let that program stay in the running for now. (Rather than throw out materials for programs you will no longer pursue, however, donate them to your department's graduate school application file. If your current academic department does not have such a student service, suggest to the department chairperson that one be started—see Appendix B.)

Next, make a folder for each program that remains of interest to you. On the front of the folder, print the name of the program and the school. List the contents of the file (e.g., letter of greeting from the program chairperson, application, program description, pamphlet describing housing options, etc.). If little cards and odd-sized pieces of paper are included (as they often are), attach them to the folder with a paper clip so that they will not fall out or get lost. Also, make sure that the name of the school is on each separate item, and when it is not, write it yourself. Many items do not have any affiliation identification, leaving you in big trouble if something falls out of its folder.

If you have sent for information from more than just a few programs, get a sturdy, file-sized cardboard carton, if you do not already have a file cabinet drawer available. This project is important enough to have its own home rather than becoming just another stack of papers on your desk or dresser. Also, list on the face of each program's folder the following important information:

1. The date application materials are due. Note that there can be more than one date per program. Applications for financial aid, for example, often are due earlier than program applications. Occasionally the deadline for the departmental supplementary application form and the university-wide application are different.
2. Test scores required, such as the GRE General Test and Subject Test.
3. Other action items, such as transcripts, essays, information that will take time or special effort to retrieve, and other specialized tasks that must be done in a specific way.

This list should be made promptly to alert you to the demands you will face and to reduce anxiety through organization. You are starting the important process of structuring what will likely be the course of the rest of your working life. Careful organization will help combat fear and confusion and a desire to stall.

Next, evaluate more methodically those programs that remain of interest to you after initially establishing as best you can how your credentials and experience match with their requirements. Does the program offer training that reflects the kind of work you want to do? Do you have a reasonable picture of the course, experiential, and time sequences? Do these meet your needs? Are the names of the faculty included? If you are applying to a competitive research scientist or scientist–practitioner doctoral program, identifying your educators is especially important. Many of the programs thoroughly present their faculty and include research interests, citations to selected publications, and sometimes personal statements about ongoing program activities.

Knowledge of the faculty will enhance your chances of acceptance, because it can help you make a good match between yourself and the program. If faculty information is not included, plan to request or research it if the program remains of interest to you (see chap. 15).

Now is also the time to note other important information that you do not have. For example, is information included about housing and financial aid opportunities and how to apply for them? Do you get a feel for life as a student in that particular program?

How do I get the additional information that I need?

Usually the graduate office staff will be able to provide additional information. Before writing or calling the staff in the appropriate office, however, very carefully read the materials you have received—at least twice—to make sure that any questions remain unanswered. Graduate faculty and staff are generally displeased when applicants call with questions that are answered in the application materials. The very people you want to impress may note that you do not read or retain information well.

Try to lump all of your questions into as few letters or telephone calls as possible. Another common complaint about graduate school applicants is that some of them call over and over again, giving the impression that they are disorganized or have bothersome personalities.

We do not want to give the impression that graduate staff hate to hear from prospective applicants; indeed, most welcome appropriate telephone calls from students. Still, if you call a graduate program office for help, keep the person on the phone for as short a time as possible. These offices are usually very busy, so respect for the time constraints of the staff is always appreciated. Do not demand to speak to the program director or an admissions selection committee member for basic program information. Such requests are often viewed as inappropriate.

Sometimes an office staff member will suggest that you talk to a specific faculty member, but let the staff person be the one to propose that solution. (See chap. 15 for appropriate ways to contact faculty.) Finally, always be polite in your letters and calls, even if you perceive the recipient to be cold or unhelpful. This is not merely an appeal based on the desirability of displaying good etiquette but also is a way to protect your chances for acceptance. We have heard a number of accounts from program directors who excluded applicants even before reviewing their folders because of rudeness or verbal harassment toward staff.

Before offering assistance in making decisions about where to apply, we would like you to consider geographical, financial, and GPA issues. The next three chapters are dedicated to these important considerations.

CHAPTER 12

SHOULD I STAY IN TOWN OR SHOULD I GO?

A well-kept secret for boosting your chances of acceptance into a program that may be just right for you is to seek graduate training away from your current geographical area. A diverse student population is often viewed as a positive feature of a graduate class, and geographical balance is an easy way to achieve some degree of diversity. It is also a straightforward way for an applicant to gain a number of advantages. You just have to muster up the courage to do it!

Excuses, Legitimate and Otherwise

I'm hesitant to move to some strange place where I don't know anyone. It's more comfortable just to stay here.

If most students were a bit more flexible and willing to relocate a few hundred to a couple of thousand miles away, at least temporarily, we would not have had to write this chapter. Despite the disruption and trepidation that often accompany a journey into the unknown, it could be the best thing you ever do for yourself. Most students we have known found the experience of moving away to attend graduate school both maturing and exciting. They made new friends easily, and making new friends is something you will have to do anyway, even if you go to a school only a few miles from home. Regardless of where you go, your classmates will be a ready-made social group. Also, once you are accepted into a graduate program, the staff will usually provide you with contacts and information to ease your transition.

An advantage of applying to distant programs is the instant widening of options, which, in turn, boosts your chances of finding the best program to suit your needs. Students who confine themselves to local or in-state universities have to choose from a much more limited pool. Those whose interests are very specialized and who also will not consider venturing from home base may not find any suitable program.

But I don't like the cold, and I need to be able to scuba dive and eat authentic Mexican food on weekends, and my dog will miss me, and . . .

Whoa! Talking yourself out of moving away is as easy as sleeping in on Sundays. Because you are creating the foundation for your life's work, you must examine your priorities. There are very few legitimate reasons for limiting yourself to your familiar territory.

What are they?

Geographical distance is difficult on relationships, especially those that require frequent emotional and physical connections. So relationships should be considered carefully in graduate career planning. Nevertheless, we encourage you to carefully explore options and the reasons for your decisions, rather than simply giving in to the initial knee-jerk impulse that says, "I can't go very far."

Those who are in a committed relationship with a partner whose career is so well-established that uprooting would be extremely detrimental may have more limited options. The people involved need to consider priorities and longer term goals in the context of a possible relocation. Occasionally health problems or needed services may restrict geographical mobility. Still, adequate, similar services may exist in other locales.

Even the additional financial cost, due to travel and (sometimes) high nonresident tuition costs, is not always a legitimate excuse for staying close to home. As long as you do not need to visit home often (and, remember, graduate students are very busy), travel costs may not be very high. Sometimes considerable money is saved by moving away from one's local area because the cost of living is lower. Nonresident tuition is often waived as part of the support package offered to graduate students who enroll in state-supported programs.

Sometimes other educationally relevant facilities in the student's current community are an important consideration (e.g., an affiliated hospital, target population, or research institute that may closely match a student's training needs). If some unusual training opportunity related to your strong interests is local or in-state, then you have a valid reason for sticking around. However, we doubt that this condition applies very often.

The weather is frequently an issue, and emphasis on this factor should also be minimized unless there is some genuine medical rationale. People adapt to just about any weather imaginable, and you will be at that location for a limited number of years. A student of ours who was born and raised in southern California amazed himself with his relatively easy adaptation to the University of Minnesota. He found that Minneapolis was exceptionally well-prepared for the rough months and that cross-country skiing was almost as much fun as surfing.

Students often try to avoid considering a move away from home by convincing themselves that a culture clash will cause them debilitating shock. Remember, however, that your primary base of social operation will be within the graduate institution. Sometimes liberal or nontraditional schools are located in communities with a very conservative or traditional atmosphere, and vice versa. You will spend a considerable amount of time in the buildings housing your program, so you may remain largely unaware of the surrounding community. Even your living quarters will likely be close to campus.

It would only be fair to add that the social atmosphere of the community can sometimes contribute to a good match between the student and the new location, and prevailing values and attitudes are sometimes tied to specific geographical areas. Ethnic minority or gay and lesbian students may feel uncomfortable in a community that has evidenced intolerance or hostility toward these groups. If the only living quarters you can afford are dismal, in a dangerous neighborhood, or a long distance from the campus (as can be the case for schools in large urban areas), you may have to reevaluate your choices.

I heard that you should choose a graduate school located in an area where you will want to spend the rest of your life, because you will probably get a job there after you're finished. Is that true?

No. Chances are high that your first job will not be anywhere near the locale of your graduate school. For example, institutions housing graduate programs almost never hire their own graduates into a potentially permanent, tenure-track academic position. You may not even finish your training in the same community where you attend graduate school, because some types of training programs require, as the last step, an internship at a different location. If you like the area around your graduate program or internship, perhaps you may stay in the area by working for another university or agency. Most likely, however, you will return to where you originally came from or take a job somewhere you have not yet been, the location of which you cannot even begin to predict at this point.

Additional Advantages to Consider

Besides having a new experience, gaining more independence, and widening my options, should anything else convince me to apply to programs far from home?

The main problem with confining your applications to your own stomping grounds, or even to extremely desirable locations in general (such as the east or west coasts), is that so many of your peers are doing the same thing. This puts you in intense competition with the best and the brightest applicants. A solid-looking applicant from across the country does not blend in with the local applicant crowd. This person may become the Kansas applicant or the Virginia applicant, an object of intrigue that may tempt a closer look.

One California student we know received something special attached to the application materials that arrived as a result of her routine request from a Midwestern school. A handwritten note read, "We always try to find a place for an applicant from California. We hope you will apply here." It was signed by the program director, who knew nothing about the student! This 180 degree twist on the concept of "geographical desirability" will not ensure acceptance in the absence of other qualifications, nor does it pertain to every program. Yet it is an advantage in some places that too few students have apparently been willing to exercise.

Another subtle yet potentially profound advantage of applying to distant programs is that you and your peers are seeking references from a restricted pool of professors, all of whom will write letters to local programs for several of you. Therefore, even if Professor Smith wrote a positive letter, you may be rejected from a competitive program if her letters for two or more other students were more positive than the one she wrote for you. Why? Because competitive programs have very few slots open each year, and they seek a variety of backgrounds in their students. Therefore, they may take only one or two applicants from any single, local campus. When, say, five applications are received with letters of support from Dr. Smith, it is usually very easy for selection committees to spot who Dr. Smith thinks are the best among the five, even if all of the letters are generally positive.

I never thought about it that way! What can I do to keep from being a victim of that invisible trap?

The easiest way, of course, is to spread your applications around the country so that your letter from Dr. Smith is the only letter (or one of two at the most) the selection committee receives from her. Finally, we must also note that this trap is generally less likely with master's programs and some doctoral programs that are less competitive or that primarily draw from local student populations.

I think I am beginning to understand how applying to distant programs can be an advantage. I might even get excited about living someplace new.

If you find that you are actually excited about going away to school, be sure that you express that enthusiasm somewhere in your application materials. The most likely place where this point can be made briefly but comfortably is in a discussion of good match in your statement of purpose (if it fits with the essay requirements) or, otherwise, in a cover letter. As noted throughout this book, an important consideration for the evaluators is how well you and the program fit. That you are interested in a particular site and have no problem making a major move may be taken as some evidence of a potentially good match and seriousness of purpose, or at least maturity and enthusiasm about the program. If the application does not provide an opportunity to declare your interest in coming from afar, you can express it in a cover letter.

How to Find Out About Other Communities

Ideally, you should travel to the communities in which the graduate programs are located and do some firsthand exploration. There are no truly adequate substitutes for walking around the campus, stopping to talk to anyone who is willing, and driving around the town.

Obviously, most applicants will not have the opportunity to visit every distant campus of interest. There are ways, however, to learn quite a bit about these places without leaving town. Many communities have web sites providing vital statistics, places of interest, and photos of the primary attractions. Many web sites for universities provide a link to pages about the surrounding community. Otherwise, try typing the name of the community into a search engine to find relevant web sites. If the location of interest is a large, suburban area, such as New York City, Boston, or Los Angeles, tour books and newspapers from these areas are available at your local library or the travel section of a bookstore.

You can communicate directly with communities both small and large. Requesting information from the Chamber of Commerce or Travel Information in the communities housing the universities in which you are interested will frequently net relevant responses. Simply use the same town and zip code as in the mailing address of the university. You will typically receive promotional brochures, which often contain stunning photographs as well as information about housing, businesses, and other opportunities and attractions the community holds. Because these materials are designed to stir interest in outsiders, they can reduce apprehension over applying to a distant program. Simply having more information and a few visual images of the community often reduces anxiety.

Most communities surrounding a college or university have a local newspaper. Obtaining single copies (or even subscribing for a brief period) can teach you many things about a community including what problems it faces, what activities and entertainment it supports, and, from the advertisements, how much things cost and what kinds of services are available. The local Yellow Pages also provide an interesting perspective about a community including health and other services and types and numbers of businesses.

International Graduate Study

What about going to graduate school even farther away, such as Canada or a more distant country?

The main consideration here, assuming that you want to return to the United States to work, is that the degree may not allow you to qualify for jobs and compete with those who have earned their degrees from accredited U.S. universities or professional schools. This is not a problem, typically, for Canadian schools or the top-rated universities in foreign countries, depending on the career for which you are training. You should, however, research this point before proceeding, particularly if you wish to pursue a career that requires state licensure. A foreign degree in a mental health service provider program (e.g., clinical psychology) might not qualify you to seek licensure in your state.

Before applying to foreign schools, find out what language is used in the classroom. Sometimes it is English; often it is not. (Remember that parts of Canada are French speaking.) Even if you have learned to speak and read another language, being able to carry on a reasonable conversation in the language does not necessarily mean that you could cope with advanced academic studies in that language. (It can be hard enough in English!) If classes will be taught in another language, be sure that you can handle the material with which you will be working.

If you decide to apply for graduate training outside the country, be prepared for a great deal of extra preparation and paperwork required from both the university and the immigration authorities in the United States and the other country, including checks on your character and criminal record. You will need to gather certain documents and fill out a bundle of forms to receive a student, visitor, or other type of visa. If you request an application to a Canadian school, much of what you need to know to get started will be included in the materials you receive initially. Canadian schools are used to applicants from the United States and provide relatively easy-to-follow directions.

Details about the intricacies of foreign application procedures are beyond the scope of this book. Note, however, that applications to schools outside of the United States are usually due up to 2 months earlier than those to schools in this country, because immigration authorities need extra time to process students into the country. Another consideration is that financial aid is highly restricted and often not available in any form to U.S. citizens. (This is similar to the problems international students face in the United States.) Also, it can be difficult for those attending foreign schools (or their spouses) to get work permits. Proof of preexisting and adequate financial support is often required prior to acceptance into a foreign program. In short, it is clearly advantageous for those interested in foreign-based training to take care of their financial planning before leaving the country.

I'd like to think more about going out of the country to graduate school. Where can I find more information?

Information about schools in other countries can be found in a number of ways, including Internet searches. Directories of universities in the world generally, or in specific countries, provide names and addresses to which you can write for application information. Such directories may be available in university campus libraries. Another route is to write to the Educational Office of the embassy (located in the United States) of the country in which you wish to study. Many have lists (often in English) of schools with the type of programs you request accompanied by their complete addresses and, sometimes, a little extra information. The student exchange or international studies office at your own or a nearby college or university probably has publications as well as a staff member who can guide you to the information you need.

Occasionally, students express an interest in a specific foreign program because of an admired scholar or a highly specialized program. In such cases, write to that professor or to someone in the program expressing your knowledge of, and interest in, his or her work. Ask for information, including whether the program would be interested in having a person such as yourself there, and what your situation might be were you to enroll. Chances are reasonably good that you will get some sort of response that will help you determine what to do next.

CHAPTER 13

HOW AM I GOING TO PAY FOR GRADUATE SCHOOL?

Bright, well-qualified students who are severely limited in what they can spend on their educations account for a large portion of graduate school applicants. Only rarely do we run into someone who declares that financial assistance will be unnecessary. At the same time, most graduate programs do not expect that you are still totally dependent on your family for financial support. In this chapter we offer suggestions for financial survival during your graduate training.

Types of Graduate-Level Support

I can't afford to continue my education on my own. My parents struggled just to get me through college, and I haven't saved much. What kinds of options are available?

The federal government and individual states offer financial assistance programs for graduate students. Corporations, foundations, service organizations, and financial institutions are other sources of aid. The graduate institutions themselves usually have various types of funding available, often in the form of assistantships and tuition waivers.

The options available range from fellowships to loans. *Fellowships* are prestigious awards to be used to cover educational expenses and sometimes provide allotments (often called *stipends*) for living expenses. Fellowships require no work, do not have to be repaid, and are generally based on merit. *Grants* are also often given in the form of stipends, requiring no work or repayment. Grants are usually based on need (although, obviously, the recipient must also be meritorious enough to be invited into the program). "Need" is defined as the difference between the amount of money required to allow you to receive your education while living at a basic level (nothing fancy!) and what ever personal resources you have available. Your own resources include savings, family contributions (spouse or parents), and other assets. Documentation is required to substantiate need, often based on tax records and some established formulas. Many schools will require you to file a FAFSA (Free Application for Federal Student Aid) form (see http://www.fafsa.ed.gov/ for a copy on the Internet). These forms are also probably available at your local college or university.

Teaching and research assistantships are common ways to help finance graduate education, especially in traditional doctoral and master's programs. Work must be performed, but as most of us who have held such positions will attest, these activities were integral to our education and enriched it deeply. Our first scholarly publication was often a coauthorship on a research paper written by the faculty member we assisted.

Tuition waivers are common sources of support offered by graduate schools. With this type of aid you do not have to pay tuition, even if you are from out of state, although you may still have to pay the university general fee or administrative fee each quarter or semester, which is still only a fraction of full tuition.

Student loans are available from a great many sources. As the name indicates, these must be repaid. However, for some types of loans (e.g., Perkins and Stafford loans) payback schedules are delayed until after the recipient has earned his or her degree. Interest rates on these types of loans may be far more favorable than the prevailing rates for loans for other purposes, and often the interest does not start accruing until the recipient has completed his or her graduate education. Loans derive from a number of sources including the federal government, the graduate institutions themselves, and private-sector banks. Other assistance comes in the forms of work–study programs and traineeships (i.e., being paid to perform work related to your training).

Matters related to taxation of awards, need analysis, residency requirements, renewal, and so on can get complicated and are beyond the scope of this book. However, there are many resources available. A comprehensive source of financial aid information and advice can be found on the Internet (http://www.finaid.org/), and several books have been published on the topic (e.g., McWade, 1996). Perhaps the best source of information is the financial aid office at the graduate schools that interest you, because individual universities and professional schools differ considerably in terms of how much is available and in what form. Get the literature from each office and study it carefully. Applications for financial aid are often due earlier than applications to the graduate program, so attend to financial matters early.

Recent Trends in Levels of Support

I've heard that student support for graduate school is low.

Federal grant and fellowship opportunities for graduate students have declined, whereas the percentage of graduate students taking out educational loans has increased. A survey by Golding, Lang, Eymard, and Shadish (1988) described the situation for psychology graduate students specifically. Comparing groups from three decades led these authors to conclude that current graduate students were bearing a greater share of the cost of their own education than had students from previous decades. Controlling for inflation, the stipend amounts had decreased, although the number of tuition waivers had increased.

Securing financial support for graduate training may be more difficult than ever before. Most students will probably have to consider loans, at least to support a basic standard of living. Many master's programs, most private professional schools, and plenty of doctoral programs do not have much outright support to offer. However, the news is not all bad.

What's the good news?

There are educational funds out there, especially for students who intend to pursue full-time doctoral study. The money just has to be sought with some diligence. We are saddened when a very capable but financially needy student settles for a less suitable program because it is cheaper. The reason is typically a lack of information coupled with poor planning.

Seeking financial assistance on your own in the form of grants or fellowships is highly recommended. Not only might you prevail in the competition, but you would also impress selection committees if you brought in at least some of your own funding. You do not have to have been accepted anywhere to apply for most independently awarded financial assistance, although you have to enroll in an eligible program before you can actually receive any funds.

Many students miss out because they wait until it is too late to look into opportunities. Ideally, you should go to your own (or a local) college or university library sometime during your junior year (or at least 6 months before graduate school applications are due) and begin to search through the many directories that include funding opportunities for graduate school. (Note that many books are only about undergraduate funding.) There is also a wealth of information available on the Internet. Do not become overwhelmed. Just browse through one directory or website at a time, perhaps in 1- or 2-hour sessions. Write down the name, address (both mail and Internet), and telephone number or URL of each funding source that seems plausible, and contact each for information. Response time for a snail-mail request is usually 3 to 5 weeks; follow up with a second request if you do not have a response by then.

Applying for financial assistance usually requires early action and takes some time. Many of the funding opportunities require that applications be submitted well before the deadline for any graduate program applications. For example, the National Science Foundation (NSF) fellowship program is a two-stage application process with the first part due in November of the year preceding the fall you will enter graduate school.

In addition, many applications for the most competitive awards are as involved as the typical application to a graduate program. Very similar questions are asked. Often required are letters of recommendation and a statement of purpose or a short essay that provides the awards committee with information about your qualifications for assistance. (All of these aspects are covered in detail in upcoming chapters of this book. Although the chapters are couched in the context of filling out graduate program applications, the advice can be directly applied to financial aid applications as well.)

Once I am accepted into a program, does the institution take care of most financial needs?

Indeed, some doctoral programs admit only students who they are prepared to support financially. One major department, for example, states in the information packet that all admitted students are ensured a tuition waiver and at least $9,000 per year in some other form (as an award or assistantship) for each of 4 years. Usually, however, you have to declare your interest in receiving financial aid. Programs that are very interested in you will try to help you by arranging for some institutional support or by offering you a teaching or research assistantship. Many times, an assistantship and tuition waiver are offered for the first year, after which such financial aid is awarded competitively.

If you say you do not need financial aid, do you have a better chance of being accepted?

According to our survey of graduate faculty, there is little bias against applicants who state that they require financial assistance to attend graduate school. There is only a very slight overall tendency for such a fact to detract from a candidate's application, and surely it could be compensated for by other favorable attributes. If applicants stated that they did not require financial aid, they were generally rated on the positive side, but very weakly so. Other strengths are much more important. If you have the means to attend graduate school without any funding, or with minimum assistance, let the selection committee know that. Otherwise, be honest about your financial situation.

The cost of your graduate training, and your projected ability to underwrite it, are factors you must consider before deciding where to apply. Schools in the state where you legally reside may be the only viable options if you have very limited means (tuition at state schools is less for state residents than for students from outside the state). However, to attract qualified students from other states, tuition is either waived or the resident tuition fee is offered.

How much consideration should I give to finances when it comes to deciding which schools to apply to?

Your finances cannot be overlooked altogether, but do not let them discourage you. If you are an extremely strong candidate (based on the criteria presented in chap. 4) and are applying to a program that has some funding to offer, by all means go ahead and apply for admission. Applicants with modest grades, test scores, and accomplishments need to place more emphasis on financial considerations because chances are lower that sufficient assistance will be forthcoming. Those who could use funds but cannot show convincing evidence of need will also have to be more careful in their choices of where to apply because strictly merit-based funding is extremely competitive.

What happens if I need financial assistance to attend graduate school but wait until too late to apply?

If the program to which you applied wants you, officials may automatically offer you assistance along with the notification of your acceptance. If you were accepted without any financial assistance, you can inform them that you cannot accept the offer because you cannot afford to do so. If they really want you, they may come up with something. Otherwise, consider loans for the first year, and get cracking early in your first graduate term to apply for support for your second and subsequent years. The final, less satisfactory option is to work for a year before applying to graduate school, maybe build a savings account, get organized earlier, and apply again next year. This last option may be more viable if you can also use the time to enhance your credentials, perhaps by working in a setting that is related to your career goals.

Self-Sought Funding

If you have some time, look into support opportunities on your own. Loans are a little easier to apply for than financial aid, and you can do so later in the process (there is all that bureaucratic paperwork, of course). You will have to pay it all back. We could give you a long list of new PhDs we know who wish they had gotten organized earlier when they were applying to graduate school and had explored noninstitutional sources of funding more aggressively. Although they all have the income necessary to make their monthly loan payments, some of them owe as much as $60,000.

It's all I can do to keep up with my studies and worry about submitting applications. How will I ever find time to search for funding?

Applying for financial support can feel rather onerous, but here's a point that may help you find the motivation you need. It may take you less than 10 hours to locate and apply to smaller scale opportunities for which you appear to qualify (e.g., $500 each). If you apply to three and receive only one, you have earned $50 an hour. One student we know spent a full 3 days applying for several awards and grants and received only one of them. But that one was for $5,000!

OK, I'll look into some options. Can you help me get started?

Many sources of assistance, such as smaller foundations and service organizations, offer very modest one-time amounts. However, these awards are easy to apply and compete for. The applications ask only for some basic information (which you will have to gather for your applications anyway) and a letter of intent informing them about yourself and your educational plans. We know of a student who paid for most of her graduate school expenses by applying for, and winning, numerous smaller awards. Many people do not take the time to seek out these tiny pockets of patronage; thus, competition is not always intense.

Some financial aid programs are for applicants with specified characteristics or experiences. Many of the smaller, private funding sources have some specifications that might apply to you. A small sampling includes being born in a certain state, being the child of a veteran of a specific war, or having an affiliation with a designated religious group. Military veterans should carefully check on options that might apply exclusively to them.

Here are some of the resources you may wish to consult. Because most of these are updated and reissued, sometimes regularly and sometimes more sporadically, we list only the titles and publishers. Look for the most recent versions.

> *Annual Register of Grant Support*. New York: R. R. Bowker.
> *Catalog of Federal Domestic Assistance*. Washington, DC: U.S. Government Printing Office.
> *Directory of Financial Aid for Minorities*. Santa Barbara, CA: Reference Service Press.
> *Directory of Financial Aid for Women*. Santa Barbara, CA: Reference Service Press.

Directory of Research Grants. Scottsdale, AZ: Oryx Press.

Financial Aid for the Disabled and Their Families. Santa Barbara, CA: Reference Service Press.

Financial Aid for Veterans, Military Personnel, and Their Families. Santa Barbara, CA: Reference Service Press.

Foundation Directory. New York: The Foundation Center.

Foundation Grants to Individuals. New York: The Foundation Center.

Free Money for Graduate School. New York: Henry Holt.

Grants for Graduate Students. Princeton, NJ: Peterson's Guides.

Worldwide Graduate Scholarship Directory. Franklin Lakes, NJ: Career Press.

Why didn't you mention holding an off-campus job while going to graduate school as a way to make it financially?

Graduate school training is not the same as the undergraduate model wherein you attended classes and then planned on a couple of hours a week of outside work for each course in which you were enrolled. Unless the program is set up for working students (allowing for part-time attendance or holding classes geared to the working adult's schedule), we recommend against working at a job outside of your department and going to graduate school at the same time. The graduate school experience—especially doctoral programs in traditional university settings—is one that extends well beyond in-class experience. Students hang out in the labs and offices with faculty and each other and learn as much during these informal encounters as they do from classes or from books. Furthermore, the successful graduate experience requires considerable and focused energy. Students already exhausted from an outside job commitment will not fare well.

This is not to say that holding an outside job half-time or more and going to school full-time is impossible. We have known a number of students who did it that way. Every one of them, however, would tell you that it was extremely demanding, exhausting, and stress-producing, and that it diminished the quality and enjoyment of their graduate school experience.

It sounds like I will be living in near poverty. I'm not sure I will like that.

This is a short-term sacrifice for a long-term gain. It is true that you will likely be living very frugally for the duration of your graduate studies, but you will also find that the essence of meaning in your life will not be money-oriented. What is important will be there. The latest fashions, new cars, and gourmet meals are irrelevant to what you are doing and to most of the other people around you. Most of us who went through graduate school recall having trouble scraping up enough money for any nonessential purchase, yet we also fondly recall our graduate school years as an especially enriched period of our lives.

Know Your Prize

If you are awarded financial support of any type, check out the details so that you will not be faced with any budgetary surprises. Is the aid taxable? Some types are; some are not. Are there any limitations or stipulations? Sometimes, for example, accepting one form of aid prohibits you from accepting other forms of aid or a part-time job. What is included in the package? For example, is the full tuition subtracted out of the award amount, or is the award amount in addition to a full or partial tuition waiver? How many years will the support be provided? Will the level of support change from year to year? Does the school offer a medical or dental plan to students and, if so, at what rate? You do not want to seem mercenary or ungrateful, but a gentle yet thorough inquiry is in your best interest.

We again emphasize that your first consideration should be to find a graduate program that meets your needs. The second is to get yourself admitted to it. The third is to figure out how to pay for it. A program that you can afford but either does not meet your needs or to which you cannot gain admission is of no use to you.

CHAPTER 14

WHAT IF MY GRADES AREN'T SO HOT?

You may be among the many students who did not take their grades seriously until it was too late to turn around their academic records. Perhaps you got off to a rocky start in college due to a difficult adjustment period. You may lament that you did not, or could not, commit more strongly to your studies. Do not despair! If your grades do not reflect your true ability, you may still be able to attain your educational goals. College underachievers can even excel in graduate programs.

Why is the GPA so important anyway? I am very good with people, and isn't that what should count most?

Of course admissions committees are interested in your potential for making professional contributions, and how you are with people will be important in virtually any career associated with mental health services and social and behavioral science. But, first you will have to get through a demanding academic program. One of the best predictors of future academic success is past ability to complete academic work successfully. Because getting into graduate school is competitive, the GPA is an easy (as well as a justifiable) criterion for selection committees to apply.

My friend is a first-semester junior and really wants to be a psychologist, but his transcript qualifies for disaster relief. Has he already struck out?

Not necessarily. Take a look at Fig. 14.1. This is a portion of the actual transcript of a student who went on to complete a psychology doctoral program at one of the top universities in the country! As you can see, she earned a *C* in the introductory psychology course and flunked a chemistry class twice. An incomplete and a withdrawal were additional blemishes. Hardly a record that inspires faith or optimism!

FALL 1984						
BIOL	150	PRIN OF BIOLOGY I	3.0	3.0	B	9.0
BIOL	150L	BIOLOGY I LAB	1.0	1.0	A	4.0
CHEM	101	GEN CHEMISTRY	-5.0	-5.0	D	-5.0
PSY	150	PRIN HUM BEHAVIOR	3.0	3.0	C	6.0
SOC	201	CONT FAM IN SOCTY	3.0	3.0	B	9.0
SPRING 1985						
BIOL	322	POPULATION BIOL	-3.0	-3.0	C	-6.0
BIOL	360	GENETICS	-3.0	-3.0	C	-6.0
CHEM	102	GEN CHEMISTRY	-5.0		F	
PHYS	100A	GENERAL PHYSICS I			W	
PHYS	100AL	GEN PHYS LAB	1.0	1.0	B	3.0
FALL 1985						
CLAS	115	ENGL VOC-GRK+LAT		3.0	CR*	
BIOL	151	PRIN OF BIOL II	3.0	3.0	B	9.0
BIOL	151L	BIOLOGY II LAB	1.0	1.0	A	4.0
CHEM	101	GEN CHEMISTRY	5.0	5.0	B	15.0
POLS	155	AMER POL INST	3.0	3.0	C	6.0
			12.0	15.0	2.83	34.0
SPRING 1986						
HSCI	170	EMRG PROCEDURES	1.0	1.0	B	3.0
HSCI	170L	EMRG PROCDRS LAB	1.0	1.0	B	3.0
P E	127A	BODY COND. I	1.0		I	
BIOL	322	POPULATION BIOL	3.0	3.0	B	9.0
BIOL	360	GENETICS	3.0	3.0	B	9.0
CHEM	102	GEN CHEMISTRY	5.0		F	

Figure 14.1

What Ever Happened To This Student?

It was not easy for this student to turn things around. However, with tremendous dedication and commitment she was able to demonstrate to a selection committee that she was intelligent and motivated, a good risk despite her record. She cultivated relationships with professors who helped her reveal her true potential. She volunteered to help them with their research and spent many weekends running rats and processing data. Her GPA for the last four semesters was close to a 4.00.

For some students who catch themselves early on, it is a matter of repairing their records during the latter part of their undergraduate careers. It is impossible to markedly raise the numerical component itself to a figure that rivals those of students who have earned high grades all along. The student just described, despite her heroic effort during the last half of her undergraduate studies, graduated with a modest overall GPA of 3.22. However, evaluators will usually notice a dramatic upward trend, especially if the applicant has additional compensating strengths and provides letters of recommendation that describe his or her true abilities. Many programs weigh the GPA earned during the latter half of the applicant's undergraduate career far more heavily than that earned during the first half.

What about students who can't catch up because they will graduate within the next semester or two?

In a survey we conducted with undergraduate psychology majors, most wanted to attend graduate school, including the majority of those with GPAs of 1.9 to 2.9. Presumably, a very large number of students whose final academic records are average will attempt to enter graduate training programs. Some of them will actually make it.

The remainder of this chapter is devoted to students whose academic performance throughout their undergraduate career was not near the top, yet who believe they have far more ability and motivation to succeed in a graduate program than their records reveal.

What does "modest academic record" mean in numerical terms?

It is difficult to give a precise GPA range that defines "modest" because other factors influence its interpretation, such as the applicant's selection of undergraduate courses, performance in specific courses within the student's major, and the rigor or reputation of the undergraduate college or university. In general terms, however, we are talking about students with *B–* to low *B+* averages (or GPAs of about 2.7 to 3.2 on a 4-point scale). Students with GPAs below 2.7 may be able to find graduate study options (perhaps a master's program) that will lead them to a career in their general interest area; however, direct entry into a doctoral program in a fully accredited graduate training institution is highly unlikely.

Ten Strategies for Students with Modest Grades

1. *Delay Graduation*. If you think you can significantly improve your GPA by delaying your graduation a semester or two, it may be the wise thing to do. Perhaps by reducing the number of credits you take (while still taking solid courses) you will be able to focus more time and effort on your studies. This is a plausible strategy only if you are extremely confident in your ability to do better work. If your grades remain low, and it takes you longer to graduate, the plan will have backfired!

With increasing numbers of students going to school part-time, or adding a semester or more because they changed majors late, it is extremely common for students to take more than the traditional 4 years to complete an undergraduate degree. Therefore, you are unlikely to feel any embarrassment or to be discriminated against if you stay on a while longer.

2. *Take Selected Courses Over Again.* Another tactic to consider (which may also delay your graduation date) is to repeat one or more of the courses that are substantially pulling down your GPA—courses in which you received *D*s and *F*s—or key courses in your major in which your performance was mediocre. Most colleges and universities allow courses to be retaken (or at least a limited number of them). This plan only makes sense if a few courses are involved, the rest of your record is adequate, and you are convinced that you could perform significantly better the second time around. The original attempts and the lousy marks associated with them will remain on your transcript. You would repeat the courses not to hide a problem but to demonstrate that you can do better.

3. *Become a Postbaccalaureate Student for a Semester or Two.* It is usually possible to remain at your undergraduate institution (or go to another) as a postbaccalaureate (PBA) student to take additional courses. This would be done to round out your record or to improve it by earning better grades and gaining other valuable experiences. The only difference between this ploy and delaying graduation is that you graduate before taking more courses. The courses you take as a PBA student are likely to be at the undergraduate level, because graduate courses often are only open to students enrolled in graduate programs, and your undergraduate GPA will remain unaffected.

So far, these suggestions all take time but don't count toward an advanced degree. It's like standing still, isn't it?

No, you are not just marking time. You are digging out and mopping up. These strategies offer you a second chance to competitively apply to graduate programs for which you do not currently qualify. We have not finished with the list of strategies, however, and the rest of them involve moving ahead from where you are now.

4. *Score High on Admission Tests.* If applicants with very modest GPAs have exceptionally strong showings on the GRE, they will earn a closer look. Selection committees frequently use GRE scores to offset otherwise less than satisfactory credentials: That is, selection committees may try to avoid "false negatives" (i.e., making the wrong decision about a good prospect based on grades only) by allowing strong GRE scores to compensate for a weaker GPA. (This is not to suggest that one can ignore course work and make up for it with stellar test scores.) Selection committees are looking for more than just how well one can perform on tests. The admissions committees look at an applicant as a whole package of credentials. A dramatic weakness could knock one out of the process, but

a student who is marginal in one area may be able to make up for it in other ways. A student with high GRE scores and lower grades would also have to provide a plan to better apply himself or herself to course work as a graduate student. (See chap. 10 for a discussion of the GRE and how to optimize your chances of doing your best.)

5. *Take Classes at the Target Institution.* Those who have identified the program to which they aspire but do not quite meet the qualifications for acceptance may find it possible to attend anyway—sort of. Many universities, including the most prestigious and competitive ones, have *nondegree status* categories that enable students to take a few classes, sometimes even at the graduate level. These categories go by such designations as "unclassified graduate student," "special student status," "course-work-only status," "associate graduate student," "graduate study only," "special standing," "visiting student," and "limited student status." Sometimes the limitations of this status are so restrictive that this strategy would not get you where you want to go. Check out the specific school of interest for details, and then assess feasibility according to your goals.

The point of this tactic, of course, is to get to know the program by being there, to meet the faculty, and to try to attract their support. The strategy is somewhat risky, however, because there is certainly no guarantee of acceptance into the graduate program, even if you do very well in the courses you take. However, we know students for whom this route was successful.

6. *Settle for Programs with Lower Academic Requirements.* Not all graduate programs have the same high academic requirements. Many will take students with more modest grades, although they will usually want some other evidence that you are bright, committed, and well-suited to the program. The less competitive institutions may have names that are less familiar and may not be in the locale you prefer, but they are legitimate academic training programs. Some doctoral (and master's) programs will accept students provisionally and give them time to make up their GPA or course deficits.

Among the options for less competitive programs are a number of nontraditional training programs. These may not have a campus complex in the usual sense with departments representing many disciplines, a library, undergraduate as well as graduate programs, and a football field, but they may provide training that meets at least the minimal standards required by the profession. Many of these programs cannot compete for applicants with strong academic records and are, therefore, available to students with modest grades and experiences. Many are designated as free-standing professional training programs. The lesser known or very small schools of this type may provide what you need to reach your goals while having more lenient admissions requirements. Ask their staff for information about what their students do after they graduate, and be wary of vague answers. The *Bears' Guide to Earning Col-*

lege Degrees Nontraditionally (Bear & Bear, 1998) provides assistance, but watch out for degree mills and other programs that may be insufficiently accredited or may lack the rigor or reputation to qualify you for the kind of work you would like to do (see chap. 5).

7. *Earn a Master's Degree Before Applying to a Doctoral Program.* We discussed in chapter 5 the possible advantages of completing a master's program before attempting to enter a doctoral program. That discussion focused more on students whose goals were not firmly set or who believed that they needed more time to mature. Certainly, another group who could benefit from this route includes students whose grades and test scores qualify for entry into a master's program but are not high enough for a doctoral program. If you use the master's degree period as a proving ground, a way of showing evaluators in doctoral programs that you can successfully complete graduate academic work, then you may be accepted into a doctoral program and receive some credit for your master's-level work.

However, earning a master's degree is no guarantee of admission to a doctoral program; it is still necessary to stand out from the crowd while you are a master's student. It is important also that the master's program you select is rigorous and well-regarded, especially if your ultimate goal is to enter a traditional doctoral program. You may well want to take more statistics and research methodology courses than are required for graduation from the master's program.

8. *Earn a Master's Degree Instead of a Doctoral Degree.* If your grades are very modest, you may never qualify for a doctoral program. However, as we discussed in chapter 5, a number of master's programs may prepare you to do the kind of work you would find fulfilling. If you must abandon your hope of becoming a licensed clinical psychologist, for example, you may opt for master's-level counseling programs, which come in a wide variety of types. You could specialize in counseling families, persons rehabilitating from a mental disorder or physical condition, persons returning to society (e.g., ex-prisoners), or substance abusers. Settings include community mental health centers, health maintenance organizations (HMOs), halfway houses, hospitals, industry, schools, and private practice. Many states license master's-level counselors to provide mental health services somewhat independently, and there is definitely a market for such licensed master's-level therapists.

Students who prefer more research-oriented or theoretical aspects of social science can also earn master's degrees in such areas as experimental psychology, applied social or developmental psychology, human factors, or industrial/organizational psychology and find work in various public and private-sector agencies. Such positions often involve research, program evaluation, and training or supervising personnel.

9. *Fill Out the Forms Like a Professional.* Many other graduate school applicants may have better grades than you do, but nothing precludes your submitting neat, professional application materials that are as im-

pressive as those of any student with a 4.0 GPA. Carefully read the upcoming chapters on how to prepare your application forms and essay
statements, and put in that extra effort. This may not put you over the
top, but it will make you appear sincere, motivated, organized, and competent, and maybe—just maybe—someone to take a chance on.

10. *Seek Career Counseling*. Students who must adjust their goals because of their weak academic records would be wise to get some in-depth
career counseling. If you are still an undergraduate, these services are
probably available to you for free or at minimal cost. Many students report that taking one of the available vocational interest inventories provided useful insight. Find out what is available from your campus counseling or career services office.

*If I explain that I had boring and unfair professors, will that help se-
lection committees understand my low grades?*

A number of strategies will not help, and shifting the blame for your academic record onto the institution and its teaching staff is one of them.
The evaluators will more likely assume that you overuse rationalization
and are unwilling to take responsibility for your own performance.

Other useless strategies include filling up the end of your undergraduate career with lower division, fluffy, or easy-*A* courses; begging a
referee to fudge for you in describing your academic potential; hoping
that no one notices your GPA if you never mention it to your referees
or in your essay statement; and applying to dozens of programs for
which you clearly do not qualify in the hopes that you will get lucky
with one of them.

Other Pointers for Students
With Modest Academic Records

Although you should read all of this book and apply whatever you can
from it, students with modest grades may have to make a few modifica-
tions. When it comes to asking people for letters of recommendation, you
may not have the luxury of choosing professors from whom you earned
high marks. First consider any in whose classes you performed the best
(any *A*s or *B*s). Meet with them in person and discuss your academic
record openly. You do not have to apologize or put yourself down, but do
discuss your goals and how you plan to do better work in the future.
(Even better, give evidence that you are already doing better work.) The
idea is to give potential referees a flavor of your motivation and commitment that may, if they are convinced, carry over into the comments they
make about you on the referee forms.

What about asking professors who gave me a C? There was one who I think thought well of me.

Sometimes a letter from a professor in whose class you performed only average work will be effective. If you are reasonably sure that the professor knows and thinks well of you, ask yourself what else this person could say about you that would help your cause. For example, one of us (P.K.S.) once had a student who earned a *C* in our course but who did a terrific fieldwork project. He volunteered to work with high school students on the verge of dropping out. His own street smarts were perhaps the key to forming effective relationships with these kids. The school personnel thought he was superb (I told him to get that on paper!), and his long-term career goal was to work with at-risk adolescents. I was pleased to support his application to a counseling program in an educational psychology department by stressing the strengths I could emphasize even though I could not portray him as a strong student. He earned his master's degree and went on to work with adolescents in a community agency.

Perhaps something you did well or something about you that the professor admires can provide positive aspects of the letter. Your negotiations for a letter of support should address these issues directly. If you have trouble getting three letters of recommendation (the number usually requested) from professors, consider any other credible sources such as a fieldwork supervisor (see chap. 17). In our experience, many students with more modest academic records receive enthusiastic reviews from supervisors in research or practicum settings.

What should I say on the application about my grades?

In your statement of purpose (or in a cover letter), address your mediocre grade situation directly. Unless you do so and try to convince evaluators that you can do better and why, they may conclude that you are trying to hide, or are unaware of, your shortcomings.

If your grades improved markedly with time, it is obvious that you have changed, and you do not need to elaborate extensively on the reason. Simply note that your performance accelerated as soon as you decided on your goals, or mention whatever event or circumstance explains the turning point. You may also calculate (even if not specifically requested) your GPA for the last 2 years to concretely illustrate your current level of performance. If extenuating circumstances accounted for a botched semester or two, you could describe them briefly. Be cautious about going into more detail than is necessary. Include how you have since remedied the situation. Focus most of your comments, however, on your strengths—what you have done well and what about you warrants the selection committee's serious consideration.

Applicants whose grades were low and were very stable over time, or whose grades became worse over time or whose grades in their major are as low or lower than their overall GPAs, will have more difficulty convincing a selection committee that they are good risks. If you are in this group, you should take one or more of the suggestions presented earlier.

Conclusion

If you have a modest academic record but are truly motivated to earn a graduate degree and think you have the ability to do it, stick to your convictions. You will have to work hard to prove yourself. You may well be discouraged along the way, including being told that you do not deserve a letter of recommendation. The main thing to keep in mind is that your advanced training, as long as it is from a legitimate institution, will prepare you to do competent, meaningful work, and your undergraduate GPA will become a distant memory as your career progresses.

CHAPTER 15

HOW DO I MAKE FINAL PROGRAM CHOICES?

Unless you are geographically locked into a particular locale, you have probably identified at least 10 to 40 programs that seem to provide training that corresponds to your needs and interests. You may have included some schools that appeal to you, even though you suspect that your chances of acceptance into them are low. Let them remain on your list for now because the current task is to assess possibilities, and that includes long shots. If a reassessment is necessary, you can do that later when you have more information. Sometimes what you thought impossible actually materializes, so you want to leave all doors open for now.

The Difference Between Undergraduate and Graduate Training Selection Strategies

Selecting the specific graduate schools to which you will apply may start out feeling a lot like what you went through to get into college. The SAT is comparable to the GRE, and your college GPA is at least as important now as your high school GPA was then. The application forms look similar, on the surface, and you have to order transcripts and ask people to write letters on your behalf. However, it is like comparing chess to checkers. The boards you move around on look the same, but the games are distinctively different, and chess is far more complicated than checkers.

When you decided where to do your undergraduate studies, you probably settled for the school with the best to offer, given the limitations of your high school grades and activities, how far you could comfortably move away from your friends and your home town, and your parents' financial situation. You may have had only an inkling of what your major field of study would be, and you may have written that on the application somewhere. However, you also knew that you might change your mind—perhaps several times—before you graduated. Your doors were still wide open when you were working toward your bachelor's degree.

Things are much different now. Your graduate program will shape you in specific ways and in large part determine the course of your life's work. To change or add specialties later on is possible, but you might have to undergo considerable retraining. Thus, choosing your graduate training site is well worth the time and effort it takes to make thoughtful and carefully informed decisions. The nature and quality of the specific program and its individual faculty members should be your focus of interest. The overall reputation and popularity of the university as a larger entity are far less important now. Some less well known universities or professional schools may have far better programs to suit your needs than the better known or more prestigious universities. Some schools that would not have suited your undergraduate demands may have the best graduate program for you.

How about just applying to programs that I'm aware of in my geographical area, or trying to get into the schools where my favorite professors went?

It is unwise to proceed in this way. Convenient, irrelevant, or trivial criteria have no place at this important juncture. Staying close to home limits your options considerably and also places you in intense competition with others who are doing the same thing. (See chap. 12 for a full discussion of this.) And, unless your favorite professors are recently hatched, their programs have likely been modified in several ways since they were students. Undoubtedly, many of their professors have moved on, retired, or died.

Is there any way I can figure out my odds of acceptance in any particular program? Then I would just apply to those I was confident would accept me.

Unfortunately, precision is impossible. Some programs are extremely difficult to get into, with rates of acceptance as low as 1 out of 200. Other programs, however, offer good training and are far less competitive, accepting as many as half their applicants. How many students apply, and how many students who were ranked higher than you will turn down their offers, are numbers you cannot know for sure. Factors such as how much effort was put into advertising or promoting the program, how much funding is available, how well the program is functioning, differing admissions criteria (and these often vary among programs within the same department), and other factors unknown to both you and selection committee members will also affect your chances.

You must look at your record (what you have to offer) and what you want, and then avoid programs that are too far afield in either respect.

Your best bet for heightening your odds of acceptance remains careful school selection.

Serious Decision Making

Now that you have full sets of materials before you, try not to agonize over the wrong question, namely, "Can I possibly get into this place?" Applicants often waste valuable energy struggling to mold themselves into an image that they think a selection committee would like to see. If you find yourself ruminating about this, and if the materials you have before you represent programs for which you probably meet the basic admissions criteria, focus more on what they have to offer you.

Another mistake that frequently compounds decision making is that applicants become overwhelmed and use a random approach to selecting schools or superficial criteria. For example, they may make their final choices based on the ease with which the application can be filled out, the due date (usually favoring those that are furthest in the future), or the glamour or image associated with the graduate institution. Some students freeze at this point and do nothing; others fill out every application in their possession, even if it means that they could not possibly do an adequate job on any individual one. Applicants who use such haphazard decision-making techniques run the risks of impressing no one or, worse yet, of enrolling in a program that does not meet their needs.

What is a better way to go about this?

The question you should ask is, "Does this program train students to do what I ultimately want to do?" You now have up-to-date materials that allow you to scrutinize each program more carefully than was previously possible. If you have at least 8 weeks before applications are due, further assessing how well you match with each program that still interests you will markedly enhance your chances of acceptance. Focus now on two specific facets of the program when assessing how well the program and you would meet each other's needs: the program orientation and course sequence, and, particularly for competitive doctoral programs, the faculty.

Program Orientation and Course Sequence

The materials you have received in the mail or downloaded from the Internet should contain either a general description of the courses comprising the degree program or a complete listing, year by year, of the actual course sequence. Sometimes this detail appears in the all-university graduate catalog. Overview statements also may reveal a favored orientation or philosophy, such as an emphasis on a particular theoretical model or a focus on training future scholar–clinicians rather than practicing clinicians. These descriptions should help you make more finely tuned decisions.

Course sequence information provides a general feel for what components will go into completing your degree. If you see many courses that look unappealing, or if the emphasis within your interest area is not at all what you wanted, that program may not be right for you. On the other hand, if you see that the general menu is compatible with your capabilities and your longer term goals, keep that program on your list.

Identification of Active Faculty

Those of you who have already identified a specific interest within your general program area will have an easier time locating and narrowing down your program choices based on the faculty at each. Selection committees are often particularly attracted to students who will fit in and who have demonstrated, by their careful choices of where to apply, that a good match will result.

As much as selection committees want to attract the best students they can, they will decline to offer admission to someone who will probably not be happy in their program, even if that student has an extremely admirable record. If you list, for example, a strongly held career objective to work with nonhuman primates, and the university has no primate colony or no cooperative zoo program in the geographical area, you probably will not be considered further on the grounds that the program cannot fulfill your educational needs.

What if I am not really sure of what interest area within the general field I want to pursue? Should I cast myself in stone before I even graduate from college?

This question probably characterizes a majority of graduate school applicants. We are not saying that it is absolutely necessary to pick a set of research interests if one hopes to get into graduate school. However, for those students who do have a sense of what they would like to study, being clear about these interests can be important in the selection process. Even then, one's interests do not have to be set in stone.

The graduate program faculty would be delighted if the students who declared what orientation or interests characterize them currently would persist and deepen those perspectives once in a graduate program. That way the faculty's own decision making and long-term planning would be easier and more satisfactory. However, they realize that students, especially those who have only dabbled in certain areas, change their minds. Because most applicants have not had extensive experience in specific study areas, graduate-level faculty accept that students may not yet have defined interests or may abandon their stated interest for another one, possibly even shortly after entering graduate school, perhaps when they discover a particularly congenial faculty member to work with.

Why is it important to focus on faculty when making my program decisions?

If you are applying to a master's program or a professional school program with large first-year classes, your focus may rightly be on the programs' offerings. However, the heart of any graduate program is its faculty. These people determine the quality and ambiance of your graduate education. An important question, especially for competitive doctoral programs, is, "Who are these people?" It is wise to find out as much as you can about them. Often faculty research areas and recent publications are listed in application materials. If they are not, or if you have not received application materials, use literature access techniques (which have never been more efficient) to identify citations of recent works by specific authors (e.g., by using PsycLIT on CD-ROM). Also, increasing numbers of professors have their own web pages with information about their own education, current research interests and recent publications, courses taught, teaching philosophy, syllabi, and so forth.

If you are applying to a competitive doctoral program, matching yourself with one or more faculty members is one primary way to stand out from other qualified applicants. However, attempting to link yourself to any particular faculty member is a hazardous strategy unless you take certain precautions. One risk is that you will narrow yourself too much and then be passed over by selection committees because they will perceive themselves as being unable to fulfill your needs.

How can that happen?

If you fashion your application around the desire to work closely with a particular faculty member, several things can lead the selection committee to conclude that you would not be happy in their program. First, university faculty can be somewhat transient, especially newer professors in the lower ranks, and the faculty member you identified may have moved on to another position or may be in the process of doing so. Remember, faculty information that appears in books is usually based on program material that is 1 or more years old. Even departmental web sites may be somewhat outdated.

Some faculty may not be taking on new students at this time. Older faculty retire or become less active in the program, yet because they are often well known they remain on the lists. Faculty members often take leaves of absence for a semester or two, sometimes longer, to engage in special projects off campus or to teach at another university or in another country. If you are unaware of a faculty member's extended leave or semiretirement and you state that this is the person with whom you want to work, you could be excluded from further consideration for this reason alone.

Furthermore, faculty research interests occasionally shift, sometimes abruptly, rendering published accounts of their research areas highly misleading. Finally, a percentage of faculty listed as part of a program are actually involved in a very peripheral way. It looks good for a program to display many names. In reality, however, only some of them are sufficiently central to the operation, and usually these are the people on whom you want to focus your attention.

What can I do to avoid seeking mentors who will not be there?

Start with the programs' own, most recently issued materials that you have already received, as well as information posted at their web sites. These will not be totally error-free or completely sufficient for this purpose, but they are the best sources available at this point. Ask any professors in your department who are in the same area if they know what a particular graduate school educator is doing at the moment. News travels fairly fast within specialty areas. If they do not know, some of your current professors may even be willing to help you find out.

Look at each faculty member's description, noting recent publications (a likely indicator of their current interests) and any other current activities, such as directing a substance abuse prevention project or editing a pediatric psychology journal (another indicator of present interests). See if the faculty members who are listed as associated with the program also appear as involved in one or more other programs in the department. If a faculty member is involved in more than two programs, he or she may not be heavily involved in the one you have selected. Ensure that the people who interest you the most are on the regular faculty as opposed to having adjunct or part-time status. (This information is often, but not always, included. You may have to call and ask for it.)

Once you get names of some people who might be possibilities, try to find out if they will be around for the next couple of years at least and if they are regularly on campus and available to work with students. If you make a polite call to the office staff, they may be able to help you.

You could also ask for the faculty member's office hours, and call to him or her directly. As an example, one might say to Dr. Token, "I am applying to the M&M University clinical psychology program. If I am accepted, I hope to work in your behavior modification research laboratory throughout my doctoral training. Would I be able to do this?" You may only get a quick, "I plan to be around for quite a while," or "I'll be leaving M&M to take a position at the S&R Institute next spring," or "I'm afraid I do not foresee any opening in my lab for the next 2 years," but you now have the information you need. Do not keep Dr. Token on the telephone unless she extends the conversation.

If you are too shy to make this call (or are unable to reach the faculty member by telephone despite several attempts), you can put the same brief message in an e-mail message or neatly typed note with a postage-paid return envelope, so that all the recipient has to do is write a quick reply.

When to Contact Graduate Program Faculty

Is it okay for me to talk or write to some of the faculty members who are active in the programs that interest me?

Maybe, but you will have to proceed carefully and exercise sensitivity to the time and energy demands that you put on people who are working full-time with graduate students already enrolled in the program. The faculty in programs attracting large numbers of applicants, especially, are not likely to be able to accommodate your requests for personal attention.

Before contacting a graduate program faculty member, think about whether you have a legitimate need to do it. When we ask students about their motivations, a common answer goes something like, "If I can just talk to her for a few minutes then she will remember me and I will have a better chance of standing out in the applicant pool." There is no guarantee that you will be recalled by a person who, no doubt, has hundreds of brief encounters with people every year. Worse yet, if you were at all intrusive or if you failed to impress the person in a positive way, any memory that remains will work to your disadvantage.

How can I tell if a faculty member would be willing to hear from me?

There is no way to predict the receptivity of any particular faculty member. Some program materials explicitly warn against attempting to contact the program chair or faculty, indicating that the high volume of inquiries makes such contacts burdensome and unwelcome. Other programs, however, give quite the opposite message. Prospective applicants are expressly invited to call and ask questions. Several programs host open houses so that prospective students can meet with faculty and tour the facility. The most astonishing set of materials we have encountered came from a psychology department that encouraged students to call and listed the office telephone numbers as well as the home telephone numbers of its faculty members!

Take these cues as suggestive of what response you might get from a specific faculty member, realizing, however, that not every professor in the "don't call us, we'll call you" departments would turn you away, nor would every individual professor in the welcome-mat departments be delighted to hear from you. A majority of programs do not offer clues about faculty availability directly, except that individual interviews with the selection committee will be scheduled only by invitation.

Perhaps a relatively safe medium for attempting to communicate with faculty is electronic mail. This way, faculty can respond at their convenience and do so quickly and at no cost. E-mail messages also allow the faculty member the option of not responding. Note, however, that many faculty belong to one or more listservs or e-mail discussion groups serving people with similar professional interests. This results in the faculty member getting perhaps dozens of e-mail messages daily, although few, if any, are addressed personally to that individual. It is common in this case for the faculty member to delete many of these messages without reading them if the header or brief title of the message is not of interest. For this reason, we recommend that you put the faculty member's name (e.g., Dr. Token) in the header or subject line of any message you send. E-mail addresses of individual faculty members are often available in directories at the institutions' websites. Keep a record of your messages and do not attempt to send multiple copies of the same message to a list of faculty. That will be perceived of as "spamming," and your message will be deleted without a response.

What are some specific legitimate reasons for attempting to contact a faculty member?

A request for information critical to your decision to apply to a particular program that is neither addressed in the program's material nor appropriate to ask an office staff member is a legitimate reason to contact a relevant faculty member. Also, prospective applicants with established areas of interest in the discipline should be able to learn whether the program and its faculty can satisfy their needs. Examples might include the need to know if certain necessary resources or equipment to pursue a particular line of inquiry are available, or if a particular faculty member who has expertise in an area, such as the effects of early experience, also has an interest in a more specific subarea, for example, the effects of early paternal deprivation.

Students interested in working with a specific faculty member, particularly those who have already completed some work in the faculty member's specialty area, may find that their inquiries are actually welcomed. The risk, of course, is that the impression you make may not be positive if your expertise in the shared interest area is, in fact, weak or superficial. Do your homework carefully before making this kind of contact.

Regardless of your reason for contacting faculty, avoid asking for information that would take the faculty member a long time to prepare. Do not request special favors or clues to the inside track. Do not, for example, ask, "Would you please send reprints of all of your research articles?" or "What are my chances of getting into your program?"

I think I have a legitimate reason to contact a faculty member to request a meeting. Should I call or write?

An e-mail message may be the best way to open communication with a faculty member if you have questions that are not easily or quickly answered. For one thing, your chances of reaching Dr. Engram by telephone at her desk are not high. If you do catch her in, you may interrupt her. The office staff can be protective of the faculty, and the response you get, if you have to go through the office phones, may not accurately represent a faculty member's openness to being contacted. Leaving a message for the faculty member to call you back is not recommended for making this type of connection. If you call, do it during the person's normally scheduled office hours. If the person is busy, ask if a telephone appointment date and time could be arranged. Be sure to keep that appointment!

A letter or e-mail message should briefly describe yourself and your accomplishments or current activities as they relate to this professor's interests as well as the questions you need to ask. Be simple and direct about your interest in working with this person. Include your own e-mail address and your telephone number (and an indication of when you can be reached) just in case the person wants to call rather than write to you. If you are unsure about the appropriateness of your call or letter, one of your current professors may be willing to advise you.

Will my letter or e-mail message be answered, and when?

The chances are fairly good that you will get at least a brief reply, although it may not be fully satisfying. Individual professors do not make graduate admissions decisions by themselves and, therefore, are likely to be cautious about giving encouragement. The reply, moreover, may be delayed because it has to be squeezed into a busy schedule. If you receive a response that gives at least some substantive information to assist you with your decision making, it would be thoughtful to send a very brief thank-you note or e-mail message. One sentence will be sufficient unless the professor's letter was long and detailed, thus warranting, perhaps, a more elaborate response.

Normally, a professor's brief response to your initial inquiry will be the end of it. Occasionally, however, an original letter will begin a chain of exchanged letters or will lead to an invitation to visit the campus for a personal chat. However, the professor, not you, will determine the developmental course of the connection.

If I don't hear back, does that mean I should not apply to that professor's program?

No, it probably only means that messages from people the recipient does not know are a low priority, or your message was lost in the mail or cyberspace, or that this person is not good about handling correspondence or is not around campus during this period. You do not need to ascribe any personal meaning to a nonresponse.

Actual Visits to the Program Sites

You can learn much from even a relatively brief visit to the sites of the graduate programs that interest you. Visiting programs that are more than an inexpensive weekend away may be difficult to arrange, but consider the potential value of a trip carefully before dismissing the notion. The main advantage of a visit is that even if you do not get a chance to speak with any of the professors active in the program, you will get a feel for the place. With just a little assertiveness, you can probably find a graduate student or two who is willing to talk to you for a little while. (Watch what you say. The students may report the conversation to people you want to impress!)

Some departments have programs for students who ask to visit. Try to get an appointment with a program representative well in advance. If you write or call a specific faculty member, as discussed previously, ask about visitations.

What about just showing up at the department?

Visiting and browsing around campus and the graduate program area are rarely a problem. However, intruding on someone without an appointment may not go over well at all. A colleague from a major doctoral program shared what he thought was a legitimate tactic for students visiting the campus who had not made an appointment: Pop your head in during office hours and say, "Hi. I'm Gary Spiegel. I am planning to apply to your doctoral program and am here for the day looking around. I just wanted to say hello." This allows the faculty member to simply say, "Hello, hope you're enjoying yourself" (end of conversation) or, "Come back at 2 o'clock, and I'll show you around for a few minutes." Even if you do make a connection successfully, keep it brief unless the other person clearly encourages a longer conversation.

When is the best time to visit?

There is no answer that agrees with everyone. Late summer, just before classes begin, might be a good time. Faculty and students are more likely to be around, but the hassles and demands of the semester have not started yet. Prior to this period is a more relaxed time, but many faculty are on vacation or hold very limited office hours. If you visit while classes are in session, certainly avoid doing so during the "crunch" times (e.g., the first week of classes, midterm, the last couple of weeks of class).

How about waiting until after my application is submitted?

The consensus seems to be that a visit after the application deadline date is inappropriate. At that point, your status changes formally to "applicant," and program representatives tend to become involved in protocol. The selection committees begin to meet, and appointments and interviews are typically made by invitation only. Also, the staff and faculty become inundated by applicants making unwise, premature calls about the status of their applications. Well-meaning students who only want to drop by for a few minutes, and have no manipulative or hidden agendas, cannot be differentiated from the others. If you are going to visit a campus, do it before the application deadline!

Part IV

_____

The Application Process

CHAPTER 16

WHAT ARE MY FIRST STEPS IN APPLYING?

As soon as you have narrowed your choices of programs to those you find particularly attractive, it is time to appraise your plan and take care of a few business matters before you actually tackle those application forms. The number of applications you actually prepare will probably be fewer than the number on your final list. When it comes down to the wire, most students delete up to 25% of their "final" choices for various reasons.

How many applications should I actually prepare, and how do I make those last decisions?

You want to apply to enough programs to which you have a reasonable chance of being admitted, given your credentials. Generally, the better your credentials, the fewer programs you need to apply to. This advice must be tempered with practicality: Apply to those programs that prepare you to do what you want to do in your professional life, keeping in mind that applications cost both time and money.

Because the competition can be stiff, most students seeking entry into a doctoral program should apply to 6 to 10 programs, and possibly more if their interests are in scientist–practitioner clinical psychology programs housed in traditional university psychology departments. Even very strong students should not presume acceptance wherever they apply. Because it is impossible to know the competition in any given year, the program's current needs and agendas, and a number of idiosyncratic factors, even the best candidates should apply to a minimum of 4 or 5 programs, and more than that if only popular and more prestigious doctoral programs are on their lists. In our experience, even students who were accepted into a highly competitive program were not extended offers by every program to which they applied.

Students with more modest academic records and test scores may also be wise to apply to up to 15 programs, although blasting the landscape with applications is not the preferred strategy for the average student. (See chap. 14 for more constructive ideas.) Master's program applicants may decide to apply to fewer schools because acceptance rates are generally higher.

In making these suggestions we assume that you selected your final set of programs very carefully. Even 30 or 40 applications can lead to as many rejections if you apply to programs well beyond your qualifications or apply with little consideration of whether there is a good match between you and the programs.

The number of programs to which you apply will also be based on your resources, the most critical of which is your time. Although you will gain speed with each application, you will need to prepare each with individualized care. Detailed time estimates for filling out applications are discussed later. Note, however, that those carrying heavy course or work loads who must additionally meet application deadlines within a 3- or 4-month period during the fall semester may have to limit the number of programs to which they apply simply because there is too little time to adequately prepare materials.

The amount of time between gearing up to apply and the application due dates is also a factor in determining the number of schools to which you ultimately apply. Programs with December through January deadlines require a great deal of groundwork (including taking required tests such as the GRE) during the previous October and November at the latest. Many of the competitive doctoral programs have early deadlines, and it would be unfortunate to delete a choice because you failed to get organized early enough.

Finances will also play a role. Each application, with the exception of a very few schools, requires an application fee, which typically ranges between $40 and $60. If we add $25 per application to cover the costs of transcripts, materials, test reports, and postage, then the average applicant would need about $750 to apply to 10 schools. If you are applying to more than 10 schools or have completed university course work at more than one institution, you will have to spend even more. A student we know attended one summer school class at a university that charged $6 per transcript. When she later applied to 25 graduate programs, it cost her $150 to verify just a single course. If you must rush to meet deadlines and are forced to send your applications by express mail, the added expense can be substantial.

That's a lot of money, and I'm a little short financially.

Although the many little items add up, application fees and associated costs are part of your investment in your future career satisfaction and earning capacity. We strongly advise, therefore, that you not drastically limit the number of schools to which you apply solely to save money. You might consider borrowing it, assuming you have the resources to make payments. (You might consider telling your family that money for applications would be a welcome holiday gift!)

If you are truly strapped for cash and have no reasonable means of finding it, you can request an application fee waiver from the programs to which you want to apply. Sometimes the criteria and procedures for requesting fee waivers are detailed in the application materials. Otherwise, contact the university-wide Admissions Office to ask whether they have such an assistance program and to get the details. Students who have requested such help generally report that, although some documentation is required, it is not a complicated or humiliating process.

So, I shouldn't apply to a program unless I am pretty confident that I can get in?

You cannot really know who will select you and who will not. At best, you can estimate probabilities. Here is the counsel we generally offer:

Apply to from 1 to 3 "stretch" programs, that is, ones that interest you greatly but whose requirements appear to exceed your qualifications. Although your chances of acceptance may be low, we have witnessed an occasional student's acceptance into a stretch-choice program. If you have designated a school as a stretch choice, is it solely because it is a big-name school? If so, reconsider whether the program offers a good match; a top school may have nothing satisfying to offer you beyond its name.

Some students may find it worthwhile applying to one or more stretch schools just to know once and for all what can and cannot be. Even though the rejection letters may sting, they may be preferable to the nagging, unanswered question, "Could I have gotten in if I had bothered to apply?"

Finally, note that *stretch* means a relatively small reach from the qualifications that would give you a more solid chance of acceptance. It is not our intent to put anyone through an exercise in futility and sure-fire disappointment. Your faculty advisor may be able to help you assess where stretching ends and out-of-reach begins.

Apply to between 4 and 8 programs that, based on your careful assessment of all of the information available to you, appear to be good matches. If you have done your homework on the programs, their requirements, and what kinds of students are seen as attractive, and your thoughtfully prepared applications reveal that compatibility, you stand a reasonable chance of acceptance into at least one of these programs.

Given the competition for graduate student slots, we strongly advise applying to at least 2 programs that you feel reasonably confident will accept you. To make these selections, you must also carefully study the available information, assess degree of match, and ensure that your qualifications exceed those of the program. Select schools in this category that you would be willing and satisfied to attend, because it is possible that you will be doing just that. There is no point applying to programs that you would dread or regret attending or ultimately decline to attend.

It wastes your resources and places an unfair burden on graduate program staff members, who deserve the assurance that their time and energy are being devoted to sincere applicants. Although other options—such as taking a postbaccalaureate year to beef up your record—are perhaps more circuitous and time-consuming, they are far preferable to applying to any program you do not really want to enter.

I want to enter a doctoral program, but should I apply to a couple of master's programs just in case I don't make it into a doctoral program?

If your goal is entry into a doctoral program and your record of accomplishments is very strong, we doubt the wisdom of a safety-net application to a master's program. If your record is more modest, however, an application to one or more master's programs may be a good idea for several reasons. Your chances of acceptance are generally better, and you will have an opportunity to increase your future attractiveness as a doctoral program applicant while working on a master's degree, a credential in its own right.

Another option is to apply to one or more doctoral programs in less competitive areas or departments. Proceed with caution, however. Although you may be accepted into such a program, it may also lead you away from your career goals. If the doctoral program you enter reduces or eliminates your chances of doing the kind of work you want to do for the rest of your life, the master's-first option is a better choice for you. A general master's program buys you some time to mature and to qualify for the specific training that will take you where you want to go.

A friend of mine wants to go to only one school and is submitting only one application. Is that a smart thing to do?

This plan is extremely risky. Hopefully your friend is highly qualified for the program and has chosen it because the match appears to be near-perfect. We also hope that your friend has developed an alternate plan in case this single shot misses its mark.

Ordering Transcripts

Transcripts of all undergraduate courses (and graduate work, if applicable) are virtually always among the documents required in support of your application. It can take up to 6 weeks for transcripts to arrive at their destination. Some institutions are excessively slow at getting transcripts out, and some make routing errors. So, ordering transcripts, although not difficult, deserves your careful attention.

If you have attended only one institution and are still enrolled, ordering transcripts is easy. You simply visit the records office, pay a small fee for each transcript, and order them sent to the schools to which you are applying. If you have attended other schools or have been out of school for a while, you will most likely contact these previous schools from a distance. Because the office staff at the schools you have attended have a lot to do besides processing requests from former students, you must make these requests as soon as you are fairly certain of the schools to which you will apply. We recommend arranging for transcripts to be sent to each program to which you will apply even before you start to fill out the applications. You may have to request a transcript order form, which adds further delay. It is better to waste a few dollars by ordering transcripts sent to a school you ultimately cross off your list than to be missing documents necessary for your application.

That sounds easy enough. Any hidden problems?

Things can get more complicated, and you must stay on top of this process to avoid potential glitches that could diminish your chances of consideration. For one, be sure to check the application materials for the proper destination for transcripts. Sometimes you will deal with three different offices in applying to a single program.

Many students have attended more than one college or university or have taken additional classes, perhaps during the summer, at a different institution. Usually, each institution attended must be contacted directly, and every program to which you apply must receive a transcript from each institution you attended. It is not unusual for a student to arrange for the mailing of over 30 transcripts (three different schools attended multiplied by 10 or more graduate program applications). This is not a complicated task, but it requires vigilance and can be time-consuming.

Some schools to which you apply will want two official transcripts for each institution you have attended. This does not mean one official transcript and one photocopy of an official transcript. Both must arrive from the site of training with the official stamp or seal. Deviating from what is specifically requested can delay your application. While you are at it, secure a complete set of your transcripts for yourself. Some programs require that you include an unofficial copy of your transcripts with the application materials. If you are running late with your applications, or if you learn that a transcript has not arrived and the deadline is looming, you can send a photocopy of your transcript to the office you to which you sent your application. (This may not be the same office to which the official versions are being sent.) Indicate that you recognize that this photocopy is not official, and that the proper documents have been ordered. Sending unofficial copies under conditions of extreme time pressure will allow the selection committee members to get a complete picture of your academic record even though it is not yet in the form that satisfies policy.

Applicants who have changed their names between the time college courses were taken and the preparation of the application—usually women who marry and take their husbands' surname—have an additional responsibility. Unless the application form specifically requests previously used names, the staff members who receive your application may not be able to match it to your transcripts. Even if you put your previous name in the middle, such as Mindy Cooper Putnam or even Mindy (Cooper) Putnam, you must take special care—perhaps in a cover letter—to assist the staff in matching everything up. In one case, an applicant in such a predicament ended up with essentially two half applications (a set of transcripts and test scores under one name and an application and letters of recommendation under her married name). The problem was not solved until it was too late for this student to be considered. The fault for such an unfortunate glitch does not lie with the graduate program staff.

Sometimes transcripts never arrive at their proper destination. Errors could have occurred at the beginning, in transit, or at the end of the process. Follow up with each place from which you ordered transcripts (give them 3 to 4 weeks processing time) to ask if they have been mailed out. If you are still unsure, call the appropriate graduate program offices—that is, the office to which the transcripts should have been sent—and ask if they have arrived.

What about transcripts for courses I am taking now?

For programs with early deadline dates (i.e., December or January), you will have to order a second transcript as soon as your fall or winter term grades are available. Be sure to note this on your calendar, because it is a critical detail that is easily overlooked. Consider sending the program selection committee a copy of your fall/winter term grade slip as soon as you receive it, as well. This will come to you before transcripts can be updated and sent out. Although it is unofficial, it allows the selection committee to review your most recent performance. If you took any critical core courses during this period, sharing such information as early as possible could significantly impact your candidacy.

Test Score Reports

Arrange to have required test scores (e.g., the GRE) sent to the proper destinations prior to or along with filling out the application forms. Consult the instructions provided to you by the test companies and follow them precisely. For tests not using a code-ordering system, indicate the correct addresses to which the scores should be sent.

Test companies also take anywhere from 2 to 6 weeks to report to the graduate institution, depending on the test and the mode of administration. The responsibility for ensuring that all materials arrive is entirely yours. Although many programs send out postcards shortly after the application deadline date to alert applicants to missing data in their files, this is a courtesy rather than a responsibility. The graduate program staff is not responsible for tracking down items that have not arrived, as some applicants seem to assume.

Again, if you receive your own test score report well before the official copies sent by the test companies will arrive at their destination, you can send a photocopy of your report (which does not, of course, substitute for the official score report) to the program office. This way, the selection committee has something tentative to evaluate.

Negotiating for Letters of Recommendation

Finally, before you fill out your applications, you will want to identify and line up people to write recommendation letters for you. It is crucial that you fully understand the process of securing reference letters, so much so that the next chapter is devoted to it exclusively.

CHAPTER 17

WHAT ABOUT LETTERS OF RECOMMENDATION?

Virtually every graduate program will require you to provide written evaluations from others, whom we shall call *referees*, to help the selection committee assess your potential as a graduate student. This chapter lets you in on the process, which is very mysterious to most students. By gaining insight into how referees and their letters are viewed by evaluators, and how referees approach this task, you may be able to minimize some common problems that could detract from your application.

Referee Forms

Most graduate programs provide forms for you to give to those who have agreed to serve as your referees. Referees are usually requested to send a completed form and a written statement back to the program or university graduate office directly using the referee's own envelope. A growing number of programs ask, however, that the applicant collect the referee letters in sealed envelopes, with the referee's signature over the flap, for inclusion with the application materials. Sometimes special envelopes are provided by the graduate school. Only a very small number of programs contact the referees themselves, after requesting their names and addresses from the applicants.

Reference letters are a standard tool used in the higher education selection process. Although you cannot dictate what your referees will say, you most certainly have some influence on the process, especially if you have some time before it is necessary to solicit letters. Here we provide you with considerable guidance on how to achieve the best possible results from your referees.

How many letters of recommendation do I need?

The directions in each application packet will specify how many letters are required. Occasionally it is two, usually three, and rarely four or five. Very infrequently the directions will provide a range (e.g., two or three, or two to five). Sometimes the directions will specify that no more than the requested number should be solicited. Comply with the directions of each program to which you apply.

Does it help me to have more than the requested number of recommendation letters?

Most students are thankful just to find appropriate references to meet the minimum required number. An occasional student may be fortunate enough to have more than the usual three referees. If extra letters are acceptable, add an additional one or two if these will truly add power to the application. That is, all letters (including the one or two extras) should be from relevant sources. Adding extra letters just for the sake of having more of them in your file is probably not wise and could even backfire if your extra letters are wishy-washy or off-base. But, if an extra letter would better round out the evaluator's view of you—that is, the additional referee would add something positive that could not or would not be mentioned by your other referees—then it could be helpful.

What kinds of things about me do they want to learn from my referees?

In most cases you will see exactly what each selection committee wants to know, because the referee forms will be sent to you for distribution. A minority of the programs supply no forms or miniforms that include a request only for referee identification data. Usually forms contain a brief description of what the selection committee desires referees to write about. Virtually every form asks the following:

- The length of time the referee has known you and in what capacity (e.g., student, research or teaching assistant, advisee).
- Whether your academic record reflects your academic ability.
- If you would be an acceptable graduate student in the referee's own graduate program.
- Your likelihood of successfully completing a master's or doctoral program.

Very often referees are asked to rank you from high to low on several characteristics. A typical ranking scale is *outstanding, superior, good* (or *above average*), *average, marginal* (or *below average*), and *inadequate op-*

portunity to observe (or *unknown*). The following list, gleaned from a content analysis of over 300 referee letter forms supplied by graduate psychology and related field programs, illustrates the assortment of characteristics for which rankings may be requested. (Note that no program requests comment on all of these!)

- Academic achievement
- Research ability, experience, or potential
- Teaching potential or experience
- Verbal skills, public speaking ability
- Writing skills, level of writing proficiency
- Industriousness, motivation, perseverance, energy level, drive
- Quantitative ability
- Creativity, originality, imagination
- Analytic ability
- Leadership skills, level of respect accorded by others
- Sociability, social skills, ability to get along with peers
- Emotional stability, level of emotional adjustment
- Judgment, ability to make sound decisions, ability to reason
- Flexibility, adaptiveness
- Ability to work independently
- Knowledge of the field
- General knowledge base
- Desire to achieve, seriousness of purpose, initiative
- Professionalism, maturity
- Social awareness, level of concern for others
- Physical grooming, personal appearance
- Character, honesty, integrity, ethical and moral standards
- Ability to work with others, teamwork potential, cooperativeness
- Dependability, level of responsibility

The recommendation forms often conclude by asking referees for a general ranking, taking all characteristics into consideration. Typical questions along these lines are as follows:

- Overall, I give this applicant ____my strongest recommendation ____a high recommendation ____a recommendation ____a recommendation with reservation. ____I do not recommend this applicant.
- Of the ____ number of students I have taught, this applicant ranks in the top 1%____ top 5%____ top 10%____ top 30%____ top 50%____.

In addition, forms often request information about the reference population to which you are being compared (e.g., undergraduates, graduating seniors, or first-year graduate students).

Referee forms almost always request a longer statement that speaks to your qualifications (including both strengths and weaknesses), evidence of your fitness for graduate-level study, and anything else that might help members of the evaluation committee select students.

I now see why my grades on exams and class projects are only a part of the story when it comes to recommendation letters. They want to know a lot more than just my academic performance!

That's right. Some even contend that it is the referee's responsibility to extend beyond assessing strictly academic performance and to consider social behavior and even character.

The Value of Recommendation Letters

How seriously are these letters taken? Are they as important as grades and test scores?

They are taken very seriously, and sometimes they are as important as grades and test scores. It is extremely unlikely, however, that even strong and supportive letters of recommendation could compensate for academic achievements and test scores that are not minimally acceptable.

Occasionally, a student with marginal credentials may be considered because one or more referees present a compelling case on his or her behalf. The circumstances are typically somewhat unusual. One example is a foreign-born student with a serious but rapidly dissolving language barrier who has evidenced her brilliance by other than the conventional means, which rely heavily on the ability to speak and read English. Similarly, letters of recommendation could help offset instances where the numerical indicators fail to assess adequately the students' strengths. Such may be the case with some students who are physically disabled, members of a minority group, or very talented but otherwise marginally qualified applicants.

Once an applicant has made the first cut, that is, having attained the minimum grades and test scores that a program requires, the content of referees' letters can be extremely powerful. Many otherwise qualified applicants may be rejected, and some otherwise borderline candidates may be accepted, solely on the basis of their letters of recommendation.

Letters become so salient at this point because they can provide insights into how applicants attained their grades and test scores by offering descriptions of projects and perceptions of how the students conducted their academic work. Letters can also help selection committee members understand applicants' motivation and commitment and offer interesting testimony about certain areas, such as social and personality style, that could not be gleaned in any other way. They can also signal problems that might not otherwise be revealed by the applicants themselves or by objective data.

However, letters written to support graduate school applications often end up being of little consequence one way or the other. Such letters are generally positive but too short and nonspecific to tell the recipients what they need to know. An example might go something like this:

> Sammy was a student in my social welfare history class last semester. He was a good student. His grade was an A minus. As a person, Sammy seems to be friendly and pleasant, although I did not get to know him very well. Sammy wants to be a social worker in a position related to social policy and advocacy. I see no reason why he should not be able to attain his goal.

Sammy may be damned by faint praise. This letter reveals nothing about Sammy that other materials have not already substantiated, except that Sammy has no overt personality problems. Yet because the instructor admits to not knowing Sammy well, the letter may also be deficient in assessing personal characteristics. We know nothing about why Sammy received a good grade and have no idea where he placed in the class. Did half the class receive an *A*–?

Unfortunately, many students and professors do not get to know each other well enough to allow anything better than this to emerge, and many professors do not or cannot become better acquainted with their undergraduate students. Furthermore, students do not always take advantage of opportunities to become better acquainted with their educators. Even if you do not get to know your referees very well, however, you can avoid this dilemma by the way you prepare the materials to give your referees.

What kinds of letters impress selection committees?

The best help a referee can give a student is to provide specific and detailed examples of accomplishments or character traits that will validate the quality of the applicant's record. Research has demonstrated that specificity and the use of performance examples enhance the attractiveness of the applicant as well as the perceived credibility of the referee, which, in turn, further enhances the status of the applicant (Knouse, 1984). Referees typically write longer letters for students they like and admire than for students they do not like, admire, or know well, so that letter length per se becomes an indirect measure of referee attitude. Favorable letters are usually longer than unfavorable letters, and referees are well aware that they write more about students they believe to be more qualified. Too-long letters, however, may be merely skimmed by the selection committee members.

What kinds of problems can be revealed that would hurt an applicant's chances?

Because most letters are either bland or positive, negative comments stand out like a leopard coat at a "Preserve our Wildlife" rally. When raters operate under time pressures or distractions—two likely conditions when graduate school application materials flood in—greater weight may be placed on negative evidence.

Following are items that respondents in our survey of evaluators were asked to rate that were found to detract from an applicant's candidacy if noted consistently by the referees. They are listed in order, starting with the most detracting:

- Often hands in assignments late
- Is arrogant
- At age 29 is a bit immature
- Participates often in class, but comments tend to be off-target or rambling
- Is dependent and can be "clingy" when insecure
- Misses classes frequently
- Requires considerable structured direction
- Is brilliant but unmotivated
- Likes arguement for its own sake
- Is poorly groomed and unkempt

These traits and behaviors were rated as discrete entities and therefore were seen by the judges as undesirable in and of themselves. A candidate described as possessing one or more of these, yet who is very strong in most ways, may not be excluded from consideration depending on the type and extent of his or her problems.

What if the referee describes positive things about my personality, academic style, or social skills? How much does that help?

Being thought of as nice, dependable, and the like certainly cannot hurt your chances of acceptance, but the power of positive traits is apparently not as strong as the potentially devastating influence of negative traits. This is probably because most letters describe the applicants in positive terms, so these do not discriminate as powerfully as do negative comments. Following are traits and behaviors, starting with those rated the most positively, that enhance candidates' applications if consistently noted by referees:

- Is a self-starter
- Is highly motivated to achieve
- Is responsible and dependable
- Is always willing to pitch in and help out

- Has a professional manner and attitude
- Participates effectively in class
- Is outgoing and friendly
- Has a good sense of humor

Applicants whose cheeriness brightens up everyone else's mood, who are respectful toward faculty, who are very popular among peers, and who are neat and well-groomed receive slight positive credit for these characteristics. However, the most positively viewed characteristics tend to be those that reveal themselves in how students approach their academic performance.

What practical meaning does all of this information have for me?

This information could help you in several ways. If you have a semester or more before you will apply to graduate school, you know what image you must project to potential referees. If you are applying right away, this information may help you decide whom to approach (and whom to avoid approaching) for a recommendation letter. Your most recent academic performance and demeanor will be remembered more readily (unless earlier performance or behavior was dramatic), so improvements over the past few terms may be persuasive to referees.

Now that you know what kinds of things might be problematic between you and a potential referee, these should be discussed openly if possible. For example, if you did well in a professor's class despite missing class often because of illness, you might remind the professor of the difficulty you overcame and that your classroom attendance is normally very regular. If the professor praised you for your ability to take initiative or to persevere based on how you built a piece of equipment by yourself or did a very credible literature review with minimal supervision, remind her or him of those activities in the hopes that a comment about your initiative or perseverance will show up in the recommendation letter.

Finally, you can provide your referees with relevant printed information, perhaps in the form of a résumé (see Appendix A), so they can offer as specific examples of your achievements. That is, you make it easy for referees to write a longer letter!

Sources of Recommendation Letters

Most graduate student applicants do not have the luxury of choosing from among many eager referees. Indeed, many students believe that they will be lucky to convince as many as three people to write anything about them. Students often have more alternatives than they may realize, but it is also true that some students make very poor choices from among the options available.

Your best bets for referees are professors with whom you have studied or worked recently, from whom you earned good grades or evaluations, and whose own professional identities are aligned with the content area of the programs to which you are applying. A letter from a professor who instructed you in statistics or in a heavily research-oriented course and who thinks very highly of you and your work is also highly desirable, regardless of which graduate-level specialty area you have chosen. If you will be training to provide direct services to people, at least one of the letters should be from a person who teaches or works in that field and who is able, based on direct observation, to discuss your interpersonal skills, ethical sensitivity, and ability to relate to others.

The professor who is likely to be best prepared to give selection committees complete and detailed information about you is one with whom you have worked closely on a research or activity project. Because, as previously noted, selection committee members weigh specific and detailed letters more heavily than shorter, less meaty ones, try to get at least one professor who knows you well enough to write a full and descriptive letter. As discussed in chapter 8, seek out opportunities to work closely on some kind of project and, if you locate one, devote considerable effort and dedication to the task even if no monetary considerations or academic credits are involved.

If you still have the time, take another course with a professor in your major with whom you have already worked and performed well. Professors recall students better the second time around. The decision to take a second course from the same professor, however, must be tempered with a consideration of what courses you need to round out an impressive transcript. For example, a student applying to neuroscience programs should not opt for an elective course in counseling theory solely to take another course with a professor with whom she has had success.

Are there any kinds of professors I should not ask to write letters for me?

Avoid asking professors from whom you received mediocre grades or with whom you have had any problematical interactions or unresolved interpersonal difficulties. Professors who only taught you introductory or other lower division classes are relatively poor choices if you have other options. Professors from whom you only took softer elective classes, such as Psychological Profiles of Historical Figures or The Sociology of Modern Art, are usually less preferable than those who taught more substantive, demanding courses.

Is it okay to have a letter from a professor in another department?

If there is no restriction in the application instructions (and usually there is not) and you have a willing supporter in another department, consider the interactions among that professor, the courses you took with this person, and the nature of the programs to which you are applying. These elements should all readily correspond if the outside professor's letter is to support your application.

An example of appropriate congruence would be a biology professor's letter, based on her knowledge of you as a student in a biology class, sent to a neuroscience or physiological psychology program. A political science professor's letter, based on his knowledge of you as a student in a contemporary political issues class, sent to a clinical psychology program is not a good match unless, perhaps, the particular graduate program places heavy emphasis on social policy.

What about a letter from a professor with whom I never took a course but who got to know me pretty well?

Occasionally students become well acquainted with professors even though they never studied with them. Involved advisors and faculty members who are very student-oriented and have an open-door policy are probably most likely to fit this description. The problem with asking such persons to support you is that they probably do not know the information that selection committees want to learn about you. They can attest that you are pleasant and that you know how to express ideas, but they usually cannot verify your academic or research qualifications. If you find someone you like to talk to, and there is still time, perhaps you could arrange for a research or project collaboration that would strengthen the basis of a letter.

What about letters from fieldwork or job supervisors?

A supportive supervisor in a relevant and appropriate practicum or fieldwork experience, particularly if she or he is a licensed professional or has a doctoral degree (or MSW), is a very appropriate referee for applicants to clinical, counseling, applied, or related training programs (such as social work). This supervisor should have observed your work over a period of time and be able to describe your strengths clearly and specifically. If you are applying to an academic research-oriented program, a fieldwork supervisor letter is less impressive unless you were somehow involved in a research component (such as a program evaluation).

Employers or job supervisors are usually helpful only if your job bears some clear relationship to the programs to which you are applying. For instance, if you have worked your way through college as a computer programmer, and you are applying to a quantitative program, your employer's letter should greatly enhance your application. Such a letter would be of less benefit if you are applying to social work programs, and you should use a more relevant referee if possible.

Should one's personal counselor or psychotherapist ever be asked to write a letter?

Many students ask about having their own therapist submit a letter on their behalf. When asked why they think this might be a good idea, most students state something similar to one or more of the following: "I am not afraid to ask him"; "She is a professional in the same field I want to go into"; "He knows me better than anyone else"; and "She believes in me and would write a very positive letter." Not bad rationales, on the face of it. However, we recommend against including a letter from your psychotherapist.

A therapy relationship is so intensely personal that it may be largely discarded by evaluators. Worse yet, it may be interpreted as indicating that the applicant has serious and unresolved problems, regardless of the content of the letter. It is possible that such a letter would be judged positively by those evaluators who admire students who seek assistance and view sitting in the patient's chair as a valuable experience. However, it is impossible to predict if any evaluators sitting on your committee will view such a letter from that positive perspective.

We have, on rare occasion, agreed with a student's decision to use a personal therapist as a referee. In these cases, the students' academic records revealed a serious dip for a semester or two and then turned upward again. The decreased performance was caused by external life stressors for which professional assistance was sought. The therapists in these cases substantiated both the existence and cause of the problem as well as the sustained and successful effort that the students put forth to solve the problem and to come out stronger as a result. However, this is a fairly narrow path in terms of reasons and outcomes, and it is still not risk-free.

I have a cousin who is a well-known psychologist. How about having her write a letter for me?

It is certainly moderately common for students to credit their interest in the field to a relative or a friend whose career is in psychology or an allied field. Such a close relation may also be a useful source of encouragement, information, and guidance. However, that is about as far as the involvement of a close relation should extend at this point in your life.

Evaluators typically view letters from close relations as biased and, therefore, tend to discount them. Worse yet, selection committee members may assume that if an applicant needs to resort to the family or the family's social circle, there may not be sufficient support from more credible and persuasive sources.

A possible exception to the foregoing occurs when an applicant performed significant research (or other professionally relevant work) for a professional who also has a preexisting personal relationship with the applicant. For example, Gary's uncle, who is a professor at a local university, hires Gary to run research participants and enter data over the summer. Although Gary would certainly want to note this type of valuable experience somewhere in his application, we still think it would be best to choose other referees if possible.

Are there other types of people who can serve as referees?

Very rarely, schools will request or allow character reference letters. These could be from people like high school guidance counselors with whom you have kept in contact, club leaders, current or previous employers on a job not related to your career goals, or a nonimmediate family member or long-term friend. A few religiously oriented schools will encourage or even require a letter from the leader at your place of worship.

Does the reputation of the letter writer matter?

Yes, to some extent the identity of the letter writer will be influential. There is no doubt that students who have worked for, and are highly regarded by, scholars with outstanding reputations in their field will be greatly advantaged in the graduate selection procedure. If you have choices, all else being equal, a better known referee is generally preferable than a lesser known one, a full professor is better than an assistant professor, a tenure-track professor is better than a part-time faculty member or teaching assistant, and a fieldwork supervisor with a doctoral degree is preferable to a supervisor with a master's or bachelor's degree. Still, the most important criterion for a referee is the extent to which the referee knows you and can say specific, positive things about you.

One of our surveys asked respondents to rank sources of recommendation letters. The respondents were asked to assume that the letters from these different sources were equally strong and positive so that rating variations would be due only to the referees' characteristics. These sources are listed from most to least enhancing to an applicant's candidacy:

- A mentor with whom applicant has done considerable work
- The applicant's professor, who is also a well-known and highly respected psychologist
- An employer in a job related to the applicant's professional goals
- The chair of the academic department in which the applicant is majoring
- A professor from another department from whom the applicant has taken a relevant upper division course
- A volunteer work supervisor
- A well-known and respected psychologist who is a family friend of the applicant
- An employer (job not related to applicant's professional goals)

- An applicant's professor from another department in a course not directly related to the applicant's goals
- A graduate teaching assistant
- The applicant's psychotherapist

Evaluators view the top two sources, mentors with whom applicants have done considerable work and well-known and respected psychologists, as among the most enhancing factors of any type. In fact, they were rated higher than the applicant's grade point average! The next seven sources were ranked in far more modest, but still helpful, ranges. A letter from a graduate teaching assistant was rated, essentially, as no help, and one's personal therapist was the only source rated negatively.

How to Ask for Letters of Recommendation

Students typically feel extremely anxious approaching people to write letters of recommendation for them. Writing letters of recommendation is also a trying task for professors, as Philip Zimbardo (1987) described:

> One of the more important tasks that a faculty member is called upon by students to undertake is to write letters of recommendation for them—for jobs, for admissions to other schools, for awards, [and so on]. It is also one of the most onerous of teaching functions when the number of such students begins to proliferate and your knowledge of most of them is not as adequate as you would like it to be. I am always distressed when I indicate to a student that I have not had enough personal contact over a sufficient period of time to be able to write a strong letter, and he or she replies, "but no one else here knows me any better than you do!" Our large lecture sections, overworked faculty, student shyness, the diversity of courses, the necessity of after-school jobs, commuting, and the like all conspire to reduce the level and quality of personalized interaction between faculty and students. In addition, a surprising number of students are unaware of their need to secure a series of recommendations until it is too late, as well as being uninformed about the non-grade-related dimensions of such recommendations that are important. (pp. 94–95)

Despite the difficulties for all concerned, remember that the faculty members in your department want to send as many qualified undergraduate students on for advanced training as possible. It is the way that individual academics symbolically reproduce themselves, the way that a scholarly immortality of sorts is achieved. To be a component of a student's success is a very special, intangible reward for your teachers. So, these people are not your natural enemies. Most want to help you if they believe that they can.

Can I assume that if I got a good grade in a class and the professor seemed to like me I can just send that professor the recommendation forms?

Take nothing for granted! Negotiating with your referees is a very important step that must be done carefully, respectfully, and sensitively. Application forms often stipulate that you list the names of the people who will write letters in your behalf. Never list a name unless that person has agreed to write a letter for you. Unless you get express permission, the person may not follow through, leaving the evaluators to wonder how sharp you could possibly be if someone you declared would recommend you never bothers to do so. Or, the person could write a negative letter, a disastrous situation you might have been warned about had you consulted with him or her first. We know of an *A* student who confidently assumed that a professor would write a letter because they joked around regularly outside of class. However, when the student asked for a letter, he was shocked to hear the professor say, "I will have to inform them that although you are very bright, you are also manipulative and can be quite arrogant."

It is also a huge mistake to assume that all you have to do is mail potential referees the forms or leave them in their mailboxes, without checking out their willingness to get involved. Here are three actual notes we have received.

Hi. I was in your introductory psychology course back in 1988. Long time no see! You gave me a B. I graduated in 1991 and have decided to go back to graduate school. Can you believe it? Attached is the form that you need to fill out. Thank you.

Jill Airhead

Attached are recommendation forms for the seven graduate programs I am applying to. Notice that the first one is due next week, so you will have to get to it right away.

Cappy Qweeg

I am a student in this department. I am applying to graduate programs and I want to get into a good one. I have never taken a class from you, and we have never met. But a letter of recommendation from you would be very helpful. I have enclosed my personal statement. Thank you for your help.

Carl Clueless

The students' names have obviously been changed to protect the naive and the brash. Unfortunately, Jill was a long-lost memory. Although Cappy was a more recent student, he had never come by for any sort of informal chat, so all that was really known about him was the grade he earned. Carl was never even a student of ours. These students' notes are masterpieces of how not to ask anyone for a favor! Worse yet, these students demonstrated by their lack of sophistication that they may not be suitable candidates for graduate school.

Even if you know a potential referee very well and feel confident that he or she will write you a letter, you must still assume a professional stance and ask first.

Asking for a recommendation letter is unsettling. I don't feel as if I know any professor very well.

Your feelings are very common. It is scary to ask someone for help, especially if you hardly know the person and it is someone you perceive as powerful or intimidating. Most students have these feelings, especially those from large, impersonal universities. Referees are used to dealing with them, and they will usually put you at ease. If you still have at least a semester or two before you will apply to graduate school, try to get to know some of your professors (or other good reference sources) better (see chap. 6). If, like many readers, you are ready to apply now, you will simply have to plow ahead with what relationships you have developed. It is not too late to earn some points, however, and these techniques will be described in what follows.

Couldn't I ask for a letter in writing or call on the telephone? I'd prefer that to showing up in person.

Unless the potential referee cannot be reached except by mail or telephone, a situation that would arise only rarely, you should request your letter of recommendation in person. Referees like to see faces to stimulate our recollections. (Students tend to credit us with better memories than we actually have.) Referees also typically prefer a direct discussion of your situation and needs. If you want to ask a professor, an easy and convenient method is to show up during office hours. (Do not try to ask for recommendation letters in the hallway.) Otherwise, call ahead and ask for a brief appointment at the professor's earliest convenience.

If you must write—and taking off from work or traveling some distance is preferable to a letter—we suggest enclosing a recent photograph unless you know for sure that the potential referee does know and remember you. Also, enclose a resume and a letter describing your record and plans.

Okay, I admit that I can arrange to see each person face to face. What do I do after I get through the door?

Do not worry about feeling awkward; most students feel that way. Just try for the smoothest possible self-presentation. Some hints will probably help you out here. Do not beat around the bush while trying to muster up the courage to ask for a letter. After a brief greeting, let the potential referee know exactly why you are there. We suggest saying something like this: "I'm here to ask you if you would feel comfortable writing a letter of recommendation for me." (The reasons for this particular wording will be made clear soon.) Also indicate where you plan to apply and briefly describe your degree and career goals. Remind the potential referee, if necessary, which courses or other relevant experiences you had with him or her, and what grades you received. The potential referee will likely enter into the discussion at that point and have a few questions to ask you.

If the person agrees to write a letter of support, be prepared to do one of two things. Either hand your referee the forms and any other information that he or she would like to see, or indicate that you will be delivering them at some specified future time.

What if I get the impression that the referee has some reservations about writing a letter for me?

The reason you ask the referee if he or she would "feel comfortable" is to allow him or her to express any reservations. Sometimes even very sophisticated and professional people find it easier to just say "yes" than to confront someone and risk a distasteful conversation. Instead, the reservation may be revealed in the content of the letter. You could be none the wiser, but your chances for admission could be damaged beyond repair.

If you sense a resistance, interject something like, "I would appreciate it if you would tell me if you have any reservations about writing a letter for me." At this point, the potential referee will correct a message not intended or may reveal an impediment to his or her support of you.

If potential referees are direct about reservations from the beginning, it is likely that the problems may be more serious, and you may wish to attempt to discuss and ameliorate these. This will depend, of course, on what the reservations are. If, for example, a professor says, "I am unsure about recommending you to this particular program because I have no knowledge of your ability to do research design," you may provide the person with information such as a grade in a research methods course. You could make assurances that another referee will be evaluating you in that area. At that point, the potential referee may comfortably agree to write you a letter.

Some potential referees would support your application to some programs but not to others. Usually the reason is based on their view of your academic potential. That is, they might be very willing to write a positive letter for a master's program but not for a competitive doctoral program. Some will agree to write letters to all of the programs to which you applied but will inform you that some of the letters will be stronger than others, again often depending on how academically suited to each program they judge you to be.

The part that I dread the most is possibly being criticized and turned down. What should I do if a potential referee says a flat-out "no"?

Of course this feels pretty awful, but the potential referee who rejects the opportunity to get involved with your quest for advanced study has done you a huge favor of sorts. It may have been easier for the person to have agreed to write the letter and then made it short and flat (no help!) or, even worse, laced with explicit, unflattering commentary.

The main reason students receive a "no" is because professors do not know them well enough. Before giving up, however, propose your willingness to provide much more information about yourself to see if that would make a difference. Having a résumé handy, or better yet, the referee packet that is described later, is a great prop for such a situation.

Some referees, however, agree to write letters only for students they know very well and have worked with closely over a period of time. Those people will not likely change their minds. Others, particularly faculty from larger institutions with high student-to-faculty ratios, are more sympathetic to students' dilemmas and may be more willing to get involved and learn more about the student now for this particular purpose.

Another relatively common reason for being turned down is that students give the potential referees too little lead time. The referee cannot drop everything to do you a last-minute favor, especially when a number of other students are ahead of you. (How much lead time to give referees is covered later.)

If you are turned away because of a judgment that you do not deserve a letter, anger or embarrassment is certainly understandable. You may be told that your classroom behavior was unacceptable or that you have not evidenced dependability or responsibility. Here you may discover (the hard way) the hidden costs of talking excessively to your neighbor during lectures, too many absences or makeup exam requests, or too many excuses as to why you could not do something the way everyone else in the class was required to do it. A concern may be expressed that you are not capable of success in graduate school or that the referee doubts your emotional suitability to the profession. These more serious reasons for declining to write a letter are unlikely to be amenable to a reassessment. Thank the person for being frank (which is better than simply writing a scathing letter!) and excuse yourself. Remember that sometimes a rejection says more about the professor than about you. There are some biased, burnt-out, or mean-spirited teachers whose evaluations may not be accurate. Don't give up yet. Go on to the next name on your list.

It sounds like some students will not be able to find anyone to recommend them and therefore will be unable to apply to graduate school at all.

Yes, that happens.

What if a potential referee agrees to write a letter with some praise in it but states that she will have to be honest and also reveal some short-coming or deficit she sees in me?

This is a tough call. Ask for details and analyze both the degree of strength that the letter will reveal as well as the concerns. Are the strengths considerable? Would it be impossible for another referee to speak to them? Are the weaknesses minor or common to your stage in life? A selection committee may forgive or discount immaturity (if you are under 23 years old), lack of direct experience, and other minimally problematic characteristics that are very likely to be outgrown, as long as there are compensations in other areas.

Sometimes what a referee sees as a weakness may not be viewed as such by others. A colleague we know, for example, sees students who graduate without having taken any courses in the philosophy of science as possessing a serious deficit. Such courses may be highly desirable, but it is not likely that everyone will view their absence as a fatal flaw. Some characteristics, although not desirable, may not be viewed as all that terrible either. These include mild shyness, being soft spoken, and having difficult-to-read handwriting.

If a potential referee expresses concerns about you that are more obviously problematic, such as irresponsibility or insufficient intellectual capacity, proceeding with this referee obviously poses a major risk, even if he or she will also attest to positive and strong points. We recommend that you thank the person for his or her time and then move on to another potential referee.

When to Ask for Recommendation Letters

The timing of your request is very important, because, as noted earlier, a common reason for refusing to write a letter is insufficient lead time. Three weeks is a reasonable lead time for most referees. Cutting it much closer than that can be risky.

A common complication is that most colleges and universities have an extended winter holiday break that overlaps with the period (late December through January) when about a third of doctoral applications are due. This means that you will need to complete your negotiations with referees by mid-November at the latest because they will be busy getting term grades in before the holiday break. After that, they want a rest! Even for February deadlines, it is best to get everything set to go well before the winter holiday break.

As we discuss next, the task is not quite as simple as asking for a letter, receiving a "yes," and then handing a pile of forms to your referees. To write an effective letter, each referee needs some information about you. It is your responsibility to pull these materials together and deliver them to your referees either at the time they agree to write you a letter or very shortly thereafter.

Providing Referees With Information

How carefully you prepare information for your referees can actually influence the quality of their letters. Here is your chance to show yourself to be an organized, competent, careful student who is sensitive to the demands on the referees' needs and time. It is also your chance to fill your referees in on yourself. Most referees know you only in a relatively restricted sense, as their student or supervisee. Here you can display your motivation, commitment, and goals. When the referees prepare your letters, you want them to have a lot to comment on positively, and they will appreciate the way you organized your materials, making things easier for them. Accomplishments, skills, and traits that you emphasize in your materials are likely to be emphasized in the referee's letter.

What is the right way to convey this information?

Create a set of standard referee packets, one for each referee. Give them to your referees well in advance of the application due date. This packet can include the following:

- A résumé, vita (see Appendix A), or biographical statement
- A statement of your interests and career goals
- Your GPAs (overall and in your major; undergraduate and graduate, if applicable)
- A list of courses taken in your major (as well as other relevant courses completed) and grades earned, or a copy of your transcript
- A list of courses you expect to complete before graduation
- GRE scores and other standardized test scores (if available)
- Any other comments that indicate your interests, your educational record, and your strengths
- Which courses/experiences you took with or were supervised by the referee
- Relevant work or other experiences

Also include a photocopy of any significant assignment, such as a research report or term project, that you did in the referees' classes. (Some may also want an example of what you consider to be your very best work, even if it was done for someone else.) Therefore, routinely make copies of all of your larger assignments and save them in a secure place. They may come in handy now, or later if one of the programs to which you apply requests a writing sample or a discussion of your major undergraduate projects.

Make sure that everything you include in the packet is accurate and completely honest. Check it over carefully. Referees may independently verify the correctness of the information, and errors can give a negative impression.

This packet can be assembled in a variety of ways as long as it is well-prepared, complete, and neat. If you have already composed a statement of purpose, give it to referees; it will probably cover several of the points listed previously. Type everything. Staple everything together. Include your name and telephone number and, if applicable, your e-mail address.

The next crucial part of the packet is the referee forms themselves, which must be prepared properly. First, make sure that your name is typed on each form. Fill out the waiver of rights section if there is one. (This issue will be discussed later in the chapter.) If a program did not supply forms for referees, there may be a statement of what issues referees should address. If so, be sure to make copies of that statement to distribute to each referee. If there were no forms or other guidelines for referees, include a note to that effect so that your referees will not worry that something is missing or that they have lost a form.

Address (using a typewriter or printer) plain white, legal-sized envelopes for each program, double-checking the addresses. If there is an individual to whom the letter should be addressed, show that clearly. (Sometimes the application destination and the referee letter destination are different.) Affix first-class postage with a paper clip. (Some referees may prefer to use institutional envelopes and will transfer your stamp to that envelope.) Attach the envelope to the corresponding form with a paper clip. As noted previously, if the program supplied no form or guideline sheet, clip the envelope to a piece of paper that reads, "[Name of program and university] did not include a form or other instructions."

Finally, we highly recommend that you create a cover sheet that clearly lays out your entire scheme very clearly. At the top, put your name and telephone number and the date. Next list the programs to which you are applying, and the degree you are seeking. Now, clearly list the date that the referee letters are due. Here is an example:

> *Saltine University*
> *Master's in Counseling Psychology*
> *Letter due: March 15, 1991*

List programs in the order that letters are due, with the earliest one on top. This cover sheet gives referees your complete plan at a glance and indicates when they need to do their part.

If you very strongly desire to get into one or more specific programs, there is another type of information that you can supply to your referees. Because a good match between you and the graduate program is so important, a wise move is to provide each referee with a statement (which can be brief) of what attracted you to each program and why you think that you would be a good selection for that program. A sample might go something like this:

> *The clinical psychology program at Bumpers State University has several faculty members who are interested in cognitive therapy, which is my major interest area. I have done a literature review paper on cognitive therapy for depression and have assisted Professor Halfull with his research on depression.*

How your referees describe you to the Bumpers clinical psychology selection committee will likely be far more effective as a result of your sharing this information.

You may not be as focused as the student in this example. If you made your choices carefully, however, informing your referees of the basis for choosing each program could still be helpful.

Is it okay to give my referees the forms one at a time as I make my decisions and receive forms?

It is somewhat annoying when students dribble a number of referee forms in, one at a time, over a period of months. So, if at all possible, give all of your application materials to your referees at once, well in advance of the program with the earliest deadline. Most referees like to write an applicant's letters in a single sitting and get the satisfaction of completion, even though they may stagger the dates that they actually mail the letters. If you cannot give the referee all of the forms, indicate if possible that one or more additional forms (noting the names of the programs, if known) will arrive soon.

Will referees write separate letters for each program that I apply to?

Most will fill out the brief line items and checklists on the forms individually, but typically the letter will be generic. Mentors may do more individualizing for their most highly prized students. However, some referees will not do any individualized work on the referee materials and will not even fill out the line items on the specific forms. Instead, they will send only a copy of the generic letter.

It is our strong opinion that filling out each form individually gives applicants the best advantage. Selection committees can compare applicants more easily if their own forms are used, and at least partially individualized referee materials give the impression that the referee enthusiastically supports the applicant. Before we leave the impression that we are admonishing referees who do not individualize applications, however, let us add that preparing these forms and letters is an enormous task and not everyone has the time and stamina to do it the hard way. Selection committees are used to less than personalized input. For example, one major university's referee form states, "We prefer that you [the referee] use the forms provided with the departmental application, but letters on your departmental letterhead are acceptable."

Can I ask my referees to show me a copy of my letters?

This is not generally considered appropriate. Some referees may offer to show or give you a copy; others will not. That is their prerogative.

What exactly are my legal rights to know the contents of the letters, and is there any advantage to waiving them?

The Family Education Rights and Privacy Act of 1974 established applicants' rights to inspect filed letters written by their referees, and the Buckley amendment permitted universities to request that applicants waive this right. This is a pretty strange situation, which has caused profound dilemmas for students, referees, and selection committees (Ault, 1993). We offer information about this complicated dilemma, but only you can decide how you will handle your own files.

Students are placed in a dilemma because there may be some advantages to waiving their rights, and yet if a damaging letter is in their file, they might never know why they had problems getting into graduate school.

Referees may worry that if they are completely honest, they could be sued for defamation of character by students who attempt to prove that their failures are due to false or speculative comments in their files. Such suits are unlikely to be brought, especially if the writer provides supportable facts about the student's performance. Nevertheless, there seems to be a consensus that letters now are more bland and lack candor and are therefore less useful as screening devices.

Selection committee members already suspect, as previously discussed, that referee letters are too positive (inflated) and therefore to be viewed skeptically. Selection committee members may further regard letters in an open file as reflections of the referees' reluctance to disclose unfavorable comments or to be less objective and honest. Selection committee members may be right about that. Ceci and Peters (1984) used a prewarning deception technique that allowed them to test their hypotheses in actual rather than simulated circumstances. They found that letter writers rated students higher across a number of dimensions if they believed the students might view the letters. These same letter writers rated the same students lower if they believed that the students would not be able to see their letters. Our surveys also revealed that selection committee members view letters about students who signed away their rights to see their letters as less biased and more honest.

In the end, the decision is yours. It is unfortunate that anyone has to be put into the situation of waiving their rights. If you do decide to waive your rights, however, also do your very best to ensure that the people who write letters for you are supportive advocates of you and your goals.

Should I check up later to see that my referees have sent my letters?

Unfortunately, for a variety of reasons, it is rather common for recommendation letters to arrive late. Because a selection committee may drop an incomplete file from consideration, even if the deficit is not the student's fault, applicants themselves must check up on their referees. The easiest way is to stop by the referees' offices around the date when the first letter is due to gently inquire about the letters' status. (Most referees won't be offended by a polite reminder, and some may actually appreciate it.) Or, you can call the destination office staff a week or so after each deadline date and politely inquire if letters have arrived.

A Small Matter of Etiquette

As soon as you have ascertained that a referee has fulfilled the agreement to contribute a letter to your file, drop by in person to express your appreciation or send a thank-you note or card. Although assisting worthy students in their educational and career development is a professional responsibility, it is also a very demanding and time-consuming task, which referees do on their own time for no overt reward. Also, please drop by and share the results of graduate application. Referees were actively involved and are interested in the outcome. It is rewarding to hear that we played some part in a student's successful application for graduate study. If you were not accepted into a program this time around, these same people may be able to make good suggestions for your next move.

CHAPTER 18

WHAT SHOULD I CONSIDER WHEN FILLING OUT APPLICATION FORMS?

Once you have selected programs to which you will apply, watch out for an attack of procrastination. A primary purpose of this book is to help you move along until the job is done. So, hang on and let's go!

The Time Commitment

It is possible to whiz through the application process, but the chances of making mistakes that will cost you an acceptance are high. This critical task is worth the time that must be taken to ensure success.

Students often estimate that the typical graduate school application takes about 2 hours to fill out. In reality, for applications to competitive programs, it is safest to plan on 8 to 16 hours for the first one (of course, you do not have to do it in a single sitting). Plan on 4 to 6 hours each for the remaining applications. You can usually save time on subsequent forms because some of the information can be used again or adapted from the initial one, and your confidence level increases markedly with each application completed. (You will want to be careful about too much adaptation from one application to another, however. More on that later.)

Just what is included in these time estimates?

The time estimates include mapping out the line items and plugging in easily available information on practice versions of the forms, tracking down information not readily available, creating the statement of purpose or other required essay, typing or carefully hand printing the final materials, and preparing the package for mailing. Applications from some programs are more demanding than average and take additional time.

The time estimates presented here do not include asking for letters of recommendation or creating and distributing information packets to your referees, studying for and taking required tests, having someone review and proofread your application materials, ordering transcripts and test scores, filling out proof of residency or financial aid request forms, and making any major alterations of early drafts of your essay statements.

Students we encounter typically underestimated the time and energy involved in putting applications together. Many believe that their chances of getting into their favorite programs were hurt as a result. Following are two representative comments:

> I just wish that someone had told me that I should have put in every spare hour for over a month into my 10 applications. I could have planned better and certainly saved myself a bout of temporary insanity.

> Applicants need to realize that this process is all-absorbing for a while. It goes better if you are organized and know what to do. It is hell if you don't. It was hell for me until about the fourth one.

What differentiates an average application form from a difficult one?

The average application form for doctoral or master's programs will have two to four pages of brief questions on an all-university graduate admissions form and another somewhat similar form (or *supplementary departmental form*, as it is often called) for the specific department or program. You may be asked to send the two separate sets of materials to two separate offices, or you may have to send materials to the academic department in which you are interested.

Most of the requested items on the application forms are for information that you already know or is easily available to you, although plan on having to search for a few things. The university or program will also usually want a statement of purpose or some other essay assignment (see chap. 19) of about two to four pages.

Most of the time spent on the application forms themselves goes into two tasks: the essay statement and experimenting with how to fit the line item information neatly on the forms. Hidden surprises, such as requests for different ways of computing your GPA, can arise. Some applications request an overall GPA for all college courses taken; others want your first 60 units separated out from the last 60 units, or overall GPA and major-only GPA. Occasionally you may have to convert semester to quarter credits or vice versa. Even with your transcripts in front of you, it takes time to calculate these figures and ensure accuracy.

Some more difficult applications require information that most students do not have readily available or details that take considerable time to compile (such as a list of textbooks you used in certain psychology courses). More commonly, applications are more difficult because several essay statements are required or the single statement that is required is very complicated.

If you really want to attend one of the schools with a more difficult than average application, try to persevere. Those applications will scare off many less motivated students, thus increasing your chances of success.

Where do I start?

First, make at least two photocopies of every application form and put the originals in a place safe from spills and smudges. Making two copies should be enough, but some students have reported messing up several copies before getting the spacing right. Work with these copies until the very end. Some schools now offer the option of downloading their application forms from the Internet, making it possible to get additional copies easily.

Use the first working copy for penciling in information. Erase and rewrite until it seems right. The second working copy is for a quick trial pass with the typewriter you will be using (or your neatest printing) on those items that must fit into a closed space or short line. When you type or write the version that you will send, you will know how to fit the information into the space available.

Mapping Your Plan

Read all of the directions and highlight any peculiarities or elements you might overlook. Applications vary widely in their appeal and ease of use. The best ones are on firm white or cream stock, with roomy spaces provided for the requested information. The unappealing ones are printed on delicate onionskin or on bright pink or goldenrod paper, or provide such puny spaces that you are in trouble right from the start, unless your name is very short. Often little cards and other odd-sized items (which you have to fill out) are enclosed. Be sure not to lose them.

Some all-university forms require you to locate various code numbers in their scheme to indicate assorted facts about your degree plans. Some of these appear strange, but take the time to figure out each system lest you end up a candidate in the physics department!

Examine the actual forms and decide whether the line items can be typed or whether neat hand printing looks better. (Experiment with a photocopy to see what looks best.) Next, using another blank copy, start filling in the lines, being very careful to follow the directions.

Why all this fuss about trial runs?

We will soon discuss why taking extra time to create a very neat and professional-looking application is worth this bother.

What kinds of information do applications typically ask for?

Common short-line items include address (current and permanent), telephone number, social security number, citizenship, all educational institutions attended and when (some want high school as well as college), military service and eligibility for veteran's benefits, languages spoken and proficiency level, undergraduate major, professional organization or honorary society memberships, GRE information (dates taken and scores), what program you wish to enter, what student classification you seek (e.g., full-time, part-time, unclassified), what term you would begin graduate school, what degree you are seeking, a statement of intent to apply for financial assistance, and a list of the individuals who will provide letters of recommendation. These types of items are usually easy because the information is readily available to you.

Common longer line items (that is, you are provided a full line or two for your response) include scholarships, honors, awards, or other distinctions earned; academic work in progress and courses planned prior to graduation; employment history (sometimes "relevant" or "pertinent" experience is stipulated); publications or paper presentations; previous graduate work; and teaching or research experience. These items typically take a little more time and thought to compose in a way that fits the space allotted.

Less common line-item requests include dismantling your transcript into course areas (e.g., math, science, philosophy, etc.), activities since leaving college, details of any dismissal or suspension from an educational institution, and a description of any disability that would require special services. Rare Items include person to notify in case of emergency, questions about previous legal problems, and a space for inclusion of a photograph.

What other kinds of things are asked for in the application form?

A number of applications require a declaration that all statements made in the application are true to the best of the applicant's knowledge, and that any misrepresentation could be cause for refusal or revocation of admission or termination of enrollment. All forms require your signature.

Tax-supported state schools may require elaborate residency forms for residents. (Nonresidents are spared the forms but pay higher tuition and fees.) Financial aid forms also require specialized information and occasionally an essay statement.

Getting through these forms can be onerous, but most are clear-cut in terms of what they want. After a practice run, it is time to fill out the actual form. Some application packets are especially user-friendly and include checklists to ensure that you do everything right and send materials to the right offices.

Remember, there are usually two forms per program: one all-university form for all students who apply to graduate programs at the institution, and one supplemental department form. The line items on the department form will be oriented more toward your proposed area of study. Often they are miniversions of the common essay topics presented in the next chapter. For example, one program might ask you to describe your career objectives using the two lines provided, and another might ask for a 250-word essay on the same topic.

Check your final version to make sure that you responded to every item. We suggest putting NA (for "not applicable") rather than leaving any line item blank because it does not apply to you (e.g., military service dates or already earned graduate degrees). That way the evaluators know that you did attend to the item.

What if the information I meant to include won't fit in the space provided in the application?

You can use one of two strategies. The preferable one is to put as much information as possible on the application form, adding the phrase "continued on separate page" on the last line of the section in which you are working. Then, on a separate sheet, type the heading from the application section (e.g., Honors and Awards) and complete the information you started on the application.

A second strategy is to put the phrase "see attached sheets" in the relevant spaces on the application form and then provide all of the information under the appropriate headings on those separate sheets. The disadvantage here is that the evaluator has to flip back and forth between the application form and the attached sheets. You also run the risk of the evaluator perceiving that you tried to take the easy way out in preparing your application.

Neatness Counts!

Do I have to type?

The best possible impression will be a form completed on a typewriter with an easy-to-read font and a brand-new ribbon. A very neatly hand-printed application form using black ink is also acceptable. Indeed, sometimes you will have no choice because only a master typist with specialized equipment could fit the print into the tiny boxes and narrow spaces provided on some forms. However, a typed version probably helps a little in the evaluation process. Statements of purpose or other required essays should always be printed on a computer printer or typed, even if you choose to hand print the form.

It is getting more and more difficult to even find a good typewriter to use these days! However, do try. Unusual fonts, poor quality printers, and typewriters with quirky problems (e.g., a filled-in *m*, an elevated *a* and *o*, no tail on the *y*) may annoy the reader. Faint print makes the material look dreary, an impression that could be generalized to the perception of the content. Odd-colored ribbons or fonts make the application difficult to read and may suggest that the applicant is an odd person.

Use black ink and a standard Courier or similar letter-quality font. Remember that the selection committee members may read as many as several hundred applications. Imagine how gratifying it is to pick up one that is neat, clean, crisp, and easy to read. You may score your first point before they even get to your name!

Do you really have any hard evidence that neatness is, in and of itself, a factor in the selection?

Of course, a professional-looking application is not going to elevate an applicant's status to the top of the heap regardless of other considerations. Evidence suggests, however, that the appearance of the application materials influences selection. Appearance gives clues about the applicant's competence and conscientiousness. The majority of the program office staff we surveyed reported that neatness of the application was "definitely" or "somewhat" of a factor in making admission decisions. Only 4% believed that neatness of the application form itself had no bearing on enhancing the attractiveness of the candidate.

Doesn't almost everyone send in neat-looking applications, making everything dependent on other factors?

You would think so. Amazingly, many do not. In a large batch of applications, some will have been completed in pencil or using a printer with problems, and several will contain typos, grammatical problems, smudges, and crossed-out letters and numbers. Some will look sloppy overall. Others will include poorly copied materials. Clearly, these give a poor impression as to the applicant's seriousness, ability to follow directions, attention to detail, professionalism, and general competence.

Optional Enclosures

Should I include a cover letter with my application?

You do not need a cover letter in an ideal situation, that is, if your application is complete, everyone who writes letters on your behalf mails them on time, your test scores are in or will arrive shortly, and all important and relevant information about you has been covered somewhere in your application materials. You may want to include a cover letter, however, to explain any logistical problem, such as a reference letter or test score that you know will be a little late. The body of such a note may read something like this:

> If my GRE scores have not yet arrived at your office, they should be there shortly. I took the tests on December 9. Dr. Slow has just returned from Norway and has promised to write a letter of recommendation on my behalf and send it later this week.

A cover letter may be a wise idea when you believe that something about you (such as your foreign language fluency or advanced mathematical skills) is important to share, but there is no obvious place for it on the application. That is, a letter should be included when certain information may seem awkward if included in the essay or elsewhere. One such cover letter might go like this:

> Enclosed are my completed application materials. Although this information was not specifically requested, the selection committee might be interested to know that I speak fluent Spanish and have spent the last two summers in Mexico working in an orphanage sponsored by my church. This experience has been very valuable to me, both in terms of working directly with small children and in learning about another culture.

This example contains fairly significant information about this applicant that the selection committee for the MA counseling psychology program to which he is applying will likely find intriguing.

Should anything else be put in a cover letter?

Other types of information you may wish to share in a cover letter, if relevant, and if no opportunity presented itself elsewhere on the application, include the following: an explanation of a long lapse time between your last educational experience and the present (or gaps along the way), a nondefensive explanation for a lousy semester that brought your grade point average down substantially, and your membership in a minority group if you care to reveal it.

If you are applying to schools far away from your home (out of state and at least several hundred miles away), you may choose to assure the program staff in a cover letter that you are very willing (or even excited) to move to another place (or to their place in particular). (If you clearly prefer to be closer to home and are using faraway schools as backups, then do not describe any special enthusiasm about leaving home, because to do so would simply be dishonest.)

You do not want to play any games with cover letters to try to butter up your evaluators with overblown flattery. Such attempts are easy for these experienced and bright people to spot. Cover letters should be brief, less than a full page, or they may be largely ignored. Use plain white bond paper. Type neatly, single-spaced with double spaces between paragraphs.

Is there anything else that I might include in my application packet?

As one selection committee member reported to us, "Submit whatever will make your application stronger, whether it was specifically requested or not." If you have already created a fine-looking résumé or vita (see Appendix A), slip in a copy.

The inclusion of a research paper (from an independent study project) on a topic directly related to the program may leave a favorable impression. Therefore, if you have done a piece of work really well and it is relevant to the program area (or would be of interest to one or more of the graduate faculty as suggested by your research about them), you might be able to enhance your status significantly by including a copy of the finished product.

A final word of caution: Before you add anything that is not specifically requested in the application, be sure that it will indeed strengthen your application rather than detract from it. Showing the selection committee your work will be beneficial only if it is very well done. A bad or even mediocre paper or other product (e.g., computer or video production) would have the opposite effect. You may want to verify your decision to include a paper or other project in your application with an advisor or the instructor who graded it. In the end, the question to ask is, "Will the things I include with my application help me stand out in a positive way?"

We now move on to the part of the application that many students find the most difficult. The next chapter contains our advice about completing the essay portion of the application.

CHAPTER 19

WHAT ABOUT STATEMENTS OF PURPOSE AND OTHER ESSAYS?

The vast majority of doctoral and master's programs in psychology and related fields require applicants to supply one or more written statements. Sometimes these are required only by the university-wide admissions office, and the essay task is the same for all students regardless of the field to which they are applying. Often, however, the departmental or program application requires an additional essay or two.

The solicited statements vary from information about your past experiences to your future plans. Although many common essay themes among programs are readily apparent, each program will have its own subtleties and desired emphasis.

Most students find this task to be the most intimidating aspect of the application, sometimes leading to intense and immobilizing stress. Although no one but you can create this statement, there is no reason why this task should traumatize you, especially if you devote some time to it.

The Purpose of Essay Statements

What are these essays used for?

An obvious and primary use of your application essays (often referred to as *statements of purpose*) is to assess the information that you were requested to provide. The essays are also used, along with reference letters, to supplement and enrich numerical data (GPA and GRE scores). Selection committees also note how well applicants write, what applicants see as an appropriate self-presentation, how applicants view priorities as revealed by what they select for inclusion, perhaps something about the applicants' values and personalities, and how well the applicants' needs and goals can be served by the program. The personal essay may also alert evaluators to potential problems or deficiencies in experience.

How much weight does the selection committee assign to the essay statement?

The essay statement is your chance to present yourself as a serious student and a unique person. If your achievements and accomplishments are at the highest level, your essay would probably have to be poorly done or reveal disturbing information to eliminate you from the running. If your record of achievement falls well below established cutoff points, even the most thoughtful and well-written essay ever created is unlikely to help.

There are two circumstances, however, in which an essay statement may be a critical determinant of whether you remain in the competition. The majority of applicants probably fall into one of these two categories.

First, students with very respectable grades, test scores, and reference letters often are in a pool with a great many others of similar caliber. At that point, the selection committee will move to the next line of discriminators to narrow the applications to the number that they will accept. The essay statement is among the most important such discriminators. Thus, those who have created an impressive, clear, carefully reasoned, and well-composed statement that speaks to the issues requested will rise to the top of the heap.

Second, students who have marginal grades and test scores may be able to advance their position significantly if they have other strengths or characteristics that make them special or unusual. These compensating factors may be best revealed in an essay statement.

Essay Statement Content Categories

Essay tasks have some remarkable similarities from one program to another. This means that you can get started on your essay task even before you receive applications.

If essays are so similar, can't I just write one which I can then use for every application?

The generic statement of purpose is a frequently used ploy among graduate school applicants. It is also one of the very serious mistakes that applicants can make. As we shall soon see, most programs ask for a few, but never all, of the commonly requested types of information. The requested emphasis varies as well. For example, most programs want to know something about your interests and career plans. However, the wording often leaves no doubt that one of them is to be stressed over the other. For example, compare the directions for these two statements of interest from two different programs:

> *Describe in detail your academic interests. Briefly note how these may eventually dovetail with the kind of work you wish to be doing in 5 years.*

> *What career are you interested in pursuing? How did you make your career decisions, and what assets do you have that will enhance the success you hope to have with your career? How do your current academic interests fit with your career goals?*

Although both ask about academic and career interests, to send each one the same statement would not be in your best interests because the emphasis in each is different.

About half of essays request the applicant to indicate how the program or faculty match his or her individual needs. Therefore, using a generic essay statement virtually ensures that every evaluating group receiving the essay will perceive you as (a) lazy, (b) not really interested in their specific program, (c) someone who did not read the directions, (d) someone who is unable to follow directions, or (e) some or all of the above. In each case, you fail to impress those whose positive regard you are trying to earn.

Please help me get started!

The first thing you must do, if it is not there already, is to muster up self-confidence. Many students feel inconsequential or inferior as they prepare to write about themselves and their achievements. They are sure they have not done enough to impress anyone and may even turn anger inward for not having done more. Remember, no one expects you to have reached greatness. Selection committee members are aware that most applicants' accomplishments to date are relatively modest.

The search is for students with considerable potential and motivation to succeed (see chap. 4). The confidence you display and the faith you exhibit in your own ability to do solid graduate and professional work are among the ways that your potential reveals itself. However, you do not want to be arrogant or to puff yourself up beyond your actual attainments. You want to come across as someone who is very sure that, no matter what you have done (or have not done) in the past, you can succeed in graduate school if given the chance.

To help you formulate your essays, we describe the 13 most frequent content categories and suggest how they might be approached. Although you likely will not have to respond to all of these categories, sketch out some notes with respect to each category and keep them handy as you compose your statements.

What are these 13 content categories?

We analyzed 360 essay questions included in applications for master's and doctoral psychology graduate programs in the United States and Canada, as well as a selection of doctoral programs in related fields. We describe the resulting 13 categories and provide illustrative examples from portions of essay questions appearing on actual graduate school applications. Categories are presented roughly in the order of how often they appeared in the 360 applications.

1. *Career Plans*. A great many evaluators are interested in your professional aspirations. Usually the question is asked in a very straightforward way, such as, "Tell us about your long-term career goals." Sometimes the question is asked a bit more indirectly, such as, "What do you see yourself doing 10 years from now?" or "To what career do you aspire, and why does this decision feel satisfying to you?"

This is an easy one if you have developed a solid career direction and have chosen a program that is designed to train you for this career. It feels like a tough one if you are undecided. If you still sense an emptiness when you think about a career choice, and if you have time, we strongly encourage you to do some reading and to seek career counseling.

The programs to which you choose to apply (e.g., social work or clinical psychology) already determine your chosen career stage in broad strokes. Hopefully, you have a preferred work setting (e.g., university, hospital, legal system, military) and are not writing down the current "hot" job just because it is the only thing you can think of or because it has captured your attention for the moment (e.g., FBI criminal profiler or sport psychologist). Remember, your decision is not cast in stone at this point. It is alright to sound a little tentative or to offer more than one career interest, as long as they are clearly related to the program to which you are applying. You can virtually eliminate all chances of getting into a program if, for example, you describe your future self as a practicing psychotherapist to a program designed to train clinical scientists.

2. *General Interest Areas*. Most evaluators want to know what academic or professional areas interest you. This allows evaluators to learn more about you and to assess whether your pursuits are congruent with what the program offers. Sometimes the question is asked very generally, such as, "What are your academic interests?" but some programs stress the importance of focusing your interests.

Although often related to career goals, this question allows you to broaden your scope. For example, even if you want to work eventually as a psychotherapist, you may be curious about brain chemistry or critical developmental periods and desire to advance your knowledge in these areas.

If you feel stuck with this question, reflect on the most rewarding courses you had, the projects you enjoyed, and the readings that inspired you. Even a quick scan of a solid introductory text in your field could spark some ideas. Applicants who have focused on one or more specific topics in a field, especially if one or more of the faculty in the graduate program also share these interests, will have an advantage.

3. *Research Experiences*. A common type of essay, especially from experimental or scientist–practitioner-oriented doctoral programs, requests specific information about the area in which you might like to do research and about any research experiences that you have had. For a few programs, a research-oriented essay is all that is requested, for example, "Include a detailed letter (two to three pages) describing your research interests."

With regard to actual research experience, at this point either you have something to discuss or you do not. If you do not have a publication or presentation (remember that up to half or more of the applicants who are accepted into top doctoral programs do not), you may still have something to say. Did you assist a professor with his or her research project? Did you complete a research project for a class that went well? Do you have any research in progress at the present time?

Regardless of your actual experience, most research-oriented questions allow you to discuss your research interests. Therefore, you can focus on what you think you might like to investigate in the future, even if there is not much of a past. If you have some time, we recommend putting in a day's work at your local university library if you have not already firmly established your research orientations. Helpful resources are recent editions of the *Annual Review of Psychology, Psychological Bulletin, American Psychologist*, or any high-quality scholarly periodical in your specific interest areas.

Applicants who will most impress evaluators in programs that value research are those who already have relatively specific research experiences or interests. If these dovetail with the interests of one or more graduate faculty members, the impact will be powerful. Do not be afraid to commit yourself. Everyone knows that you might change your mind. If you cannot meet the ideal, however, remember that many other worthy students cannot either. Do not ever try to create the false impression of a firmly planned research agenda from hastily gleaned fragments of ideas. More likely than not, the presentation will be unsophisticated, possibly even laughable, to experts in the area.

4. *Academic Objectives*. This question may be asked in a variety of ways, but the request is basically for a statement of how you see graduate training as necessary to your overall goals; for example, "State why are you undertaking graduate study at this time, and describe your proposed program of study." Selection committee members will attempt to

learn about both your level of understanding of graduate training and the goodness of fit between your expectations and their own.

If you know why you are applying to the programs you chose and have read very carefully everything that has been sent to you by each program, writing about it should come easily. Consider what skills and experiences are important for you to acquire. These probably should not be restricted to fulfilling the requirements that lead to a good job. Graduate school offers far more than vocational training. There is much you can learn to better conceptualize problems and build your knowledge base—in short, to mature intellectually. There are role models to observe and appreciate. Graduate school provides these unique opportunities, and you should indicate that you appreciate the larger benefits of graduate training beyond acquiring the specific skills necessary for employment.

5. *Clinical or Other Field/Practicum Experience.* If you are applying to a clinical or other mental health or applied training program, you presumably have something to discuss here. Report on the setting and population as well as your duties, the nature of the supervision you received, and what you learned from the experiences.

6. *Academic Background and Achievements.* A common essay request involves an overview of your history as an undergraduate (and, if applicable, graduate) student. Sometimes the focus is on what courses or professors you liked best or influenced you the most or any special projects you worked on. Sometimes the question is very general, such as, "Tell us what you think we should know about your previous educational experience."

Make a list, noting your most memorable academic experiences, special classes and projects, strong areas, volunteer or related paid work experiences, any awards or honors, related group membership, and associated activities (e.g., Psi Chi, Student Social Workers of America). However, because these background questions often have twists unique to each program, you need to attend to such essays one at a time.

7. *What Do You See in Us?* An important consideration among graduate program evaluation committees is your reason for applying to their specific program. The question may be phrased in various ways; for example, "Why did you choose Plum Tree University and how can our program contribute to your long-term professional goals?" or "What do you want from this program specifically, and what do you expect from us?" This question, perhaps far more than any other, must be answered very thoughtfully and will require a highly individualized answer for each program application.

To prepare for this question, jot down "good matching points" in the margins as you review the program materials. For example, if you are interested in clinical research ethics and the program offers a related class with an instructor who has written extensively in the area, you could mark that with a highlighter.

Sometimes a second part to this question is, "What do you think you can bring to this program?" This is really the other side of the same coin. If the match is good, the faculty will enjoy having you around because you will be satisfied, motivated, and enthusiastic about being a productive and cooperative member of their academic family. (Sometimes program evaluators will try to make a better match for you. They may think that you would be happier in one of their other programs in the department and transfer your application to it for consideration. This is not a routine practice. We mention it, however, because every year some applicants will be surprised to hear that they have been accepted into a different program than the one to which they applied!)

8. *Motivation.* A fairly common question involves why you seek advanced training. Examples of specific questions are, "What experiences shaped your current aspirations?" and "Why did you choose clinical social work?"

Here perhaps you can cite exciting theories or research, inspiring books, special professors, or enriching learning experiences. Why have you chosen your specific area of interest over other related areas? You may need to sort out the roots of your current goals and, from those recollections, briefly outline the most salient influences.

9. *Personal Material.* Many programs do not directly request personal, nonacademic information. Some do but refrain from requesting what could be called "sensitive" material. Rather, they stick to hobbies, nonacademic interests, and related scholarly activities outside of your undergraduate academic institution (e.g., attendance at workshops or conventions).

Some program applications, however, either directly request or enthusiastically invite disclosure of highly personal information. With very few exceptions, personal statements are requested by programs training mental health service providers (e.g., clinical and counseling psychologists, educational psychologists, and social workers). Professional schools, especially, ask for personal disclosure essays.

That programs training mental health service providers ask for more personal information should come as no surprise. A competent and effective clinician is more than just a bright person who has learned some specialized techniques. A therapeutic or counseling relationship is an intimate one, and the kind of person the therapist is will largely determine the quality of that relationship.

The specific wording of the request for a personal disclosure essay varies widely. A selection of typical ones follows:

Is there anything in your background that you think would be relevant to our evaluation of your application? If so, please explain.

Please describe your life up to now, your family, friends, home, school, work, particularly those experiences most relevant to your interest in psy-

chology and your personal and professional development. In addition, feel free to tell us anything else that you feel we should know or that you want us to know about yourself.

Briefly describe a person known to you. How would this person describe you?

Please provide a written statement of relevant personal life experiences and background including something about your outlook on life, events that led you to become who you are today, and the kind of person you find yourself becoming.

Write a personal statement of not less than 500 words. Include a discussion of significant events and influences that have helped develop your present values and approach to life.

Because the personal disclosure question can be asked in a number of ways, do not formulate a single, all-purpose essay in this area. Select material carefully and keep it relevant to the purpose at hand rather than launching into self-disclosure for its own sake. Also, we suggest that you not disclose information about traumatic experiences (e.g., sexual abuse or chronic illness) or involvement in mental health treatment. These experiences may have indeed shaped your choice of a profession, but you do not have control over the images such information might conjure in the minds of evaluators.

10. *Autobiography*. Less frequent is the brief autobiographical statement. Sometimes the applicant is left to decide what an autobiographical statement should contain; for example, "We would appreciate the inclusion of a brief biographical sketch." At other times the requirements are specified; for example, "Forward a typed autobiography that includes the following. Where you lived as a child and teenager. Describe these communities. The significant facts about your immediate and extended family. Any other background data that would help another person to get to know and understand you as a unique person."

The majority of programs do not request an autobiographical statement. However, if you apply to a program that does ask about your life, compose the statement carefully, ensuring that you have responded to every specific request. Weave in anything that makes you stand out as an interesting person (such as living abroad, musical abilities, etc.), but do not worry if your life to date has been ordinary.

11. *Specific Graduate Faculty of Interest*. Some programs ask that you identify, from among their faculty members, someone with whom you might like to work. For example, "Cite your specific interests and long-term goals in psychology, and indicate two faculty members whose research interests correspond most closely with your own," or "Please in-

dicate which of the interests of various faculty members you find most in accord with your own or most attractive to you and why."

If you chose your programs based on the faculty and their current research interests—the ideal way to go—this question will be a welcome opportunity rather than a chore. However, if you were not able to follow our suggestions about selection strategies, and this question is on one or more of your applications, it means extra work now unless each faculty member and his or her work is carefully described in the application materials you received or on the program's web page. Go back to chapters 11 and 15, which describe how to find out about faculty in programs of interest to you, and do the best you can.

Your answer to this question is important. Clearly, evaluators will use applicants' responses to assess fit, not only between students and the overall program but between students and the individual faculty members who are active in the program. You can make yourself stand out in the selection process if you do your homework well.

Try to verify that any faculty members you choose will be around for the next few years and that they participate in the specific program to which you have applied. Applicants have been rejected solely because the only person they expressed an interest in working with was on an extended leave or was not involved in the program to which the student applied. Also, unless you have been focusing on someone for a long time, consider faculty members other than the most popular and well-known, because many other students will also be selecting those "superstars." Your chances of admission may be heightened if you are interested in working with someone in your interest area who may not yet have so much name recognition.

There is usually a perfectly legitimate way to avoid the pitfalls we have just illustrated. If the number of faculty you are allowed to identify is not firmly limited to one, pick two or three (but no more than four). The extra work involved in learning more about several faculty members is a good investment of your time and energy.

12. *Anything Else We Should Know?* Some application essays leave the door open for you to express anything else you think the evaluation committee should know about you. An example is, "Use this space to convey anything you would like us to know about you."

Keep a list of anything that seems important about you that does not appear in other content categories or elsewhere in your application. Include on your list anything that substantiates your commitment and strength of character. For example, evaluators may be at least somewhat impressed with applicants who held a full-time job while also going to school full-time. You will not know how to answer this question, however, until you see what else is asked for on each form; avoid repeating information.

13. *Special Skills.* A small number of programs explicitly request a list or description of special skills that you have cultivated, such as, "De-

scribe your preparation for your proposed program of study including mathematics/statistics, computer, and laboratory training."

Other examples might include foreign language or sign language proficiency, specialized assessment or research technique training, relevant equipment-use skills, and so on. Here you simply provide basic, honest information. Indicate the level you have attained by using examples. For example, you might say, "I have taken two advanced teaching technology courses and have a basic mastery of *Macromedia Director* and *Authorware Attain*," or "I learned to do content analysis as a result of working with Dr. Words on her achievement motivation research." Do not exaggerate your actual skill level. If you are selected because of reported skills that you, in fact, do not have, the fallout would be devastating.

Could you give examples of the most difficult essays? I'm sure that the top-rated doctoral programs ask for very complicated statements.

Although the essay requirements for a few of the top-ranked and most competitive programs are somewhat difficult, most are indistinguishable from those of other programs. Essays can be more difficult than average for three reasons: (a) A number of questions are posed with multiple categories, including some unusual ones; (b) the question itself is so elaborate or oddly worded that you are not certain what is being asked; and (c) you cannot answer the question adequately because it does not apply to you.

The first category of difficult questions can be managed; it simply requires more work. The second category feels overwhelming, but with some consultation you can usually settle on an approach. (Remember that other applicants will also probably have the same trouble you do with ambiguous or complex essays.) Consider these examples:

> *Discuss your particular interests, be they experimental, theoretical, or issue oriented. The statement could be much like a proposal for graduate studies in the more specific context of your professional objectives.*

> *Ours is a program for developing scholar–clinicians. We try to understand thoroughly both normal and pathological experiences. How would you as a scholar–clinician approach this enterprise? What modes of thinking about human behavior are most compatible with your own style? Least compatible? Why?*

The most dispiriting kind of essay, however, is the one you cannot answer because you have virtually nothing to say. When you get an application requesting such an essay, you should probably downgrade your chances of acceptance if this is the only essay requested, going on the assumption that they would not ask the question if the answer were not important to them. If you have a strong record in other areas, however, do not give up entirely. Instead, try to use the essay responses to emphasize your strengths and the assets you would bring to the program.

Here are some examples of questions that are simple and straightforward for those who have something to include and deflating for those who do not.

Describe your experiences related to conducting an independent investigation or playing a major role in a research study, preparing an honor's thesis, writing computer programs, contributing to a scientific publication, or teaching and designing a course.

Describe your human service experience such as serving as a psychiatric hospital aide, hot-line volunteer, VISTA or Peace Corps volunteer, program evaluator, legislative advocate, or consultant.

Essay Length

Most programs indicate a desired length for essay statements. Generally, they are to be quite short. The typical requested length is 500 words (or two double-spaced typed pages), although essay requirements may range from 100 words to "not more than 10 double-spaced typed pages."

Some programs do not specify length requirements but suggest that the essays should not be very long by using directives such as "in a few paragraphs," "in the space provided," or "briefly describe." Sometimes limits are stated in terms of minimums or maximums. Common directives in this category include "in no less than 300 words" or "in no more than two pages." This is confusing because it seems to leave open the possibility that one can go as far as desired in the other direction. We advise proceeding with these types of directions as if the limit specified also represents about the length they want to see. Thus, "no less than 300 words" should result in an essay of about 300 to 400 words and "no more than two pages" should result in a two-page essay (or one only slightly shorter).

If I cannot fit what I want to say into the requested length, can I just ignore the stated limit?

It can be very frustrating to attempt to crunch your past, your current interests, and your future plans into two double-spaced pages. However, we strongly advise against straying very far from any stated length requirements. A very long statement, unless it is for one of the rare programs asking for an extended discussion, may actually harm your ranking. Aside from indicating that you did not follow directions, a long statement may be casually skimmed over by the evaluators rather than carefully considered. It may also be too-inclusive and interpreted as signifying a lack of ability to focus and set priorities. Evaluators are often particularly interested in learning what you see as important, and limiting the length of the essay statement requirement is an easy and effective way for them to assess that.

What about the programs that do not specify length? How long should these essays be?

If length is not specified, you have more leeway. We advise, however, keeping essays lean and clean, not extending beyond 1,000 to 1,500 words (or four to six double-spaced pages) maximum, even for a complicated statement of purpose.

It's good to learn that essays should usually be short. Does that mean they are going to be relatively easy to write?

You do not, in most cases, have an opportunity to go into very much depth about any one topic. On the other hand, you will be challenged to make every word count. Be careful, however, not to save words by offering vague generalities. It is probably wiser to cover fewer points (choosing the most significant ones) in more depth rather than saying only a few words about too many topics. Well-constructed, concise essays result from careful drafting, editing, and revision, so allow plenty of time for this process.

How many essays does the typical program ask for?

Although the number may range between the extremes of none and eight, the typical request is two. Sometimes you will have to write one essay for the department or program to which you are applying and another more general statement of purpose for the university-wide admissions committee.

Getting Started Writing

It is time to get to work on those essays. We promise that it gets much easier after the first one! Because the statements of purpose or other essays are so important in the selection process, creating the only chance you have to tell the committees who you are, you must fight procrastination tooth and nail. We have known students who had to wait until the following year to apply to graduate school because they just could not get moving with the essay task. It really is not that bad, however, if you can get started.

Only you can create your essay statements, because your past, who you are now, and your goals for the future are yours alone. Do not try to describe yourself as the person you think the selection committee wants you to be. That person you describe will come off as phony, superficial, exaggerated, and boring.

Start out with just one essay. If time is a factor, you will have no choice but to pick the one that accompanies the application with the nearest deadline. If you have the luxury of a choice, pick the essay required by the program that feels the most comfortable to you.

Read each essay question very carefully, several times, until you feel confident you understand the question. One of the most common complaints about applicants' essay statements is that they do not respond to the question that was asked. Evaluators assume that such applicants sent the same essay to every program or they did not read the question or cannot understand what they read. Not an impressive start!

While writing the first draft, just let yourself go. The result may be garbage or, perhaps with some fine-tuning, it will be fresh and original. Take a chance at this point. Try to get into a motivated, upbeat, and creative mood.

Even if you are a superb writer, your essay will need to go through several drafts to reach its full potential. If you get bogged down or frustrated, don't waste time being immobilized. Take a break and come back to it in an hour, or even after a good night's sleep. Get others' opinions on your essay.

I could use more pointers about how to approach writing the essays.

A common complaint from evaluators is that essay statements are too vague and general. Judicious use of specific examples of what you have done and what you hope to do will greatly enhance your essay statement, giving it distinction and personality.

Your motivation will be best portrayed by use of examples. For instance, rather than saying, "I am interested in doing jury selection research," mention what led up to that interest, such as visiting a courtroom, reading, writing a literature review paper, or attending a presentation by experts. Even though none of these components is a monumental achievement, this approach puts your interests into a context and reveals you to be someone who has sought out information and exposure.

With regard to focus, applicants who have already identified an area within their field, especially those who have also done some work that they can describe, are definitely at an advantage. They have specific information to use when answering typical questions on interest areas, research experience, and career goals. The only way this type of applicant could conceivably fail is if there is a problem at the other end of the application process; that is, no one in the graduate program is the least bit involved in the student's interest area. This is why you must carefully research the faculty of graduate programs before applying.

Many students do not have a specific direction yet (and many who do ultimately change it). However, even if you do not, your chances of acceptance may not be significantly reduced. You will have to be a little more creative in presenting yourself, focusing on what interests you have developed, presenting your accomplishments in the best light, and demonstrating your motivation to learn and grow.

When discussing career goals, show that you understand what you can realistically accomplish with the degree you are seeking and that you are aware of the components and structure of the careers that you might pursue. Too many applicants either are only marginally in touch with the opportunities associated with psychology and related fields or have picked up inaccurate information. To reveal misunderstandings about your chosen career will raise a red flag, because the evaluators will be unsure of your reaction when reality finally hits you. Read and talk to people in the field about your career interests. It is only through such exposure that anyone learns what a particular field actually entails.

Applicants who think they can cure the world of all of its emotional ills within the next 10 years may be dismissed as childlike idealists. This is not to say that you must thoroughly understand all related careers in social science and mental health—indeed these may change substantially by the time you complete your advanced degree—but you should be sophisticated enought to indicate that you are not operating in a vacuum. In other words, demonstrate that you have some working knowledge of the general field in which you want to study. Chat with professors in your present department and browse through articles about psychology or related careers before tackling the career aspiration essay question.

One way to focus and condense your essay is to eliminate everything that has already been put on a line item or somewhere else in the application. For example, if you listed your Psi Chi secretary position on the line asking about honor society membership, there is no need to mention it in your essay. Exceptions to this advice would be if there was good reason to further elaborate the line-item information. For example, if you listed a publication on the line asking if you had any, describing in the essay the work you did to earn the authorship credit would certainly be appropriate, particularly if comments on your research experience are specifically requested.

Any advice about tone and writing style?

Write clearly and succinctly. Avoid both generalities and overelaboration. Do not use gimmicks or try to be cute. These could backfire or suggest immaturity. No psychobabble! If you say, "I want to learn to help people get their heads together," you will probably have to learn it somewhere else.

Do not inflate yourself or put yourself down. You want to impress the readers but not at the expense of creating the image of an arrogant know-it-all. On the other hand, many students struggle with their emerging self-confidence and tend to sell themselves short. Stick to what you have done and what you have learned from that, and how you are willing to work hard to move ahead.

If there is some obvious deficit in your record, do not try to minimize its impact by ignoring it. If appropriate, briefly address it, including any feasible plan to remedy the weakness if it persists.

Do not try to impress your readers by using enormous words you find in a thesaurus to replace perfectly serviceable common-use vocabulary. Stay away from overly complicated sentences. A clear, focused, easy-to-read essay will earn favor. Generally, avoid discussing politics and religion or dwelling on high school experiences or anything else off the track of what is being asked. However, if you have something unusual in your background that others might regard positively, note that if there is a comfortable place for it.

Do I dare show my essay to anyone before finalizing it?

Absolutely! Have at least one respected person look over it, checking the spelling and grammar as well as the content. This person might be a professor or a trusted fellow student who is sharp and interested in your success. Your essay statement will be viewed as a sample of your writing skills and as evidence of your ability to articulate your thoughts. Make sure it is your work, however, and that others only make suggestions or general editorial corrections. How you write, as revealed in the personal statement, is of great concern to selection committees.

A supportive professor is a good source of general criticism, although you should not expect this person to do heavy editing or to go over each essay for all of the schools to which you are applying! Because your essays will be more alike than they are different, feedback on an early version should let you know if you are on target.

Convince those who are willing to look over your essay that you want frank feedback, even if it is unflattering. This is no time for them to protect your feelings. If you get negative feedback, do not let it deflate your confidence. It's only an essay, but it is one that you want to be as good as it possibly can be. Take critical comments as they are almost certainly intended—to help you improve your writing and your presentation.

Should essays always be typed? No exceptions?

Only one condition overrides our strong advice to always machine print or type application essays. This single exception occurs very rarely. A handful of programs specifically request, for reasons that are not entirely clear to us, that the essay statements be handwritten by the applicant. An example reads, "In your own handwriting, prepare a statement dealing with your motivation to become a counseling psychologist." Follow the instructions, and muster up your best penmanship. It is possible that the program somehow evaluates your handwriting in an attempt to determine something about your personality or conscientiousness. Use black or blue–black ink.

Many applications specify the desirability of a printed statement or specifically indicate that a hand-printed statement is acceptable. Even if handwritten essays are acceptable, do not use handwriting. Hand-printing usually has a childlike appearance, and you want to appear mature. Typed or machine-printed materials appear more professional.

Use a good quality, 8 × 11 inch white bond paper. Number and put your name on each page (perhaps as a header). Clerical staff often make copies of these essays, and it would be unfortunate if the pages got mixed up or out of order.

Word processors are incredibly convenient, but they can open the door to mistakes. If you start with a basic statement and adapt it for each program, proofread each version very carefully to ensure that you did not leave in information that is only relevant to another program. As one graduate admission committee member remarked, "When I read how much the applicant wants to attend the University of Vermont, and I'm sitting here in my office at the University of Southern California, it kind of puts a wet blanket on the whole thing."

When a space is provided on the application form for an essay statement, we advise using it rather than attaching a separate sheet. It is frustrating to find a question that requires more space to answer than the tiny one provided, so attachments are sometimes absolutely necessary. However, do the best you can with the spaces provided and limit your use of attached sheets (unless it is specifically indicated that they are acceptable). As one of the graduate staff survey respondents said:

If we wanted attached sheets instead of our spaces filled in we would have designed our application differently. It is especially annoying when students say "see attached" several times causing us to have to shuffle through a bunch of pages looking for information that should have been put where we wanted it.

I guess I am ready to get started.

That is usually the hardest part—just sitting down with a commitment to keep at it until a draft is done. Here's the good news. Once the task is started, it often goes better and faster than you had anticipated. More good news: Essays get easier as you go along.

CHAPTER 20

I'M READY TO SEND MY APPLICATIONS. NOW WHAT?

The vast majority of doctoral programs specify a single date each year by which applications must be received. The due dates typically fall somewhere between December 1 and March 1 for entry into a program the following fall. A few doctoral programs have application deadlines falling in March or April, and due dates for master's programs tend to be a little later than those for doctoral programs. Very few graduate programs offer rolling deadlines (meaning that you can send in your application any time) or both fall and spring admissions (meaning there are two deadlines each year).

Very carefully note the deadline for each program on your calendar. Things can get tricky: The due date for the program or departmental supplementary form may differ from the due date for the all-university application form, and programs within the same academic department sometimes have different deadlines!

Do they really mean it when they list a deadline date?

The most accurate answer to your question may be "not necessarily." Some programs will not consider an application under any circumstances if it arrives after the published deadline. However, many more appear to view their deadline as firm but will consider a special circumstance or allow a couple of extra days for straggling applications to trickle in. Still other programs may allow a week, or even a few weeks, past the deadline during which late applications will be processed and added to the pool of eligible candidates.

There are at least three reasons why applications should not be late. First, lateness creates a negative impression of you as an applicant. You have enough competition as it is without handicapping yourself from the start. Many staff involved in the graduate application process have heard a wide variety of excuses and pleas for late materials; yours may be irritating or judged to be insincere, regardless of the actual circumstances. Second, late applications are likely to lead to acceptance into the program only if the applicant is particularly strong already. That means that the tardy applicant must be better than (or at least as good as) the well-regarded applicants who submitted their materials on time. Third, one does not know which programs are strict with their deadlines and which are more forgiving of late applications.

Does sending the application in early help, or is meeting the deadline good enough?

Your chances of acceptance can sometimes be enhanced if you submit your application 2 to 6 weeks ahead of the deadline date. The program's published deadline date is the latest an application should arrive, and most students are happy to make it in under the wire. Making the deadline date is good enough, but there is an even smarter way to apply.

Many admissions committees start reviewing and making admission decisions before the published deadline. Several students we have known were accepted (with financial aid) into doctoral programs weeks prior to the program's application cutoff date! Program faculty are as eager to attract good students as you are to be accepted, so many of them will move as fast as possible on promising candidates, hoping that an early acceptance will result in an early commitment to the program.

Also, graduate admission evaluators frequently have other responsibilities, such as teaching, research, and committee work. Because most applications will arrive near the deadline date, there will be a mountain of materials to review at that time. If you send your materials early, evaluators may review them during a time when they are less pressured and less liable to be in a negative frame of mind.

Another benefit of an early application is that the office staff can process early arrivals more carefully, thus helping to ensure a neat and accurate file. The early applicant is also more likely to be viewed as responsible and well-organized, two characteristics highly admired in graduate students. Finally, when more than one office is involved, which is almost always the case, applications may have to make rounds from office to office, and the program itself may be last on the list. Early applicants benefit because their folder gets to the program office in plenty of time for a careful review.

Comments from staff involved in the graduate application process illustrate the ways late applicants are often viewed:

They wait too long and then want special considerations. That behavior indicates a style of operating that we don't need around here.

Materials come in the day applications are due that look like they were prepared in 15 minutes. It looks both figuratively and literally like 'writing on the wall' to us.

We can tell when an applicant didn't get organized until it was too late to do things well. That hurts his or her chances.

The conclusion is clear. Never simply assume that application deadline dates are negotiable; if at all possible, be among the first in line by sending your materials 2 to 6 weeks early. Note that one does not want to be too early. That is, the risk associated with submitting an application before the program staff are ready to process it is that the application might be lost in the shuffle.

Should I send in individual items as I finish them so that at least part of my application materials will arrive earlier?

No! Send an application only when it is complete. Dribbling items in makes staff members' jobs more difficult and increases the possibility of confusion and misfiling.

How to Send Applications

When everything is ready to go, make a copy of the entire package. You may be sorry if you skip this step. Although it is unlikely that any of your applications will get lost along the way, such mishaps do occur. Also, a friend might appreciate the copies as examples to review when he or she applies to graduate programs next year. The most likely reason that you should keep a copy, however, is that you may receive a telephone call to discuss your candidacy. In such a case, you should have a copy of your materials right in front of you. Or, you may receive an invitation to be interviewed in person. A careful review of what you said in your application is critical in preparing for a preselection interview (see chap. 22).

What should I check before sending my application?

Despite the excitement (or relief) that accompanies dropping a completed application in the mail, take a few minutes before sealing it to make sure that everything requested has been included. It is very easy to skip small items, especially when the task itself is so anxiety provoking. Be sure you signed the application. Trying to rectify this oversight is very cumbersome after the application has been sent.

Did you include your check or money order to cover the required application fee? That is another item that is sometimes overlooked and can delay processing of your application. Do your application materials look neat and professional? If anything strikes you as sloppy looking, it will probably strike others the same way. If possible, remedy it.

Is there anything I should know about packaging my application materials for mailing?

Mail your materials flat. Place your application materials in a 9 × 12 envelope (or larger if the materials are exceptionally bulky). Folded materials have two drawbacks: The folds sometimes fall right in the middle of a printed line, rendering it difficult to read, and the bends and humps make the materials look tacky and unprofessional. Plus, flat materials are easier to file.

How can I make sure that my application arrives safely?

Many applicants worry, sometimes obsessively, about whether their materials have arrived at their destination on time. Office staff complain that applicants tie up office phone lines within a day or two of putting their materials in the mail, even though the materials are still obviously in transit.

Staff members typically request that if you must call, wait at least a week after mailing the application before checking on its arrival, and if you sent it in around the deadline date, wait for 10 working days. (Many programs include or request a self-addressed postcard that is to be sent to you when your file arrives. Give that procedure a chance to work before getting worried.) It takes the staff time to sort and file the material, and applicants should understand this process.

A miniscule percentage of applications may be lost or misdirected in the mail, and it is understandable that you might be worried about this. You are not entirely at the mercy of chance, however. You can do several things to increase the probability that your materials are delivered to the right office on time without burdening the graduate program staff and risking the possibility of irritating them.

First, make sure you have used the correct mailing addresses exactly as stated on the application forms themselves. (If there is any confusion here, a call to the receiving office for address information is acceptable.) Even one aspect slightly off (e.g., "Department of Psychology" when it should have been "Department of Educational Psychology, or "Admissions Committee" when you meant to write "Graduate Admissions Committee") can result in a piece of mail floating around the campus for days or even weeks!

Next, make sure that the address on the envelope is very neat and readable and that you have included an equally neat and readable return address in the upper lefthand corner. This will reduce the potential for error by every human being who has to sort it along the way.

Now, take the package to the post office and get in line. This trip will reduce additional sources of routing error that could materialize if you left the package for pickup in your own mailbox. By getting it one step closer to the destination yourself, you know for sure that no one rifled through your mailbox and that the package did not fly out of the mail carrier's vehicle. If you choose not to send it by priority mail, get it weighed so that you know that the postage (first-class, of course) is correct. This is no time to trust your ability to estimate ounces! You do not want to be like one teary-eyed student we knew who came in 8 days after a program's deadline and held up her undelivered application envelope with "Not accepted, postage due" slashed across it in bright red.

Finally, ask the postal clerk for a certificate of mailing. This is an inexpensive little insurance policy that at least proves that you sent something—it does not specify what—to a particular office on a certain date. We know of two instances when the certificate of mailing was judged as adequate evidence that an application received late had, in fact, been mailed by the applicant in reasonable time to reach its destination prior to the due date.

What about sending my application "express mail" if I'm running late?

Try to avoid having to make such an expensive decision. Although, for a stiff fee, your material does arrive to large cities in a day, the bold colors on the special envelope announce loud and clear that you were running late and getting desperate! But worse yet, many graduate school programs are located in smaller towns where overnight mailing is not guaranteed.

Are there other ways I can ensure that my materials arrived without having to call the graduate program staff?

Of course, a more precise way of ensuring delivery of your application materials is to mail your applications by certified mail (return receipt requested) from the post office. We do not recommend this option, however, because it is expensive and takes up staff time at the receiving end (because someone must sign for the package). Unless you will not sleep a wink from worry, consider instead the other options.

Application materials often indicate how feedback regarding receipt is handled. As already noted, some programs provide their own forms or postcards that will be sent back to you as soon as your file is complete. If postcards are included, address them neatly to yourself, affix postage if appropriate, and include them in your application packet. Many programs also have other built-in ways to inform you of missing items. Work with each system individually, and try to operate in the way each prefers.

If postcards or other techniques are not part of a program's plan to provide feedback, you can include a postcard of your own. Make sure that it is clearly self-addressed with postage affixed, with a statement on the message side that states something like, "Dear Staff of [name of program] at [name of school]: Please drop this in the mail so that I will know that my application has been safely received. Thank you. [Your name]."

What if my application gets lost anyway?

If you follow the other safeguard suggestions, you should be able to relax because the chances that something went awry are remote. However, consider the worst-case scenario and imagine that your materials have been misplaced along the way, despite your own careful and timely efforts. You need help to resolve this serious predicament. Ironically, many students undermine their major resource for assistance. The graduate program office staff either can be helpful or can discount your plight, depending largely on how you interact with them at this point.

It is understandable that an applicant would be distraught over a missing application, but you should not simply assume that the graduate office is to blame and take your frustration out on the staff. Explain to the staff what you sent and when you sent it, and ask for assistance in locating the material. A worried but polite and appreciative demeanor will be more likely to inspire someone to track down the application at the receiving campus. You can pose the idea of sending off a copy of the materials, although this may or may not be acceptable depending on program policy or if the staff believes your story. In the meantime, you could call your local post office for ideas, because it is possible that the material never got to the receiving campus. Chances are, however, that you will never have to confront this dilemma.

Part V

The Postapplication Period

CHAPTER 21

IS THERE ANYTHING I CAN DO OTHER THAN WAIT?

Everything is done, so what should I do now?

What a great feeling. After you complete such a mammoth task, it would be wonderful if the relief and pride could last for a while. However, the pleasure is often quickly replaced with a new kind of uneasiness. You might start mulling and ruminating: "Do they like me? How many other students applied? How many of them are better than I am? What is the selection committee doing right now? If they moved fast, they could have made their decisions already. Maybe I should call and ask. Or, maybe I could have Dad do it. He sounds authoritative. Maybe . . ."

The Wrong Reasons to Make Contact

You do not control the situation, which means that impulsive or inappropriate thoughts may surface. You must avoid doing things that apprehensive applicants frequently do at this point and, without realizing it, thereby reduce their chances for acceptance.

The respondents in one of our surveys gave concrete examples of counterproductive behavior by graduate school applicants after mailing their applications. When we asked, "What do many applicants do that is inappropriate?" the majority of answers referred to errors committed between the application deadline and the dissemination of decisions! The most frequently cited improper acts on the part of applicants included the following:

- Calling to inquire about their status within a week after the application deadline.
- Requesting an interview with the program director to discuss their status.

227

- Having a parent or spouse call requesting feedback about the applicant.
- Seeking information about the competition (How many? Average GRE score?).
- Showing up at the office wanting to discuss their status with someone.

Such improprieties were sometimes accompanied by an overbearing or rude manner. Graduate programs hope to attract bright, motivated students, but not at the price of enrolling a disrespectful bully who lacks common sense and good social judgment. Unfortunately, some applicants apparently make the grossly incorrect assumption that an office staff member is a powerless, timid individual who will not mention these offensive experiences to those who make the selection decisions.

Does the program faculty support the staff's rights to polite treatment and listen to staff complaints about applicants? You bet they do! In our survey of evaluators, behaving inappropriately after submitting an application emerged as one of the worst things an applicant can do. Respondents also reacted negatively to applicants who accused the support staff of losing materials or who called the staff too frequently to check on the completeness of their applications.

Legitimate Reasons to Make Contact

Are you saying that I shouldn't, under any circumstances, contact the faculty or office at the schools where I applied?

Definitely stay in touch with the graduate staff office to ensure that your application is complete. Applicants often are dropped from consideration for reasons of which applicants are unaware. That means that some applicant files never get considered because of missing information or other little problems, and the unsuspecting student does not necessarily know that anything is wrong! You might think that this situation represents a cold attitude toward applicants. However, as one graduate staff person bluntly put it, "We get more qualified applicants with complete files than we can accept, so why would we consider an applicant with an incomplete file?"

An appropriate call to the graduate program office at this point would be to verify, if you have not yet been notified, that your application file is complete. Remember, it is your responsibility to track down any missing items. Just be sure to wait a reasonable time before you call, and do not call several times a day.

When will I learn about the selection committees' decisions about me?

We would tell you if we could. Each selection committee has its own way of doing things and moves at its own pace. Some selection committees start reviewing applications as they arrive and begin making decisions early. As we noted in a previous chapter, it is possible for an applicant who submitted his or her application early to be accepted even before the application deadline date. These early-bird committees also do a favor (albeit a stinging one) for those who were not a good fit with their program by informing these applicants early of their need to focus their hopes and energies elsewhere.

Most committees, however, get moving around the time when applications are due. How quickly they process the applications depends on a number of factors, most of which you cannot know. Aside from how difficult the applications are to process, other factors include the number of applications received, how many people are on the selection committee (and their other commitments and how well they work together), interference due to final exam and grading duties or other academic demands, holidays and winter breaks, and the efficiency of the committee's operating procedure. To add even more variation, things can change from one year to the next for a given program. One psychology program director noted that one year the deadline date had to be extended by a full month to attract enough qualified applicants, but the following year more than twice the number of qualified applicants that could be accepted had applied by the usual deadline date!

Typically, there will be a period of time when nothing seems to happen. If you have verified that your applications are complete, the best advice at this point is simply to wait and try to divert your attention to other things. Focus again on school work. Get your body back in shape. Reinvest in your friends and other relationships.

After what may seem like an eternity, you will notice a hint of something in the air. You learn (or maybe it is just a rumor) that Stevie Smart was accepted into the program of his choice 2 weeks after the applications were due, but Annie Droop already has received a rejection letter from one of her program selections. You have not heard anything from anyone. What does that mean? Probably nothing. Friends may hear one way or the other as the weeks crawl by, and you get only one rejection letter. Others around you may receive an invitation to an interview. It is all over for you, right? Not necessarily. It is almost April and you have not heard a word from your favorite program. No news is simply no news.

When we monitored the dates of rejections and acceptances from graduate school applicants in psychology, we found just about every pattern and outcome possible. Some received acceptances and rejections early, whereas others were notified of decisions on precisely the date indicated in the application materials. Some students heard good and bad news weeks after the earlier announced feedback date; some knew they had made it into the finals because they were invited to an interview. Some students were placed on alternate status and did not learn their ultimate fate until the early summer, and sometimes later than that; others were placed into an acceptance-pending category awaiting notification of whether financial aid would be available or whether permission to take more students was approved. One applicant was rejected from her favorite program only to be reconsidered and accepted 2 weeks later!

Most doctoral programs are committed to informing applicants of their final status by mid-April, although things can get complicated at this time, as we describe in chapter 24. Master's programs often have later deadline dates, so the decision dates tend to be later as well, but these can vary tremendously. Some master's programs inform the applicants of their status within a month after the deadline, and others wait until well into the summer.

Is there ever a time when I should call because I haven't heard a word?

There are essentially two reasons why a call would be entirely appropriate. One is that the published decision date period has passed and you have not heard anything at all from that program. The most common reason for the delay is that the selection committee is running late. You, however, have a right to know that. Hopefully you will learn the revised target date when you call, but do not communicate any opinions about the committee's competence level or push for more information than is readily offered.

You may also find yourself in a not altogether unhappy bind. One program accepts you but you are also very interested in another program that has not yet informed you of your status. You may call the still-silent school, if the date that feedback should be available is very close or has passed, in the hopes that someone will be able to give you some information. You can objectively mention your situation as the reason for the call, but do not be manipulative by hinting that they had better move fast or they will lose you to the other program. Remember, the selection committee will, completely on its own, respond as soon as it possibly can.

In chapters 23 and 24 we discuss further how to handle offers and communicate with programs about your decisions. However, before notification of your status, there is a chance that you will be invited for an interview if you have applied to a mental health service program. In the next chapter we consider issues involved in the preselection interview.

CHAPTER 22

WHAT SHOULD I DO ABOUT INTERVIEWS?

Many programs include a face-to-face interview held at the graduate training site as an important and integral part of the final selection process. Programs that interview are most likely to be clinical psychology and other mental health provider training programs.

These interviews are by invitation only. However, expenses associated with the travel and other incidentals are almost always the applicants' responsibility. Occasionally host programs will offer to assist especially promising applicants with their travel expenses if they could not otherwise attend, but in these times of tight budgets it is not realistic to expect such an offer. Some programs arrange for graduate students to pick up applicants at the airport. Sometimes applicants can stay with graduate students to avoid the cost of commercial lodging. A few schools transport their faculty interviewers to central locations (such as Los Angeles, Chicago, or New York), where applicants may attend more economically.

What does it mean if I am invited for an interview?

An invitation indicates that you are among the serious contenders for acceptance into the program. Interviews are time-consuming and expensive for both students and the faculty, so no one will be included who is not in the final running. Your chances of acceptance should you make it to this point, all else being equal, are between 25% and 50%. This is exciting news to those who aspire to enter a program that attracts 400 applicants and accepts 12!

The Rationale for Interviews

They already have a full file on me. What else are they looking for?

They have an image of you on paper, and they do indeed have most of what they want to know about you already. They may be interested in elaboration of material from your application or recommendation letters, such as how well you speak Spanish (e.g., you said you were "fairly fluent") or exactly what statistical techniques you perform with ease (e.g., your professor described your mathematical abilities as "quite broad-based"). They may be curious about your background and seek further details (e.g., you mentioned only briefly that you spent a summer working on a Native American reservation and that your childhood was "difficult").

More important than filling in informational gaps, however, is assessing traits that cannot be tapped by other measures. Evaluators do not know from your file how you interact with people, how you express yourself verbally and how well you think on your feet, how you react under stress, what you communicate nonverbally (including appearance and grooming), how you listen to and absorb information, and your social style.

Interviewers ask themselves questions: How does this applicant come across as a human being? Will he or she fit in here? Will he or she successfully complete the program and contribute to the profession? Is there some problem with this applicant?

Can they really find out everything else they need to know with an interview?

Interviews are subject to a number of problems such as interviewer prejudices and the possible influence of first impressions. Interviews are typically conducted unsystematically, and certain questions may be leading or particularly difficult, resulting in an inaccurate picture of the applicant. Applicants who are similar to the interviewer in certain ways, or who are physically attractive, may be inaccurately evaluated in a more positive light. Despite research suggesting that personal interviews have limited value as an assessment technique, other work reveals that evaluators rate the interview as a very important (sometimes the most important) tool for making final selection decisions.

The debate over the merits of preselection interviews will likely continue. In the meantime, interviews are widely used. Although all interviewees do not have the same records, the distance between you and whoever is left in the running is far smaller than the distance between you and most of the original applicant population. Thus, other more subjective factors, such as personal impressions, will play an increasingly important role in the final selection.

Who will interview me?

The interview formats can vary from a half-hour meeting with one or two faculty members to an entire weekend of planned events involving many people, including the other finalists. Graduate students currently enrolled in the program often participate in the interview process. You might speak individually with a number of people in succession or be interviewed by up to six people at once. Small group discussions are sometimes a part of the experience.

You will likely be told what format will be used. If you are not offered that information and such knowledge would help ease any apprehension, a polite telephone inquiry may satisfy your need to know. Do not expect, however, to be informed who will interview you.

Sometimes telephone interviews are used instead of on-site interviews. Selection committees for more research-oriented programs tend to use telephone interviews more frequently than in-person interviews. Obviously, both the applicant and the program faculty obtain far less of certain kinds of information on the telephone than they might through a face-to-face meeting, but this format is far less expensive and easier to arrange.

Will a telephone interview hurt my chances?

If a program only interviews by phone, then you stay on a level playing field with everyone else. If, however, the program offers the option of an on-site visit, a telephone interview may be perceived as an inferior substitute. We urge applicants to take advantage of an on-site interview opportunity.

What if I'm invited to an interview but cannot afford to go? Or I can't go because of some important scheduling conflict?

If you are seriously interested in a program, you should make every attempt to attend the interview. The faculty is certainly aware of, and sympathetic to, the financial status of most students. Refusing an interview opportunity because of a scheduling conflict will not sit well with the evaluators unless the circumstance that received your higher priority is exceptional (e.g., your own wedding, which had been planned well before the interview invitation was extended, or a need to remain close to a gravely ill parent). In such extreme cases, an alternative date may be offered, and it should be accepted if at all possible.

If you decline an interview invitation, the faculty may assume, regardless of your excuse, that you are not sufficiently interested in them to invest the time and money to visit. Therefore, if you are invited for an interview at a place that very much interests you and absolutely cannot attend for financial or other reasons, be sure to express, enthusiastically and clearly, your continuing interest.

What if I get an interview invitation, but it is plainly stated that attendance is not mandatory?

If you are very interested in the program and believe that you will make a good in-person showing, by all means go. If you decide not to go, write a letter that indicates your reasons for passing on the invitation (they should be valid and important ones!), express your continuing interest (if it exists), and thank the committee for their interest in you. If you live close by and the interview schedule is flexible, you should definitely go even if it is not mandatory. Otherwise, it will appear that you are not truly interested in the program because there were no apparent barriers to your attendance.

I'm beginning to feel a little nervous already. I'm concerned that I might blow my chances.

No one can wave away the stage fright you are likely to feel during an interview. No one can tell you exactly what questions will be asked. No one can predict precisely what tactics would make you shine brilliantly and what ones would flop. The art of interviewing is inexact and is heavily influenced by the personalities of the interviewers, who may not even be trained in selection-interview techniques.

The following sections, however, should greatly assist you with your preparation, which, in turn, will greatly enhance your self-confidence. Also, keep in mind that everyone knows interviews make applicants very nervous and no one expects you to be otherwise.

What applicants often overlook is that interviews offer you the best opportunity to evaluate faculty, to ensure that you would like to spend a significant phase of your life with these people. You can get a feel for the social climate, extent of match, student–faculty interaction, faculty availability, and program morale. (Try to talk to graduate students already enrolled in the program. They tend to be remarkably candid with applicants, although one should expect somewhat of a positive bias in their perceptions.) Some applicants rule the program out of further consideration after the interview experience.

Finally, most of the students we have queried right after their interview said, "It wasn't so bad after all." Many actually found the experience beneficial.

Preparing for the Interview

The program extending the interview invitation will likely have some helpful hints for mode of travel and accommodations if the site is a considerable distance from where you live. Make these arrangements as early as possible. If you are invited to stay with a current graduate student, you should accept the invitation not only for financial reasons but because it is an excellent way to learn a lot about the program from a student's point of view. Always keep in mind, however, that the student might be asked by the selection committee members to share his or her impressions of you. Present yourself as an appreciative, well-mannered, mature guest.

What questions are they going to ask me? Maybe I could memorize my answers in advance.

It is impossible to know exactly what questions you will be asked. Even if you could have prior knowledge, you would not want to memorize answers because your resulting delivery would be stilted and dry. It is possible, however, to consider common questions, allowing yourself the opportunity to formulate general answers and to familiarize yourself with the topics that are often fair game. Here is an overview:

- Why are you interested in our program? (Or, why do you think that our program may be the right one for you? Or, what qualifications do you possess that would make you successful in our program?)
- What do you already know about our program?
- What are your career goals? (Or, what do you see yourself doing 10 years from now?)
- What are your research interests? Strengths? Weaknesses? Experiences?
- Why did you choose psychology [or whatever field] as your major?
- Where are your academic strengths? Weaknesses? (For the latter, be sure to formulate how you plan to remedy them, if appropriate.)
- What do you like best about yourself? What do you like least about yourself?
- What psychologist has influenced you most? Why?
- What books (psychology or other) have influenced you the most? *Postmodern*
- What outside interests do you have? (Or, what do you enjoy doing in your spare time?)
- How would you describe yourself to someone wanting to know about you? (Or, how do you think a friend of yours would describe you?)
- What undergraduate courses (or professors) did you like the best and why?
- What family or other influences had the greatest impact on your life? On your choice of psychology [or whatever field]? (Refrain from talking about your own experiences as a therapy client, a person with a particular condition, or the survivor of some form of abuse.)
- What do you think is the most important social (or political) issue today? *multiculturalism, w/our changing demographics*
- What theoretical approach to the field do you identify with?
- If you had to choose a topic for a research project at this time, what might it be?
- What is the single accomplishment of which you are proudest?

- If we were to invite you into our program but were unable to provide you with financial support during the first year, would you still be able to accept our invitation?
- Do you have any questions you would like to ask us?

The next three questions are most likely to be asked by evaluators for clinical, counseling, or other applied or service-provider training programs.

- Have you had any clinical volunteer or work experience? How would you describe your performance? Strengths? Weaknesses?
- Why do you think you are personally suited to provide clinical (or counseling) services to others? Do you see areas that need work?
- What is the greatest disappointment you have had to face, and how did you handle it?

If you had a choice and opted for a telephone interview, be prepared to answer the question, "Why did you choose to interview over the phone instead of visiting us in person?" Your honest answer should reveal a valid conflict rather than mere inconvenience.

Again, we strongly argue against rigidly memorizing answers. You can easily become confused, especially if the wording of the actual question is just a shade different than the samples presented here. For example, "What undergraduate classes did you like the best and why?" could be asked as "What undergraduate classes influenced you the most and why?" which calls for a slightly different spin on your answer. Be flexible enough to adapt to variations on the themes as well as to respond appropriately to any follow-up questions to your answers.

After you get some ideas about how to respond to the relevant questions, plan some time to practice answering them aloud. Ask a friend who is serious, trusted, and interested in your future to participate in one or more role-playing sessions. You may find that you giggle a lot and often want to start over, but the practice and experience will pay off if you stick with it.

Your practice interviewer can offer some helpful feedback. Did you mumble? Did you speak too softly? Abrasively? Did you engage in distracting behaviors with your hands? How was your eye contact and posture? Did an answer come off as silly? Pompous? Arrogant? Did you look too grim? Or smile or giggle too much? Did you put yourself down? Were answers unclear? If you can, videotape these practice interviews and critique them.

Some common interviewing problems, particularly errors committed with a lack of awareness, can be overcome with just a little practice. Behavioral rehearsal also helps to neutralize the jitters that often accompany the real thing.

If you cannot find anyone who will do this with you, practice delivery in front of a mirror, to a tape recorder, or in front of a sofa with a propped-up stuffed animal or pillow audience.

Can I do anything else to prepare for this experience?

There are three important activities that should not take too long if you have followed the application selection suggestions made earlier in the book. If you were unable to do that, you should try to do some of it now.

First, carefully review the copy of your own application to the program for which you will soon be interviewing, especially the statement of purpose or other essays and short-answer questions. Some individualized interview questions may be based on what you wrote in your application materials. A review will also remind you of the kind of information that this particular program views as relevant and important.

Second, because you may now meet the faculty about whom you have hopefully already learned something, you should review their names, interests, and research areas. If you have time and have not already done so, locate some of the recent publications by the faculty, especially if you have already identified one or more faculty with whom you would like to study. Read this material and get involved with it. Look for information about the faculty on the Internet. Some departmental web pages include photographs of faculty and descriptions of their mentoring philosophy. Should an opportunity arise to interact with these individuals, you will be very effective if you are well-prepared.

Third, read again all of the information that has been sent to you about the program and the university, perhaps making brief notes on key aspects of the program and the faculty. You will want to present yourself as a person who knows as much about this institution as is possible for an outsider. This exercise will help you with two favorite interview questions: "Why did you apply to our program?" and "Is there anything you would like to ask us?"

What kinds of questions should I prepare to ask them?

Because the quality of your questions during the more formal interview session may bear on how you are evaluated, be sure to formulate at least a few questions in advance. Do not ask anything that is clearly and completely answered in the materials you already have. However, follow-up questions based on those materials are certainly appropriate. An example could go something like this: "I read in your program description that a course in child assessment is required, but I couldn't tell for which program. I would appreciate a clarification on that."

You may also have questions about the latest faculty research activities, laboratory or computer facilities, where students do their practica or internships, access policies to the departmental facilities on weekends, and so on. Avoid silly questions (e.g., "Where does one get a good beer in this town?") or questions that stray too far from the likely knowledge base of those you are addressing (e.g., "What is the cost for room and board in graduate housing?").

You may find, somewhat to your surprise, that the main reason for your presence is to give you an opportunity to interview program representatives. Asking about what is currently going on with the faculty and students (programs, research, etc.) is wise, because people enjoy talking about their own activities. The next section will get you ready to travel and will offer hints to get you through the interview itself. Try to think of this as an adventure.

The Interview Experience

The interpersonal encounter you are about to experience is an important event but one that should not confuse or defeat you. Remember, these people are interested in you. They did not invite you to their site to belittle or expose you. They just want to get to know you a little better and give you an opportunity to get to know them. (Remember how important the notion of a good match is?) They are not your adversaries. In fact, they hope you like what you see during your experience. They realize that, although it is a difficult concept to describe, the feel of a program is one of the major determinants applicants use to make their final choice. The interview is where the faculty hope to make the greatest positive emotional impact on you.

What should I wear?

Physical appearance, which includes both attire and grooming, will influence attributions made about you. Plan your interview outfit, try it on, and lay it out well before the interview to be sure that it fits and is clean and in good shape. If you are invited to a weekend event, you will need more than one outfit but probably no more than two. (Clever mix-and-match items can offer a little variety without adding too much bulk.) If you must travel some distance, pack carefully so that you will not look wrinkled.

Where you are going for the interview and the weather, of course, will bear on your choice of what to wear. A very conservative school commands more traditional dress. However, the opposite is not true. Even those applying to a laid-back southern California campus should not show up for an interview looking too casual. Still, both men and women should avoid excessively formal and fancy attire and accessories.

In cool weather, a sport coat and slacks with a shirt and tie are always appropriate for men. A nice sweater may substitute for the sport coat. The absolute minimum for men is slacks and an attractive dress shirt. Wear reasonably dressy shoes. Longer hair and a beard or moustache require special care to ensure a well-groomed look.

Women should choose attractive but professional attire, such as a business suit or tailored dress with sensible shoes. Whether women should wear slacks is debatable; some evaluators still believe a skirt is appropriate for female interviewees for such an important, professional occasion. A natural look, provided by the skillful use of cosmetics, is preferable to heavy-handed makeup.

For both men and women, it is not the cost of the outfit that counts but rather the look and the impression it makes. Appropriate clothing is available from most outlets advertising modest prices.

Some students have adopted a trendy look that often deviates from the middle-aged style of most faculty interviewers. Here you will have to decide what risks you are willing to take to maintain your individuality. Even though it may be unfair, a very unusual look can work against you. We recall an extremely bright and very pleasant young student who sported a punk look. Despite our expressed concerns, she insisted on retaining her black leather jacket and skirt, a nose ring, and the purple stripe in her hair. She was invited to several interviews and promptly received a rejection letter after each of them.

Your visual impact is the first characteristic that interviewers will consciously or subconsciously evaluate. Although preselection interviews are not (thankfully) beauty contests, you do want to project the image of a mature, competent student as you walk in the door. Your physical appearance will be the foundation for the rest of the attributions made about you. A well-groomed, professional-looking candidate may even get away with a few stumbles during the interview, whereas an unkempt or rhinestone-flashing candidate may have to play catch-up the entire time. Our suggestion is to cover tattoos and remove jewelry from piercings located anywhere other than the ears.

What other last-minute items must I take care of?

Know exactly where you are supposed to be and how to get there. Keep these directions safe, and check just before you leave to be sure you have them with you. Also, make sure you have a telephone number for an office that you could contact should any emergency arise.

Interview Day

If you will travel a long distance, arrange to arrive at your destination a day ahead of time, especially if the interview is in the morning (be aware of differences in time zones). If you are unfamiliar with the campus, build in extra time. Should anything happen to preclude your timely arrival, contact the appropriate office as soon as possible. You must avoid having your interviewers wait for you to show up. It is difficult to recover from the impression that your lateness or absence would make, regardless of the legitimacy of your excuse.

Allow plenty of time to get from where you live or are staying to the university and the specific meeting place. Many schools have complicated ground plans and congested parking areas that are far from where you need to be. If you are too early, you can sit and relax or look around a little.

I think I'm going to faint, and my hands are so clammy that I am sure I will become permanently welded to anyone or anything I touch. Help!

You can try breathing deeply and using a handkerchief on your hands, but do not concentrate on the effect your nervousness is having on others. It will only increase the somatic symptoms. It is expected that your hands may be cold and damp or sticky. No one will hold that, or any other visible or audible signs of nervousness, against you. Most applicants relax once their attention is diverted to the task at hand.

You look good, right? So smile as you are asked to enter the room. Take your cues from those conducting the interview. Shake hands if others extend theirs or are standing close by and seem like they might be receptive to your extended hand. Remain standing until offered a chair or until others begin to seat themselves.

Chitchat about the weather or your trip may precede the formal questions. Interact on that level comfortably, but allow it to subside as soon as it is evident that it is time for business. That will usually occur within a minute or two. The interviewers will usually start off with the sorts of questions that we have already presented.

Rarely, a stress interview technique is used to see how you function when left hanging on your own, such as not asking you anything at all (also known as the pregnant pause). No problem! After a reasonable wait, you can say something like, "I'm pleased to be here and am ready to answer your questions. I have a few that I would like to ask later." That should open up the discussion. If not, you could just start interviewing yourself. For example, you could say, "I imagine that you want to know why students are interested in your program. Well, I like . . ." The chances of this happening to you are very remote, but prepare just in case. Some interview experts suggest that you develop a 90-second mini-speech about yourself and your goals, which you can pull out whenever an opportunity presents itself or whenever you are called upon to do so.

When you are asked a question, take a few seconds to get comfortable with it and to draw together the information you have already thought about. Try not to talk too fast if that is what you tend to do when under pressure. Stick closely to the material that is requested and refrain from wandering off the point. Even if an interviewer should provide a provocative statement or question, possibly to see how you respond to unexpected comments, try to remain calm and pleasant, and take some time to formulate your response.

Should I try to embellish my answers and stretch the truth a little?

Terrible idea! Interviews allow for follow-up questions on the topic at hand, and unless you actually know what you hint that you know, you will unravel like a cheap sweater. Any enhancements on your application are fair game for scrutiny as well. Although it may have seemed easy at the time to express your interest in a certain field or a particular person's work, imagine your humiliation if you cannot comfortably discuss these topics now. The truth always has many advantages, including in the pursuit of graduate training.

If a question comes up that baffles you, do not panic. Let it sink in for a few seconds. If you understand the question and nothing comes to mind, and the question was fact based, say something like, "I'm stumped. An answer just isn't coming to me." Admitting ignorance under these conditions is usually better than embarrassing yourself in front of people who know a lot more about the subject than you do. If you have an idea that you think may be acceptable but are unsure of yourself, go ahead with it. As long as it is clear that you are doing the best you can, you can get by with a few less than adequate responses.

If you blank on a question requiring an opinion or reflection, you may consider responding with, "Nothing is coming to me at the moment. Could we come back to that a little later?" If you did not understand the question, politely indicate that and ask that it be repeated or reformulated. Everyone assumes that applicants are somewhat nervous, so pointing it out may come across as a plea for extra kindness or consideration.

What else should I do or not do?

Do not smoke during the interview even if others do or tell you it is alright. Do not chew gum. We recommend that you not accept a beverage that is offered to you if you are feeling nervous. It is a distraction you do not need, and accidents can happen. (Imagine spending the rest of the day wearing a large coffee stain.) Also, there is often that awkward moment at the end of an interview when you have to decide whether to take the beverage or container with you or dispose of it there. It is better to not have to deal with these issues.

Maintain eye contact with the interviewer. If you are being interviewed by more than one person, favor the one who asked the question you are answering, but also glance at the others. Monitor your body language, particularly any repetitive, nervous behaviors you sometimes exhibit such as body rocking, hair stroking, foot tapping, hand wringing, or face scratching.

Do not trash your current or previous academic institutions and their instructors. Regardless of how reasonable your criticisms may be, you run the risk of being seen as a difficult person.

Your demeanor is very important. Do not try to show off. Your chances of out-thinking your interviewers are remote, and you are not expected to know as much as they do. Remain alert without appearing too tense. See (and present) yourself as a bright and motivated person who is seeking the opportunity to learn more. Smile when appropriate, but do not paste on a toothy, rigid, panicky grin and leave it there. A little humor is fine as long as everyone is enjoying it, but do not take on the inappropriate responsibility of entertaining your hosts.

What if I am asked something that I think is too personal or inappropriate?

If a question strikes you as improper, quickly evaluate its possible legitimacy to the task at hand. Some questions about your personal circumstances may be relevant in deciding what kind of funding you may require, whether you would have time for an assistantship, and so on. Some interviewers may simply be very frank people, and although they do not mean to be inappropriately intrusive, they may come across that way given how vulnerable you already feel. We all have our personal boundaries, some extending further than others. Trespassing can occur without intent.

We have heard of a few instances of totally inappropriate questions, which revealed sexism, racism, ageism, or very deep intrusions into the applicant's personal life that would violate just about anyone's limits. Should this happen to you (thankfully, the probability is very low), stay cool but firm with your own standards of propriety ("I'm sorry, but I am uncomfortable answering that question"). You have been put unfairly at risk of jeopardizing your status should you protest. However, as a result of this episode, you may not want to involve yourself with this program anyway. Seek counsel with a trusted advisor after the incident. Regardless of your decision about the program and theirs about you, you might want to write to the program director or some other school official to alert them to the inappropriate behavior you were subjected to.

Will I be able to tell if my interviewers like me?

Some interviewers or teams may be easygoing and even a little playful. Others may remain glum and humorless. The reasons for the differences, however, will probably have far less to do with you than with the personality styles of, and relationships among, the interviewers themselves. So, do not automatically think that you blew it if your group seemed remote. More likely than not, the real reasons are that Professor Sneeze is feeling poorly today and Professors Cain and Abel do not like each other.

How do I leave the situation?

Termination of the interview will be determined and made apparent by the interviewers. Don't ever look at your watch! When the time comes to part, shake hands and make your exit gracefully. If you felt that things went well, you may want to say something like, "Thank you very much. I enjoyed meeting you," or whatever conveys your genuine, positive feelings without overdoing the flattery. Parting with, "You are the most brilliant and thrilling group of people I have ever spent time with" will probably be viewed as manipulative even if such an enthusiastic outburst is completely genuine.

If the interview felt rather cool (which is not uncommon), or you felt that it did not go all that well, you might try something like, "Thank you very much for giving me this opportunity to meet with you." Then, smile, maintain erect posture (head held high), and leave the room.

Is it time to go home yet?

That depends. As noted earlier, some programs are introducing innovative twists well beyond the typical 1-hour formal interview. You may finish one session only to have lunch and go for another one or more sessions. You may find yourself in a group interview or discussion with the other finalists. If so, always remain focused and alert, even if you are not speaking, because you are being watched. Try to contribute at least a couple of times. Do not envy your competitor who loudly asserts himself at every turn and upstages each previous speaker. Chances are he or she will not be viewed as positively as the applicant whose body language and reactions were always in the moment and who made several thoughtful verbal contributions. Purely social events may also be part of the interview process.

How can I enjoy parties or dinners? Or should I even try to have fun?

Parties, dinners, picnics, and the like are not held strictly to make you uncomfortable in a social situation or to assess your coping style. Truly, the purpose is to give applicants a nice time and to allow faculty, current graduate students, and the finalists to get to know each other a little better in a less formal setting. Graduate programs are often tight-knit communities and, should you be admitted to the program, much of your socializing will involve these people. So a party or social setting is another opportunity to see how you might fit in.

The best approach is to relax a little, because a stiff, humorless stance at a party will suggest an inability to adapt to the setting or a lack of social skills. This is not to say, however, that you should forget for even one minute where you are and why you are there. Do not cross any professional boundaries (e.g., asking Professor Smug if you can call him by his first name, or challenging the other candidates to a beer drinking contest). Stay in complete control of your senses and sensibilities. Let your hosts guide your demeanor, but trust your own instincts as well. You might be wise to forego any alcoholic beverages. For your purposes, the party is still all about business.

When you converse in social or informal situations with faculty or graduate students currently in the program, answer any formal questions as best you can. But, if they seem to prefer lighter conversation, do not always bring the conversation back to the program or your candidacy. Informal conversations may get into more personal matters, so remember that whatever you disclose at the party could be shared during the discussions about you at subsequent meetings held in the sober light of day!

Any other surprises?

There is one other moment of discomfort that you are likely to experience somewhere along the way. A program representative will probably ask you where else you have applied or if you have already been accepted by any other programs. Depending on the facts, you may or may not feel embarrassed by this question. Such a question may give evaluators information they can use to calculate both your perceived worth elsewhere as well as the probability that you might accept their offer should they extend one. Tell them as much as you feel comfortable in revealing.

An occasional candidate may be extended an acceptance offer during or soon after the interview, before leaving for home. If this happens to you and you have decided that this is the place where you want to be, it is a happy day indeed. However, if you are not yet sure, resist any urge (or pressure, no matter how pleasantly expressed) to answer immediately. Express much appreciation and promise that you will let them know your decision as soon as possible. If nothing like this happens to you, do not feel disheartened. Most programs do not engage in this practice, preferring instead to wait until formal postinterview discussion meetings.

After the Interview

If you are like many applicants, you will replay the interview experience in your mind. It is all right to do this once or twice, but to obsess too much is not good for you.

But I should have smiled more. My answer to Dr. Medulla's question was incoherent. And then there was that little snarling noise that my stomach kept making. If I had only read Dr. Tron's last article on arti-

ficial intelligence. He probably thinks that I have an artificial brain. And . . .

Whoa! There is nothing you can do about it now, and beating yourself up for real or exaggerated shortcomings is a no-win game. Postinterview stress responds well to physical exercise and getting out with friends.

Should I send a thank-you note to anyone?

The effect of writing thank-you notes to one or more members of the interview team is difficult to predict. Such notes are generally viewed as indicators of thoughtfulness and good taste, but they could also be perceived as manipulative. Unless a single person took considerable time with you and you think things went well, we do not recommend writing a note. If the program staff put forth a lot of effort (e.g., a meal or an extensive tour or a weekend experience), a single thank-you note directed to the entire group is appropriate. If you stayed with a current graduate student, a note of appreciation for his or her hospitality is certainly appropriate. If you write a thank-you note, make sure it is exactly that—a gesture of appreciation for the time your hosts spent with you. Do not use this as an opportunity to promote your candidacy.

CHAPTER 23

HOW DO I ACCEPT
(AND REJECT) OFFERS?

If you are an exceptionally strong candidate and mailed your applications early, some unusual events may occur. You could find yourself treated like royalty, with prestigious faculty wooing you with phone calls and invitations to the campus to chat and look around. You could be offered fellowships or assistantships and other gestures to help with your transition to a new locale. You may have to handle considerable attempts to get you to commit immediately to an offer (a pressure you should certainly resist if you want to assess your other options). All this could happen while your friends are still working on their applications for the same program because the application deadline date has not yet arrived! However, not every program processes applications early, and very few students will experience such majestic treatment.

I doubt I will be like the rare applicant you have just described. How are acceptances typically communicated?

Most doctoral programs will communicate their decisions in March through April for fall-term entry. Each program to which you applied should have indicated the feedback time frame, which can vary considerably. If the decision date is not indicated, assume it to be 6 to 12 weeks after the application deadline date, or call to the office to politely ask the staff member for a rough estimate.

It seems like things could get confusing at this point, with so many offers flying around.

If no policy existed across graduate programs, dealing with acceptance and rejection decisions would be far more chaotic than it actually is. Programs would push to attract their favorite applicants, possibly engaging in aggressive, competitive practices. The students who were thought to be successfully enlisted might simply change their minds as more attractive offers arrived from other programs. A destructive cat-and-mouse game among accepted applicants and programs (with the designation of "cats" and "mice" left quite unclear) could persist for months, leaving the graduate program faculty guessing up until the very end as to who will actually come through the doors on the first day of classes.

Thankfully, the process has some structure. In 1965, more than 300 universities agreed to abide by a resolution created by the Council of Graduate Schools in the United States. This policy, revised slightly in 1981 and again in 1988, allows students until April 15 of the semester prior to the fall entry period to make up their minds, even if an offer was extended to the student months earlier (see http://www.apa.org/ed/accept.html for the actual resolution and the amendments).

Students who accept an offer prior to April 15 are allowed to change their minds and cancel their acceptance if another offer comes in, as long as they do so by April 15. After April 15, however, accepted offers left in force must stand unless the student negotiates a release from the institution to which a commitment has already been made. Similarly, any offer extended after April 15 is conditional pending the student's release from any previously accepted offer. Any offers accepted on or after April 15 cannot be rejected later to accept a new offer without a similar release.

Getting a release doesn't seem so hard.

For psychology (and many related) graduate programs, it is not as simple as it might appear. In 1981, the Council of Graduate Departments of Psychology (COGDOP) strengthened the 1965 resolution, to which the majority of programs subscribe, making it far more difficult to negotiate post–April 15 shuffles. The resolution reads as follows:

> An acceptance given or left in force after April 15 commits the student not to solicit or accept another offer. Offers made after April 15 must include the proviso that the offer is void if acceptance of a previous offer from a department accepting this resolution is in force on that date. These rules are binding on all persons acting on behalf of the offering institution. (www.cgsnet.org/publications/resolut.htm)

Note, however, that not every graduate program adheres to the more stringent resolution. A complete listing of psychology and related programs that have pledged to uphold the resolution is printed in every edition of *Graduate Study in Psychology* (published every other year by the APA). If any offer you receive falls under the jurisdiction of the resolution, the offer should be clear and should be acted upon in good faith. Although no formal monitoring mechanism is currently in force, the APA requires the department official to sign an oath that the program conforms to the April 15 policy and indicates that evidence of violating the agreement can result in deletion from future editions of *Graduate Study in Psychology*.

What if I am pressured to decide before April 15 and before I have heard from other programs that interest me?

It is not appropriate for program representatives to be pushy before April 15. Rather strong tactics have been reported, however, and these constitute unfair practice. Unless the offer is exactly what you wanted all along and no others could possibly come in that might be better for you, we advise that you stand your ground by responding to any pressure from a school you are actively considering. You might try something like this:

> I very much appreciate your interest in me and I remain interested in your program as well. I have decided to wait a little while longer, however, to see how another program [or three other programs or whatever your situation is] evaluates me before making a final decision. I will let you know as soon as possible.

Should program representatives contact you to notify you of your acceptance, it is reasonably common for them to also ask you what other programs you applied to or where their program stands on your preference list. Although this is a very personal question (sort of like asking someone who they voted for), it is easy to understand why it is asked. It helps representatives understand where they stand with you and assess their own chances of signing you. Refusing to answer is certainly your right. However, we advise naming at least two or three of the programs you applied to that you believe, based on everything you know to date, have (or will likely have) an interest in you as well.

It sounds like the shoe is on the other foot now, like I'm the one with some power.

That is absolutely correct. Few students apply to only one program, and every program wants the best students it can attract. Now the staff is a little like you were a short while ago: waiting for letters and calls and crossing their fingers. They will even be disappointed if you turn them down!

This powerful position in which you may now find yourself can be abused, however, not only at the expense of the graduate program and its staff and faculty but also at the expense of other hopeful students just like you who very much want to further their education.

Besides beating someone out of a slot, how can I hurt my peers?

You should not characterize yourself as hurting anyone by earning an acceptance into a graduate program—you worked for it and deserve it. You do hurt your peers, however, by holding on to offers that you will not accept. Because half or more of the students who are on the first-string list of acceptances may ultimately decline their offers, a ranked list of alternates is waiting to be contacted. Invitations will be extended to alternates, one at a time, as each of those accepted before them reject the offer. (Remember, you might be an alternate for a program that you prefer.)

Therefore, you could have the power to destroy someone else's lifelong dream. Because you were too busy or forgot to let Midstate University know that you were accepting another offer, Lonnie Crumble (the next alternate at Midstate University who wanted to go there for as long as he could remember) committed to a less preferred option rather than risk ending up without any program at all. You would never know, of course, what hardships were caused by your lack of considerate responsiveness, but such a scenario is very likely. Consider that your best friend, or someone just like him or her, will be the beneficiary of your prompt response. This will keep you sensitized to the importance of notifying as quickly as possible programs whose offers you will decline.

Exactly how soon should I decline offers?

As soon as you have two acceptance offers, use a play-the-winner design. Choose between the two, and send a note within a few days to the less preferred program informing them that you have chosen not to accept their offer. (Unless your choice is easy, we recommend this brief waiting period to ensure that your decision feels firm to prevent later regret.) Retain the preferred choice and play it against the third acceptance, and so on, until you are left with two finalists. Then decide between the two as soon as you can. Remember to inform the less preferred programs of your decision to decline their offer each time you complete the paired-comparison task.

Are the choices always that simple?

The play-the-winner design can be clear-cut if you already have firmly established and ranked preferences. For example, if you applied to several master's programs as your "insurance policies" in case a doctoral program failed to accept you, letters of regret or withdrawal of your application should be sent to all master's programs to which you applied as soon as you get your first acceptance into a doctoral program. Choices are particularly straightforward if you have a single, favorite school and you are accepted into it. The game is then over, and all of the less preferred schools should immediately be notified, even if you have not yet heard from them.

Often enough, however, the boundaries will be somewhat blurry due to a variety of factors. Usually it is because two or more programs that accept you hold equal attraction. Another common choice obstruction is the oddly balanced results of a pros-and-cons analysis. For example, Dr. Incredible, the professor you would really like to work with, is at Palm Tree University, but the financial support offered there is very low compared to the generous offer by Oaks University. Palm Tree University is much closer to your family, which means you could go home sometimes on weekends. Oaks University, however, has the best reputation of any program you explored, and the curriculum itself strikes you as particularly attractive.

If faced with a difficult choice, make lists of the positive and negative features of each program. Upon reviewing the lists, carefully challenge any of the positives that are not directly related to the quality of the program itself and its place in your long-term goals. Items to challenge include the amount of financial support, access to a hobby or extracurricular activities, distance from home, physical attractiveness of the campus, and even the prestige of the school per se. Instead, you want the program that will best prepare you for what you will do for half of your waking hours for most of the rest of your life. This may require budget tightening, temporary forfeiture of outside interests, and more difficult access to your current relationships and home surroundings for the next several years. You will make some sacrifices wherever you go, so you might as well make them at the place that will serve you best in the long run.

If the list comparison does not reveal an answer, seek more active input. You might request counsel from your current professors, treating their input as one possibly valuable point of view rather than as infallible, even if they express themselves in a particularly all-knowing way. Although input from others can be valuable, do not be overly reliant on outside opinions. We sometimes give away our own best interests when someone else is willing to make a challenging decision for us.

If part of the difficulty of the decision involves a lack of information or something that is unclear about the programs, take an active approach to resolving the problem. You are now in a position where telephone calls to specific faculty members or the program chair of the graduate programs you are considering are quite acceptable.

If you have not yet visited the campus of a program to which you have been accepted, seriously consider it now. Again, because your status is now quite different than it was when you were a mere applicant, you can very likely find someone willing to show you around and spend some time with you. Some programs arrange an orientation for students they have chosen in the hopes of attracting acceptances of their offers. If you receive such an invitation from a school that greatly interests you, attendance is highly recommended. You will meet those who could be your professors as well as those who could well be your classmates, all without any pressure on you to perform. The financial outlay to take these trips (even if you must take out more loans) is small compared to the valuable long-term implications.

I understand your point that money and leaving home shouldn't be major issues, but isn't that sometimes unrealistic?

Financial and relationship considerations must, indeed, often prevail. Our point is simply that it is important to at least seriously consider alternative possibilities to the simple conclusions, "I can't afford it" and "I can't leave."

No one wants to go into debt, and if we were talking about a new car or a big-screen television set, our advice would be quite conservative. However, incurring additional debt now may be the best way to invest in your future. Most professionals who have been in the field for a few years have been able to pay back every penny without enduring great discomfort, including what we borrowed from family members.

There is no doubt, of course, that there comes a point when the cost of your favorite choice exceeds your resources. You should express this problem to the program staff before rejecting their offer. Sometimes they will give you ideas you had not considered or offer extra funds.

What if I still cannot decide among my offers?

There may well come a point when any of your two or more alternatives would be as right as possible for you. Pick one, and do not dwell on your choice afterward.

What should I say when I turn down an offer from a graduate program?

Here is a suggested model for the body of your rejection letter. However, we must stress that what you say, as long as it is polite, is less important than when you write your letter.

Dear Members of the Graduate Evaluation Committee [or a specific person you know to be in charge or the exact name of the committee if you know what it is]:

I am responding with my decision about my graduate school plans. I very much appreciate your interest in me, but I regret to inform you that I will not be accepting your offer.

Thank you again for your time and consideration. [You can end the note simply or continue with something that personalizes your feelings a little more such as, "Dr. Booster was especially helpful and I will always remember his kindness to me," or "It was a very difficult decision for me to make because I was very impressed with your program."]

Type your name below your signature (or print it if you handwrite the letter) so that there will be no doubt as to your identity. If you want to, you could certainly use a telephone call to submit your polite rejection; this may save the department and their alternates several days of uncertainty. Even so, send a follow-up note as well, because telephone messages sometimes get lost.

About programs I haven't heard from yet . . . Even though I have already accepted another offer, can't I just wait and see to relieve my curiosity?

Your curiosity is certainly understandable, but think of students like yourself who will benefit immensely from your small sacrifice of not having complete outcome information. It could make a big difference in someone else's life, so our earlier advice stands. If you have made a firm, confident decision and other programs have yet to give you their decision about your candidacy, take a few minutes immediately to write a brief note or to call each place you have not heard from and ask that your application be withdrawn. The program faculty will appreciate it, and they can then focus on still-viable candidates. (Remember, those alternates are still out there waiting.)

CHAPTER 24

WHAT IF I'M AN ALTERNATE FOR A PROGRAM?

It is unlikely that everyone who is accepted will take a program up on its offer. To make sure that there will be enough acceptable students to take the slots vacated by the ones who reject them, every program creates a waiting list of alternates.

Alternates are ranked in some preferential order. Invitations to alternates will be issued as higher ranked applicants decline offers. Alternates will receive apology letters should the class limit be reached when students who are ranked ahead of them accept offers. Alternates are highly regarded applicants; the program faculty would be pleased to have them around should any higher ranked applicants decline. A person would not be selected as an alternate unless he or she was also a truly suitable candidate.

It must feel strange to be an alternate. If that happens to me, should I just sit and wait it out?

Letters informing you of your alternate status evoke odd emotions. Your future options no longer rest with selection committee members but rather with a group of anonymous people who also applied to the program and who do not even know you exist. (If you become an alternate, you will clearly understand how much it means when applicants ahead of you are considerate enough to make prompt decisions.)

Do not, however, just sit uneasily on the announcement that you are in limbo. Rather, ask yourself whether you want to remain on an alternate list. The answer is yes if you are very interested in the program and are not yet obligated to make a decision about another school's offer. In this case, fire off a brief letter acknowledging your desire to remain in the running. If you have already made other plans or are no longer interested in that particular program, promptly call or write to request that your name be withdrawn from the alternate list. (Again, you are doing others a kindness by enhancing their opportunities.)

Do not send additional materials at this point in an attempt to further bolster your candidacy unless you have just heard that your submitted manuscript has been accepted for publication in a major journal, you have just won some prestigious student award, or you have made a similar monumental achievement (in which case you could zip off a brief letter alerting the evaluators of the information). Remember, you have already been ranked, and your place is resistant to tinkering at this point.

Surviving Alternate Status

How do you survive being in limbo? Basically, you wait. As time goes by, you may get a call from the program staff asking if you are still interested in remaining an alternate. If you do not hear anything as the weeks pass, time may begin to close in on you. This pressured feeling may arise if you find yourself in the following situation. You have one or more outright offers in hand, and you remain as an alternate in two programs that interest you more than the programs into which you have been accepted. The date when you should commit to a program lies dead ahead. What should you do? In this case it is permissible to call the offices of the programs listing you as an alternate and ask if there is any new information. (It is okay to gently nudge them now, because you need information and there is little to lose at this point.)

Try not to get upset with the staff if no news is available. They have virtually no control at this point either. They will probably tell you everything they know, but it may not be much more than, "We still have to hear from four students and you are currently the third-ranked alternate." You can be assured that the program staff are doing everything they can to facilitate decisions, because if the first-stringers are not going to accept the invitations, they most certainly want you to have that opportunity.

Unfortunately, some of the first-stringers may sit on more than one invitation for as long as they possibly can. They may even be alternates at their favorite schools. Some may have made up their minds to decline the offer weeks ago but have not been considerate enough to inform the graduate program staff. Others are in the enviable position of having several attractive options and experiencing genuine trouble making a decision. This impasse often stays in effect right up to the wire (which is usually around April 15 for many doctoral programs, as discussed in the previous chapter).

How often do alternates eventually get accepted?

No one can accurately answer that question. Based on their own historical trends, the program staff may have a rough idea of how many first-round accepted students will turn the program down, but anything could happen in a particular year. Sometimes even the top-ranked programs in the country end up going into their alternate list to fill half of their available enrollment slots. On the other hand, we have spoken with students who were notified in early April that they were the first-ranked alternate (that is, only one person had to decline an offer for this student to get in), but every initially extended offer was accepted and there was not a slot for even the first alternate.

If programs get lots of highly qualified applicants, why can't they just accept a few more students?

Graduate school involves an enriched model of training. It is based on intensive, individualized work with students as they become professionals and colleagues. To add extra students beyond those a program is capable of educating properly at this level would undermine the entire structure of the program and stretch the available resources too thin.

What if I cannot wait any longer without jeopardizing my chances of going to graduate school?

Often push comes to shove. The programs accepting you need to know right away, and the programs in which you are an alternate still have no news. You will need to say yes to someone or you will run the risk of starting the whole process over again next year because your alternate status never materialized into an offer. So, you will have to make a decision.

What if I commit to a program, and later one of my more preferred programs accepts me? Can I change my mind?

This dilemma does occur. Should you accept an offer that was extended after you accepted an offer from another program, even if it's before April 15 (see chap. 23), it causes hardships on the program you now plan to reject. They were counting on your enrollment and may have made some of their own late alternate decisions based on where you were going to fit into their program. However, if you are dealing with a school adopting the April 15 policy resolution and you are within the acceptable time frame, you may follow your own wishes and still be playing by the rules.

For programs not adhering to the April 15 resolution, the student is not bound by any agreements. However, because late changes disadvantage the program faculty, who assumed that you would honor your commitment, we recommend evaluating your decision very carefully before accepting a late offer from another program. Unless there are compelling reasons for breaking a commitment (e.g., you need financial aid badly and the latest offer is not only a better program for you but also helps pay your way, or there are major differences between the programs), strongly consider leaving things the way they are. If the differences between the two programs are relatively minor, chances are each program would be equally as good for you.

Does anyone ever violate the rules by switching after April 15?

It does happen sometimes—usually because of the ambiguity of alternate status—even though it should not. Such action does constitute a violation of an agreement instituted to help keep the process manageable and fair. If you decide to attempt to violate the April 15 resolution, inform the school you will now attempt to accept of your dilemma and ask for their guidance. They may or may not help you, depending on their own commitment to the resolution.

Will I be informed of my current ranking on the alternate list as time goes on?

Staff members in some programs have permission to inform alternates of their current ranking on the list. Other schools, unfortunately, insist on holding this information confidential, which means that you will not know whether you are next in line or so far down on the list that you should definitely make other plans.

What if I am left holding only alternate status options? When will I know my ultimate fate?

As incredible as it sounds, you can be left dangling up until the first week of classes. If someone who was expected to enroll does not show up, you may be offered his or her place. This is a crazy situation, and obviously anyone sitting on a waiting list needs to develop a backup plan. If you have not been accepted by early summer, assume that you will not be and proceed accordingly. Your backup plan could include signing up for more advanced undergraduate courses, getting relevant work or volunteer experience, or taking a job (see the next chapter). If you ultimately receive no offers, reapplication the next time around may bring about earlier and more satisfying results. In the next chapter we offer advice for those who have been rejected as well as those who will start graduate school in the fall.

CHAPTER 25

I'VE RECEIVED THE NEWS. NOW WHAT?

I didn't get in anywhere. How do I handle getting rejected?

The emotional reaction to being told, in effect, "We have chosen not to ask you to be one of us," is strong. It would be one thing if applicants did not really care in the first place, or if they had not invested much effort to be accepted. Because neither of these conditions applies, intense feeling is likely to well up. You know that, statistically, you have lots of company, but somehow that does not offer much comfort.

Rejection letters are usually written in a considerate and compassionate way, because the selection committee members are well aware of how the recipients will take the news. Those who evaluate applicants get no pleasure from this unavoidable phase of their work. The letter will often explain that there were a great many qualified applicants, that a small number of enrollment slots were available, and that it was very difficult to make decisions under such circumstances.

That's all bull, right?

Most competitive doctoral programs receive from 10 to 50 times more applicants than they have room to accommodate. Do you think that the few applicants invited into their programs are the only ones who were judged as qualified? Of course not! Many applicants were no more than a hair away from a very different kind of letter, and still many others were impressive to the committee members but were seen as less suitable for their specific program for reasons other than ability and perceived potential.

What are common reasons for rejection other than one's academic record?

Sometimes files are incomplete or applicants did not follow directions carefully in preparing the materials, and these applicants are disadvantaged from the beginning. Often students did not read the program materials carefully. Had they done so, they either would have prepared their application much differently or would not have applied to that particular program. As examples, sometimes applicants indicate that they are interested in doing research with a certain professor, but that professor is not active in the program to which the student applied. Or, an applicant's personal statement focuses heavily on a commitment to becoming trained in behavioral therapy, but no one teaching in the program focuses on behavioral techniques. Or, the applicant stresses an interest in becoming a practicing psychotherapist but applies to a program that aspires to produce research scientists. These possibilities suggest a bad fit between applicant and program, and the resulting rejection says little about the quality of the applicant.

Indications that applicants would not be happy in a program, or that the program itself could not satisfy the students' stated needs, can often be seen far more clearly by the evaluators than by the applicants themselves. In such cases, a rejection is a service to the applicant, although the applicant probably does not understand or appreciate the favor.

Sometimes factors that have no personal relevance at all affect your acceptance or rejection. Examples are geographical, gender, and ethnic balance factors. Given the context of the total applicant pool, you could have been right last year, and maybe right next year, but wrong this year.

Should I write a letter demanding to know why I was rejected?

We strongly recommend against sending off any irate or indignant letters. First, the office staff members, not the decision makers, usually receive the brunt of such reactions. Second, should those who were responsible for the decisions receive the letter, they will only feel more assured that their initial decision was correct, particularly if the communication is seen as rude, abusive, or immature.

Should rejected applicants write a nice letter asking for feedback as to why their application attempts failed? The program faculty and staff do not relish dealing with such letters because there could potentially be scores of them. Some schools explicitly state that they will not under any circumstances provide individualized explanations of their decisions to reject applicants.

Generally, seeking such feedback should not be necessary. You know that the program had many suitable applicants and that the successful ones simply had an edge or seemed to fit better with the program. You may also be fairly certain of other reasons, such as if you rushed through statements of purpose, or your grades or test scores were borderline compared to the program's stated minimum requirements.

Very occasionally, however, we do support a rejected student's desire to request feedback. Occasionally the students are totally perplexed, and others who know the student share their puzzlement. Such students and their mentors were certain that the applicant would be snatched up readily because all credentials seemed strong. An inquiry may only bring a response that shares the reasons for ranking below the cutoff line; it is rarely any deficit in the applicant but rather some brief explanation as to why those who prevailed ranked even higher. Although it has happened only once in our graduate counseling experience, such an inquiry was the catalyst to the discovery that the student had been sent the wrong letter and had actually been accepted into the program!

The most common legitimate reason for requesting feedback about an unsuccessful application is if the applicant appeared well qualified for the program and would like to apply again next year. Here the major focus of the inquiry would be to learn what could be done during the next several months to strengthen the reapplication. A helpful response may be forthcoming. The recipient, typically the chair of the program, if he or she believes that the applicant might prevail on a second pass, may reply like this:

> I received your letter requesting information about your application evaluation and your chances for next year. I cannot, of course, make any promises. I can tell you, however, that although your grades and test scores were quite adequate, we were concerned about your background in research methodology. Although we were impressed with your work in Dr. Moreau's laboratory, you have taken only the basic level design course. Therefore, it might be wise to take an advanced methodology class to demonstrate your expertise. I also thought that your statement of purpose was too general. I did not get a firm impression of where you wanted to go in the field. Finally, I might suggest that you try to get involved in another research project at your college or a nearby university. I hear that Dr. Nod is starting a large sleep study and is looking for volunteers to monitor the participants.
>
> Because you were not interviewed, and you may not have visited our campus, I think it would be wise for you to make that trip if you could. I would not have a great deal of time to give you, but if you were to drop by early in October I could give you a quick tour and we could chat for a few minutes. Call Ms. Scribe for an appointment if you decide to visit us.

This generous letter (adapted heavily from an actual one received by a rejected student) offers a rather detailed plan of action, although it rightfully avoids any guarantees. Many responses may not be so caring and thorough, but you could get some useful ideas about how to strengthen your case or gain a realistic appraisal as to why you should direct your interests elsewhere.

I was accepted into a good program, but the one I wanted more than anything ever since I became a psychology major rejected me. I feel like I crashed.

This is a tough situation that, unfortunately, we see fairly often. You tried. You could try again next year if you receive any encouragement from the kind of inquiry previously discussed. However, take a good look at those who want you. They could well be your ticket to where you want to go in your career. Sometimes we overromanticize our goals and plans of action and blind ourselves to better (or at least comparable) paths.

What's the hardest rejection to take?

Rejection hurts however it occurs, but one circumstance appears more difficult than any other. Applicants who are invited for a preselection interview are clearly aware, intellectually, that the probability of not receiving an acceptance letter is as high as 75%. However, they are still markedly stunned when a rejection letter actually arrives.

There are at least two reasons for the heightened disappointment. First, they felt as if they were so close because they were, for weeks, finalists rather than just applicants. Second, on paper these applicants were good enough to be interviewed. Up close, in person, and intimately exposed, however, they failed to impress anyone . . . or so it feels. As one rejected applicant put it, "In the role of student and test taker I was seen as just fine. My application materials were good enough for them. It was me, the me that I am, that was judged to be unworthy. How can I get over something like that?"

Although nothing can take the pain away completely, the facts of what actually happened during the postinterview evaluation session likely bear no resemblance to the images that rejected applicants hold. Perhaps an occasional interviewee was a major disappointment in person, but most are not found significantly lacking or contradictory from what was already known about them. It is highly unlikely that any evaluator would state, "Lord, I'm glad we had interviews so that we could catch this loser." Rather, very difficult choices were made among a larger number of attractive applicants than could be accommodated within the program.

What if I am not accepted to any program at all? That must feel pretty bad, too.

To be rejected from every program you applied to requires a reassessment, but not necessarily an abandonment, of your graduate school plans. First, if this happens to you, resist the temptation to run away and hide. Now is the time to seek support and comfort from others, including professors and peers who took an interest in your quest for advanced study. It is easy to feel too embarrassed to face your supporters, afraid that these people will think to themselves, "I must have drastically overestimated this student." Please know that this is never the case. We make our own judgments, and the fact that you were not admitted into any program does not alter our opinion of who you are and what you have to offer. In addition, we are the very people who can offer you some constructive ideas.

Many reasons could account for such a disappointing conclusion to your graduate school search. It is important to consider each one. On your own, or with knowledgeable assistance, carefully review the entire process and seek to discover why things went awry.

- Did you select your schools as carefully as possible, paying special attention to how your academic record and goals matched the programs you chose?
- Did you apply to an adequate number of programs?
- Did you rush through your applications, knowingly leaving out some requested information or spending too little time on your essay statements? Incomplete or hastily prepared applications can be at the root of across-the-board rejections.
- Did your record indicate absences of certain important experiences? That is, did you lack research or field experience in the area of your interest?
- Were you not well acquainted with your referees? Is it possible that their letters were not detailed and strong enough?
- Were most or all of your applications to programs with huge application rates and tiny acceptance rates? If so, your chances were slim from the beginning.
- Was your motivation high? Students who are either ambivalent or apathetic about their graduate education plans often make many mistakes, mostly by not taking the time to do the best possible job with their choices and applications. They often have numerous excuses as to why they could not do research or get involved in departmental activities. Unfortunately, their unclear priorities and low energy levels show through.

Occasionally, applicants reveal something in their application, interview, or other communications with the graduate program faculty and staff that raises a red flag. It may be something that the evaluators see as indicating poor judgment or raising a concern about the applicant's suitability to the profession (such as a history of serious emotional problems).

What if none of the reasons for across-the-board rejection discussed so far fit me?

We believe that poor school-selection strategies and inadequately prepared applications are the primary reason students are unsuccessful. However, we believe that another phenomenon also occurs, and it is best described as just plain bad luck. Some solid students may consistently be ranked just below the number of applicants who accepted offers to each program to which the student applied.

What you cannot know is the caliber of the other applicants. When being compared to stellar students, even outstanding students may be rejected. The unfortunate thing is that you may never know for sure how close you were. For this reason, you must trust your own vision of yourself.

Reapplication Strategies

If I am rejected from every program, is it all over for me, or should I try again next year?

Those who are committed to their goals and are willing to build their records and scrutinize and remedy their deficiencies should consider reapplication in the future.

You can improve your academic record if it lacks certain desirable courses by taking them as a postbaccalaureate student. A few more solid courses with strong grades may convince evaluators, the next time around, that you are definitely a serious student.

Seek field or research experience if your current record is weak in these areas and you applied to programs that rate such experience highly. Get to know a professor or two better, thus enhancing your chances for stronger recommendation letters. Select schools more carefully. Study for tests and retake them if your previous scores were marginal. Make sure that next time you include graduate programs that are realistic given your aims and qualifications.

Another viable possibility if you were rejected from doctoral programs is to apply quickly to a master's program in your interest area for which the application deadline still lies ahead. This works well for those who suspect that they may not yet be ready for a doctoral program. For example, interests may still be diffuse, grades and commitment to study harder may have been weaker than desirable, and so on. Even if the deadline has recently passed, you can call the office and ask if late applications are being accepted; sometimes they are. (Also see http://www.apa.org/ed/gradopen.html for information on psychology programs that did not fill all of their slots.)

How often do students get accepted the second time around?

We are not aware of any data on this issue. However, our own experience reveals a respectable acceptance rate when the students were willing to buckle down and bolster their records, although the acceptances the second time around were not necessarily to the same programs that had earlier rejected these students.

Several years ago, one of us (P.K.S.) picked several students who we thought deserved admission to competitive doctoral programs, but whose initial applications failed, and carefully followed them for several years. Two of them earned their master's degrees first and worked exceptionally hard to do outstanding academic work. Both also became involved as research and teaching assistants. While still master's students, one of them coauthored two publications and the other became a paid instructor who received glowing student reviews and praise from colleagues. Both worked extremely carefully on their reapplications to the same schools that rejected them 2 years previously. The one who did research was accepted (with financial support) into all eight programs that had earlier rejected her! The other one was accepted into three of the six programs that had previously rejected him.

Two other students stayed on as part-time unclassified graduate students, taking a few hard-nosed courses and helping professors with their research. They also planned their strategies for filling out forms much more carefully. Both reapplied to several programs and made first applications to several others the following fall. One was accepted to two of the programs to which he reapplied, although both students ended up attending programs from among their new selections.

Only two students did not get accepted somewhere the second time around. Although both were bright, early on it appeared unlikely that their second round of applications would be successful. One had said that he wanted to "kick back" and would take a course or two but in "topics that would be fun." The other one lost his focus when he became more involved with a job than with his earlier goal to continue his education.

Sounds like a lot of work to turn things around.

It usually takes considerable effort and determination. Those who do not find this process attractive should explore other options. If you are still associated with an academic institution, check with the educational and vocational counseling services for guidance. Life affords many opportunities that do not require graduate training, and one of these possibilities may be right for you.

Isn't there such a thing as being rejected from every graduate program just because you don't have what it takes?

If you have gotten this far with this book and followed the advice carefully, it is difficult for us to believe that such a description fits you. However, of course there are students who would be better suited to a different path.

Some students who are unhappy with the results of their applications should certainly consider other life options, especially if reapplication strategies have been carefully followed but with disappointing outcome. Sessions with a career counselor are worth exploring.

There is no dishonor in a decision to redirect your interests and goals. You and advanced study in a particular field just might not be right for each other. Your studies completed so far will come in handy for a vast variety of other careers; social science degree holders are attractive to many employers, including those in business, human relations, and not-for-profit organizations. Such degree holders often have analytical skills and can work well with people, both of which are valuable and applicable in many careers. So many students we have known, now leading happy and productive lives engaged in a wide variety of careers and work settings, did not go to graduate school in any field or waited and continued their studies in another field altogether. Many students are ultimately employed in fields quite removed from those which they studied in college.

Taking the Next Step— Starting Graduate School

What about those students who were accepted into a program and who will make the transition to graduate school life?

The term *commencement* usually conjures notions of the end for students. However, the word actually means the beginning. Just as this chapter marks the end of the graduate application process, acceptance into a program signals the beginning of your advanced training.

Graduate school is typically a unique chapter in people's lives. Although you will be enrolled again as a student, your experience will be markedly different from undergraduate school. Classes are typically much smaller, perhaps only you and 4 to 10 other students. You will have many more opportunities to work closely with faculty. In some sense, your professors will serve as intellectual parents who help you to begin thinking like a professional. Rather than just memorizing material as one member of a mass of students, you will be expected to develop the mind of a professional in your chosen field, to begin taking on a professional identity.

When working with graduate students, faculty often make assumptions they do not necessarily hold about undergraduates. These assumptions include the belief that you, as a student, want to learn just about everything you can about your chosen field, and that you enjoy learning and are eager to become a professional. Accordingly, you will be expected to be prepared for class and to not ask questions like, "How long does the paper have to be?" and "Is this going to be on the test?" You will be expected to invest in both your own work as well as the work you perform as part of an assistantship or collaboration. Overall you will be expected to be genuinely committed to what you are doing; your education and training are your top priority.

Perhaps because of these assumptions, graduate school is more demanding than undergraduate study. There will be much more reading, and you will have to process and integrate material in meaningful ways. Because your classes are much smaller, there will be much more discussion and everyone will be expected to contribute, both informally as well as through assigned presentations to your classmates.

You're starting to make it sound like it's all work.

Although it is a lot of work, you can almost feel yourself growing and expanding your intellectual and human capital. Graduate school is also a unique time socially. This may be the last period in your life during which you have a built-in social support system of people who are about your age, who are also bright and interested in the same field that you are, and who are going through the same trials and tribulations. Many times intense friendships are formed so that, despite the poverty and the feeling that you don't "have a life," most of us recall our graduate school years fondly.

Of course, the largest determinant of how rewarding your graduate school experience is may be whether you enjoy learning, especially about your chosen field. In other words, how rewarding do you find the intellectual stimulation of advanced schooling? Especially for those of us who chose to remain in academia for the remainder of our working lives, these intellectual rewards are greater than any other we receive from our profession. Along these lines, we will leave you with a passage B. F. Skinner wrote to students for the previous edition of this book, just weeks before his death:

> The thing I found the most rewarding in my graduate career in psychology was not the degrees, prizes, acclaim, or frequency of my being mentioned in books, but the immediate and reinforcing consequences that came to me in my research and at my desk when I was writing. One of the great advantages of the operant technique is that results are immediate. Change contingencies of reinforcement and the fascinating happens, often something surprisingly new. This is the excitement of real science, and there is no substitute for it. When it comes time to write theoretically, the great rewards are also discoveries; you say something that seems for the first time to be new and important. I have been very lucky, and it is not what I can say you will be sure to have, but if you are the right kind of person, it is there for the asking.

CONSTRUCTING A CURRICULUM VITA

A *résumé*, often referred to in academia as a *curriculum vita* and sometimes shortened to *c.v.* or *vita*, is a written summary of who you are and what you have done; it gives the reader an idea of the direction you are headed. You will probably be required to supply a résumé at many points during your lifetime, and it comes in handy more often than you might think.

If you have no relevant work or volunteer history, have not joined any professional organizations, have no awards, and have not been involved in a research project, then you are not yet ready to produce a vita. However, those with even very few accomplishments in one or more of these categories would be wise to get one started.

Uses and When to Begin

Résumés are highly useful as documents to supply to referees (letter of recommendation writers). A résumé gives your referees an impression that you are a serious student with professional habits, and it helps the referees compose their letters. What you think is important about yourself will often be reinforced in the referees' letters because they may contain material taken directly from your vita.

Résumés are almost always appropriate to include in your application package, even though few programs specifically ask for one. Some graduate school application forms request a very limited amount of information, and the essay assignment may not give you the opportunity to include some of the interesting items that can be contained in a résumé. Informing the selection committees about yourself by slipping in a vita is strongly advised in such instances.

It is, however, extremely inappropriate to refer the reader to a résumé instead of filling out lines on the application form. "See vita" is irritating to evaluators who must then spend extra time seeking out and matching up information. (When scores of applications are piled high for review, the evaluators' tolerance for applicants who made the job easier for themselves at the expense of the reader is very low. Conversely, making things easier for the evaluator may work to your advantage.)

Résumés may also be useful if you decide to make preapplication contacts with prospective graduate program faculty. A vita, along with your letter, helps the recipient to better understand your background and experience.

It is never too early to start a vita once you have at least a few items to list. Constructing a vita will also make you think about your career development and what things you need to do to round out your experience. Building and updating a résumé become a process by which you see yourself expand, and every new entry feels rewarding. Keep your vita on a separate computer disk and update it regularly. Also keep a backup file, because recreating a vita is a real headache!

Format

Sometimes well-intentioned professors share their vita with students for use as a model. However, unless a student has accumulated a reasonable number of relevant items, such as publications and relevant work experiences, the typical professional's vita does not offer a suitable format to model. Students, who usually have a limited number of entries, benefit from a strength-focused annotated model in which their major accomplishments and activities appear closer to the top of the résumé (right after personal information and educational background). Each relevant entry is very briefly described rather than simply listed. The three sample résumés illustrate some of the different ways résumés can be constructed to show off the candidate to his or her best potential.

Beware of modeling after how-to-do-a-résumé books or using résumé writing services whose clients are primarily job seekers. Often the emphasis is on selling oneself as one would designer jeans, and the effect of such a glitzy and often grossly exaggerated self-presentation is counterproductive for applying to graduate school.

Start your résumé with a list of basic identifying data. Graduate school evaluators expect to see the following:

Name (your full name, not nicknames or diminutives)
Permanent address
Telephone number and e-mail address

Jennifer Padgett
Permanent Address: 100 Gun Fury Road
                    Sedona, AZ 86340
Telephone: (602) 555-5555
E-mail: JPadgett@Bumpers.edu

Educational History

High School Diploma, Sedona High School, June 1995

Bachelor of Arts degree, Bumpers State University
   Major: Psychology
   Anticipated June 2000

Relevant Work Experience

Teaching Assistant. Introductory psychology course. Bumpers State University, Fall 1998, quarter-time. Prepared and delivered lectures on long-term memory research, classical and operant conditioning models, and jury selection research. Graded short essay exam questions and consulted with students about their term projects. Led tutoring session for an hour each week. Supervisor: Neil Mancuso, PhD

Research Assistant. Participated in a programmatic team effort teaching computer applications to children. Saltine Institute, Flagstaff, Summer 1998, full-time. Co-taught the six-session training sessions to 4- to 7-year-old children. Entered data. Supervisor: Bettina Clarence, PhD

Tutor (volunteer). Fischer Drug Rehabilitation Center, June 1996–May 1997, 3 hours per week. Helped teenage residents with their algebra and English homework. Participated in weekly staff meetings.

Relevant Academic Activities

Assisted the department chair, Dr. Robert Smith, at Bumpers State University in setting up the computer laboratory in the Psychology Department, Spring 1998.

Served as peer advisor (volunteer) to undergraduate students, Psychology Department, Bumpers State University, Fall 1998–Spring 1999.

Other Work Experience

Retail Sales Clerk. Halsey Department Store, Flagstaff, AZ. June 1995–June 1997, 20 hours per week.

Extracurricular Activities

Chess, music (play organ and piano), and running.

Gary S. Brian

College Address
Claremont College
Box 1000
Claremont, CA 91711

Permanent Address
9951 Login Avenue
Northridge, CA 91324
(818) 555-5555

Education:	**Claremont College**, Claremont, CA (September 1995–present). Specialized course work included advanced physiological psychology, advanced statistics, philosophy of science, upper division chemistry and biology, advanced mathematics, and computer science courses. (Graduation with BA degree in psychology anticipated May 2000.)
	Chatsworth High School, Chatsworth, CA. Graduated with Gold Cord ("Highest Academic Honors") in June 1996.
Relevant Work Experience:	**Stone Tools**, Reseda, CA (May–August 1997 and January 1999). Assistant to the vice president of operations. Created computer inventory control system. Worked in many capacities during the research and development phase. Conducted consumer preference studies. Supervisor: Steve Anderson
	Midstate College Foundation, Los Angeles (May–August 1999). Research assistant for a funded survey project. Selected 2000 survey respondents and prepared surveys to be mailed. Supervisor: Dr. Kenneth Christ
	Veterans Administration Hospital, Sepulveda, CA (September 1995–June 1996). Volunteer on psychiatric wards one-half day per week. Supervised patient recreational activities. Supervisor: Judy Walter, MSW
Skills:	Data entry and analysis. Proficient in SPSS.
Other Interests:	Politics and current affairs, basketball (college varsity team).

Abby Gerald
71386 Tenth Street, Apartment 6A
Chestnut Hill, MA 02167
(617) 555-5555

Educational Background

June 1986, High School Diploma, Bon High School, Bon, MA

June 1991, BA, cum laude, in biology from Bowl State University, Midtown, VA

June 1994, MA in psychology from Weston University, Weston, NY

Master's Thesis

Gerald, A. (1994). Memory strategies, test performance, and text anxiety in college freshmen. Advisor: Marcus D. Fillipson, PhD

Research Publication and Paper Presentation

Gerald, A., & Racimora, A. (1994). Memory strategies of college freshmen. National Journal of Educational Psychology, 11, 3–6.

Gerald, A. (1993, October). Practice effects on the motivation to succeed. Paper presented at the Rocky Mountain Undergraduate Research Conference, Boulder, CO.

Professional Group Memberships

Elected to Psi Chi, 1989. Chapter vice president, 1990. Organized Chapter Graduate School Forum, Fall 1990.

American Psychological Association, student affiliate, 1989–Present.

American Psychological Society, student affiliate, 1989–Present.

Awards and Honors

Golden Triangle Scholarship, 1990. Awarded annually by the Midtown Community Psychology Society.

Honorable Mention, Bowl State University Annual Research Competition, 1990. For paper on memory strategies listed above.

Work Experience

Claims Adjuster, Tri-City Insurance Company, Boston, June 1986 to August 1987.

Miscellaneous

Speak fluent Spanish.

Next, under a category titled Educational History, describe your schooling, starting with high school graduation. Include all higher education institutions attended in chronological order (including summer school), any degrees or certificates earned, and your anticipated date of graduation if you have not yet earned your bachelor's degree. Also list your major field of study. Include any field in which you earned a minor.

After that, the headings you use should not be rigidly adapted from someone else's form. Rather, headings should describe whatever presents you best. For example, if you took an impressive number of harder science and mathematics courses in college, work that in somehow. If you have research publications or presentations, list these right after your educational history.

If applicable, a category titled Relevant Work Experience might follow educational history. Include the name of the agency or employer and the city. Paid or unpaid experiences can be included here, although volunteer activity should be identified as such. Any relevant positions, even if held briefly, should include short descriptions of the duties you performed and the name of your supervisor. Examples of relevant experiences that graduate applicants might list include field placements from classes, teaching or research assistant positions, and summer jobs related to your career goals.

Sometimes agencies that take in volunteers offer fancy-sounding titles (e.g., recreational therapist or psychiatric apprentice) to help offset the lack of monetary rewards. Do not use such titles unless you actually have the specialized training that would justify the image created by the title. Selection committees members may be put off by designations that are obviously contrived and too overblown for your training and experience.

Generally, do not include events that occurred before you started college. An occasional exception might include a high-powered award or honor, such as being National Merit Scholar, being class valedictorian, or receiving a major scholarship award, or a highly unusual or impressive related activity (e.g., tutoring inner-city children three afternoons a week for a year). An intense multicultural experience, such as spending a summer in Uganda, might be of interest. (Do not include a six-countries-in-2-weeks trip to Europe.)

Applicants who have been out of school for a while or who have worked steadily at a job while going to school should include something about their work histories even if they are not relevant to their chosen educational and career goals. Rather than leave a blank 5-year period in your life (were you in prison?), indicate the position you held and your employer's name during that time, although you need not describe your duties if the title adequately conveys the type of work you performed and the job was irrelevant to your intended area of study.

If you have worked steadily while going to school, note that and give the title that best describes the functions you performed. This alerts selection committee members and others to your heavy schedule. We recommend putting work history that is not related to your professional goals in a separate category immediately following the Relevant Work Experience category and labeling it Other Work Experience. Do not include nonrelevant jobs that were held only for a brief time (e.g., waitress for a summer) or prior to high school graduation.

Most graduating seniors do not have any publications in scholarly journals or presentations at professional meetings, nor do they often have any in progress. However, if you do have at least one such project on your record or in progress, create a category called Publications and Paper Presentations. Poster sessions count as paper presentations. (If you have more than one publication and more than one paper presentation, you can create two separate categories.) You can include publications in press and papers accepted for presentation as well as completed papers submitted for publication or presentation in the same section. Be sure, however, that their status is clearly conveyed (e.g., "submitted for presentation at the Midstate Psychological Association meetings"). See the *APA Publication Manual* for current citation styles.

Ongoing work can also be listed and should be in a separate category titled Projects in Progress. However, do not list too many ongoing projects, especially if you have not yet completed anything. You might be perceived as a person who starts things but never finishes them.

Membership in professional associations (including relevant student organizations such as Psi Chi or your department's psychology club) should be a separate category if you are a member of two or more. Include any offices held or special projects in which you played a central role. If you are a member or affiliate of only one relevant organization, list it in a Miscellaneous section at the end of your vita. We do not advise that you list memberships in organizations that are completely irrelevant to your professional goals, such as social fraternities or the Ski Club.

If you have received two or more academic honors or recognitions (not including high school or earlier unless they were major ones), list them in a separate section titled Honors and Awards. Examples may include a scholarship, research competition award, departmental achievement award, or selection into an honors seminar. Include the full name of the honor or award, date conferred, and any detail that would enhance its meaning.

If you have received only one award, include it in a Miscellaneous section unless it was a major award. In that case, it is appropriate to have this accomplishment as the only item in the category.

A category called Extracurricular Activities is optional and could include a list of two or three hobbies or favorite pastimes. Such a category rounds you out as a person and may even be helpful under quirky circumstances. One colleague confided that he broke the tie between two equally qualified applicants by choosing the one who shared his own favorite pastime of tennis!

Do not offer too many entries here, however, or you may be seen as an overly active or scattered person who may not have enough time for or commitment to education. This category is one that you will drop from your résumé once you are a graduate student or start looking for a professional job. However, for now, selection committees are looking for bright and interesting students, and a short list of favorite nonacademic activities should not hurt you and could be slightly advantageous.

You may have other achievements and activities that would be relevant to include in your résumé, such as serving as a student editor for a professional journal or one of your professors, building a research apparatus, serving in some capacity in your undergraduate department, or other special skills such as fluency in a second language or facility with data analysis or particular software. You may have done an interesting independent study project. Sometimes these types of accomplishments or activities are very impressive to selection committee members. Check with your advisor as to the appropriateness and most effective placement of such items on your vita.

Appearance

Do not underestimate the importance of the look of your vita. Two résumés with exactly the same information, one using a barely visible dot-matrix printer or hastily duplicated crooked and the other prepared on a laser printer, come across almost as if they were describing two different people. Use a readable, nonflamboyant font. This is analogous to the impact of grooming and dress when it comes to assessing a person one has just met.

Proofread your résumé very carefully. Typos are easy for their creator to miss, so enlist a friend to seek out errors. Computerized spell checkers are helpful but should not be the sole source of assistance. The computer only knows whether your letters spelled words correctly, but they may not always be the words that you wanted. Such unfortunate or unintentionally humorous (with the laughter at your expense) mistakes can be avoided only by calling in a competent human proofreader.

Spacing should be liberal so that your résumé is easy to read and attractive, but do not try to make it seem longer by making too-wide margins or leaving extra space between lines. Those evaluating you will not take kindly to your trying to deceive them with such a conspicuous trick.

Résumés can be duplicated by a photocopier, if it makes clean, sharp copies. We suggest avoiding colored paper; white or off-white paper looks more professional. A good-looking résumé is noticed, and traits such as caring about your work and self-confidence are attributed to you as well.

A Final Note

Do not feel bad if your vita is quite sparse. Many student résumés do not exceed one page. Remember, no one expects you to have a number of high-powered professional experiences, especially if you are young and still an undergraduate. The worst thing you can do is to try to compensate for a short vita by filling it up with tangential or irrelevant items or by making it wordy.

WHAT ACADEMIC DEPARTMENTS CAN DO TO ASSIST THEIR STUDENTS WITH GRADUATE SCHOOL PLANS

The research we conducted for this book indicated that undergraduate academic departments can provide a great many resources for their graduate school–bound students that may be difficult or even impossible for students to access by themselves. Fortunately, most of the resources are not expensive or even very time-consuming to collect and maintain, although one or more dedicated faculty are typically needed to keep things going from year to year. A student club or honor society may also be willing to pitch in.

Ways to Assist Students With Graduate School Plans

1. Start a graduate school application materials file, consisting of catalogs and applications donated by your graduate school applicants who do not need them anymore, as well as information downloaded from the Internet. Replace items as newer versions are contributed. This resource requires a couple of file cabinets if the collection is extensive (i.e., materials from around 400 programs) and is easier to maintain by instituting some type of monitoring system. This resource also helps encourage students to consider programs in other geographical locations.

2. Create a small resource library that students can use, containing books such as a current copy of APA's *Graduate Study in Psychology*, relevant Peterson's and Educational Testing Service (ETS) graduate program directories, and other helpful information, such as the most cur-

rent GRE pamphlet put out by the ETS and the MAT pamphlet put out by the Psychological Corporation (see chap. 10).

3. Encourage faculty members to communicate clearly their requirements for writing letters of recommendation for students (e.g., should students submit a résumé or statement of purpose or list of courses taken in their majors and grades received, how much lead time is needed, etc.). This allows students their best opportunity to impress each referee and also makes letter writing much easier for referees.

4. Encourage faculty to submit on time the letters they agreed to write for students. Reference letters are often late, which can jeopardize the students' chances of acceptance because their files are incomplete while the review of complete files is already underway.

5. Encourage faculty to involve as many students as possible in their research projects and provide incentives for faculty to sponsor students for independent research. The data clearly show that a student with research experience, particularly if the student co-authors a publication or presentation, is greatly advantaged regardless of the kind of program to which the student applies.

6. Sponsor an annual workshop on how to get into graduate school. The best time for such a function is the spring, when second-semester juniors can learn what to do over the summer to get a jump on the application process. The best alternate time is at the beginning of the fall term when first-semester seniors will need to learn what they should do right away. Consider inviting faculty from nearby graduate program facilities to participate. If possible, invite past students who were accepted into graduate programs to share their experiences.

7. Develop an honors program in your department for the most promising students. Participation in such programs is viewed favorably by selection committees. (These can work alongside any all-university honors programs.)

8. Support the student clubs and honor societies (such as Psi Chi) in your department. Encourage faculty involvement and attendance at these functions.

9. Encourage faculty to watch for unusual opportunities for undergraduate students. These may include paid jobs, calls for student journal referees, chances to meet colleagues from departments that might be of interest for graduate study, student research competitions, and summer research programs.

10. Motivate students to attend professional meetings, especially those that traditionally offer considerable programming to meet students' needs such as APA, APS, and the regional associations. Post the information about such meetings.

11. Create a bulletin board to display information of interest to aspiring graduate school students. If your campus is very large, include the names and locations of on-campus resources that students may find

valuable (e.g., career counseling, financial aid, and placement services). Encourage both faculty and students to contribute items for posting.

12. Encourage faculty mentoring of the most promising students. Data clearly support the mentored applicant's advantage in the selection process.

13. Institute an awards program to honor students who have attained high academic honors or significantly contributed to the department. If possible, bestow these awards just before or just after the winter break so that the recipients can list their awards on their graduate school applications.

14. Make a list of faculty and their specialty and current research areas readily available to students to facilitate mentoring and project collaboration.

15. Encourage your students to participate in undergraduate research conferences (if there are any in your geographical area). If there is no such opportunity nearby, consider putting on your own annual departmental research presentation session.

16. If your campus is very small or not well-known, consider creating a concise handout about your institution and department, indicating their strengths and unusual features, suitable for inclusion in your students' graduate school application materials. Applicants from better known colleges and universities usually have an advantage, an edge that may be as much from name recognition than anything else. With additional information, the selection committees may soften any bias.

17. Make students aware of the various financial resources that they can apply for, such as the National Science Foundation (NSF) Fellowships or student internal grants available on campus. Keep recent copies of applications and other information downloaded from the Internet on file and available for potential applicants to view. In addition, post the titles of funding guides and catalogs that are probably available in your college or university library or financial aid office. Help students find financial support specifically for undergraduate research. Some schools have their own internal programs; however, outside support is available as well.

18. Try to get the word out early (on bulletin boards or in class announcements) that graduate school planning is not something that should wait until the senior year. Students who begin an active plan in their junior year (or even earlier) have many advantages.

19. If your department has a graduate program, ensure that undergraduates understand any policies regarding their applications to your graduate program. That is, are internal applicants viewed and treated any differently? Also, are there ways current graduate students in your institution (or nearby ones if yours has no graduate program) can share their expertise concerning the application process?

REFERENCES

Ault, R. L. (1993). To waive or not to waive? Students' misconceptions about the confidentiality choice for letters of recommendation. *Teaching of Psychology, 20,* 44–45.

Bear, J. B., & Bear, M. P. (1997). *Bears' guide to earning college degrees nontraditionally.* Benicia, CA: C&B.

Bloom, L. J., & Bell, P. A. (1979). Making it in graduate school: Some reflections about the superstars. *Teaching of Psychology, 6,* 231–232.

Bonifazi, D. Z., Crespy, S. D., & Rieker, P. (1997). Value of a master's degree for gaining admission to doctoral programs in psychology. *Teaching of Psychology, 24,* 176–182.

Ceci, S. J., & Peters, D. (1984). Letters of reference: A naturalistic study of the effects of confidentiality. *American Psychologist, 39,* 29–31.

Fowler, R. E. (1985). A student's guide to negotiating the higher education maze. *College Student Journal, 19,* 352–353.

Golding, J. M., Lang, K., Eymard, L. A., & Shadish, W. R. (1988). The buck stops here: A survey of the financial status of PhD graduate students in psychology, 1966–1987. *American Psychologist, 43,* 1089–1091.

Hines, D. (1986). Admission criteria for ranking master's-level applicants to clinical doctoral programs. *Teaching of Psychology, 13,* 64–67.

Huitema, B. E., & Stein, C. R. (1993). Validity of the GRE without restriction of range. *Psychological Reports, 72,* 123–127.

Ingram, R. E. (1983). The GRE in the graduate admissions process: Is how it is used justified by the evidence of its validity? *Professional Psychology: Research and Practice, 14,* 711–714.

Keith-Spiegel, P., Tabachnick, B. G., & Spiegel, G. B. (1994). When demand exceeds supply: Second-order criteria used by graduate school selection committees. *Teaching of Psychology, 21,* 79–81.

Knouse, S. B. (1984). The letter of recommendation: Specificity and favorability of information. *Personnel Psychology, 36,* 331–341.

Korn, J. H., & Lewandowski, M. B. (1981). The clinical bias in the career plans of undergraduates and its impact on the profession. *Teaching of Psychology, 8,* 149–152.

Liddle, B. J., Kunkel, M. A., Kick, S. L., & Hauenstein, A. L. (1998). The gay, lesbian, and bisexual psychology faculty experience: A concept map. *Teaching of Psychology, 25,* 19–25.

Lunneborg, P. W. (1988). Women in psychology: Career issues. In P. J. Woods (Ed.), *Is psychology the major for you?* (pp. 108–110). Washington, DC: American Psychological Association.

McWade, P. (1996). *Financing graduate school: How to get the money you need for your master's or Ph.D.* New York: Peterson's Guides.

Mayne, T. J., Norcross, J. C., & Sayette, M. A. (1994). Admission requirements, acceptance rates, and financial assistance in clinical psychology programs. *American Psychologist, 49,* 806–811.

Minke, K. M., & Brown, D. T. (1996). Preparing psychologists to work with children: A comparison of curricula in child-clinical and school psychology programs. *Professional Psychology: Research and Practice, 27,* 631–634.

Morrison, T., & Morrison, M. (1995). A meta-analytic assessment of the predictive validity of the quantitative and verbal components of the graduate record examination with graduate grade point average representing the criterion of graduate success. *Educational and Psychological Measurement, 55,* 309–316.

Pearson, C. S., Shavlik, D. L., & Touchton, J. G. (1989). *Educating the majority: Women challenge tradition in higher education.* New York: Macmillan.

Rosovsky, H. (1990). *The university: An owner's manual.* New York: Norton.

Sayette, M. A., Mayne, T. J., & Norcross, J. C. (1998). *Insider's guide to graduate programs in clinical & counseling psychology* (1998/1999 edition). New York: Guilford.

Scheirer, C. J. (1983). Professional schools: Information for students and advisors. *Teaching of Psychology, 10,* 11–15.

Steinpreis, R., Queen, L., & Tennen, H. (1992). The education of clinical psychologists: A survey of training directors. *The Clinical Psychologist, 45,* 87–94.

Sternberg, R. J. (1994). *How to prepare for the MAT.* Hauppauge, NY: Barrons' Educational Series.

Stewart, D. W., & Spille, H. A. (1988). *Diploma mills: Degrees of fraud.* New York: Macmillan.

Tidball, M. E., Smith, D. G., Tidball, C. D., & Wolf-Wendel, L. E. (1998). *Taking women seriously: Lessons and legacies for educating the majority.* Phoenix, AZ: Oryx Press.

Williams, D. A. (1989, May 1). The confessions of a gatekeeper. *Newsweek,* pp. 62–63.

Zimbardo, P. G. (1987). Reducing the agony of writing letters of recommendation. In M. E. Ware & R. J. Millard (Eds.), *Handbook on student development: Advising, career development, and field placement* (pp. 94–95). Hillsdale, NJ: Lawrence Erlbaum Associates.